BOLLINGEN SERIES LXII. 2

Researches on the I Ching

BY IULIAN K. SHCHUTSKII

Translated by
William L. MacDonald
and
Tsuyoshi Hasegawa
with
Hellmut Wilhelm

With an Introduction
by Gerald W. Swanson

BOLLINGEN SERIES LXII. 2
PRINCETON UNIVERSITY PRESS

THIS WORK IS PART TWO OF NUMBER SIXTY-TWO IN A SERIES OF BOOKS
SPONSORED BY BOLLINGEN FOUNDATION

Library of Congress Cataloging in Publication Data will be found
on the last printed page of this book

Translated from Ю. К. Щуцкий *Китайская классицеская
«книга перемен»* (Moscow, 1960)
Composition in Hong Kong by
Asco Trade Typesetting Limited
Printed in the United States of America by
Princeton University Press, Princeton, New Jersey

Contents

79- 1739

Acknowledgments

Our thanks go to the former Far Eastern and Russian Institute at the University of Washington, the Graduate Research Board of the University of Illinois (Urbana-Champaign), and the Center for Asian Studies at the University of Illinois (Urbana-Champaign) for financial support; to Margaret Karzmar, Barbara Thayer, and Barbara Manning for the typing; to Howard Goodman for help with editing and research; and to the many friends and colleagues who helped out with advice and consultations.

T. H., W. L. M., H. W.

Introduction to the English Edition

The details of Iulian K. Shchutskii's academic life are sufficiently outlined in the Russian biography by Konrad. Left untold is the story of Iulian Shchutskii, the man. Some impression of him was conveyed to the present writer through an interview he and Dr. David Knechtges had in August 1974 with the famous Mongolian expert Dr. Nicholas Poppe, a friend of Shchutskii's who had been best man at his wedding in 1928.

Iulian began his studies in 1920–1921, and he finished in 1926–1927. According to Dr. Poppe, his primary concern was the Chinese spirit and its manifestations. He had a great poetic gift, and was at home in both poetry and philosophy. He studied under A. I. Ivanov, an expert in history, philosophy, and the Hsi-hsia language.[1] He considered himself,

1. For a brief history of Soviet sinology, see B. G. Gafurov and Y. Y. Gankovsky, eds., *Fifty Years of Soviet Oriental Studies* (Moscow: Nauka Publishing House, 1968). Characterizing Soviet sinology in the twenties, Gafurov and Gankovsky have the following observations: "At that time there existed a definite gap between the Sinologues of the so-called classical school, whose stronghold was in Orientological establishments of Leningrad and who dealt mainly with the problems of philology and old literature, and the school of Sinologues of a new denomination, mostly Muscovites, for whom the scientific problems of the Chinese revolution were of primary importance" (p. 6). The same essay has this to say about Shchutskii: "I. K. Shchutskii's posthumously published translation and essay 'Chinese Classical *Book of Changes*' (1960), which by analyzing different layers of that extremely complicated philosophical treatise lays bare its inner meaning, was doubtless a momentous event in Soviet science" (p. 24). I wish to acknowledge the assistance of Hellmut Wilhelm, Frederick Mote, David Knechtges, Robert Daniels, Luther Martin, Wang Ching-hsien, Martha Powers, Sanford G. Thatcher, Polly Hanford, Alan Berkowitz, Tim Phelan, Crispin Wilhelm, and especially Dr. Nicholas Poppe.

however, a student of V. M. Alekseev (1881–1951), the leader of the Leningrad school of sinology.[2] Shchutskii's excellent command of the Chinese language, both spoken and written, was remarkable since he had never been to China. He also studied Annamese, and even published a manual of this language, and in addition was aware of the importance of Japanese scholarship. He knew Manchu and used to make up humorous nicknames for others in Manchu. He was a deeply religious man, and Buddhism played a great role in his religious beliefs. According to Dr. Poppe, "Shchutskii was an idealist and believed in the soul and spirit of man." At the same time, he was an eclectic, not accepting any dogma 100 percent. He was a great admirer of Western psychology and had studied Freud. He and Poppe both had to read Marx against their will. "It would not be correct to label him a Marxist," said Dr. Poppe, in a very deliberate and emphatic tone.

Shchutskii was gay and very sociable. "This was possibly his downfall," related Dr. Poppe, "as he used to tell political jokes." He was fond of a particular joke about an American capitalist visiting Leningrad during the Depression. The American capitalist came upon a strange man sitting on top of a forty-foot flagpole, scanning the horizon with an imaginary telescope. He was able to get the man's attention and shouted: "What are you doing on top of that flagpole?" A voice answered: "I'm waiting for the revolution." "Well, then," returned the American capitalist, "since you seem to be a man of discerning judgment and keen insight, why don't you come to America and solve our Great Depression?" The

2. V. M. Alekseev was appointed head of the Chinese Department of the Institute of Orientology of the USSR Academy of Sciences in 1929. He was not bothered in the purges of the thirties, possibly because of his international reputation as a scholar. See L. Z. Eidlen, "Akademik V. M. Alekseev kak istorik kitaiskoi literatury," *Izvestiya Akademia Nauk/Otdelenie literatury i iazyka* 5 (1946), 239–244; English trans. Francis Woodman Cleaves, *HJAS* 10 (1947), 48–59.

man on the flagpole paused awhile, then continued to scan the horizon. "I cannot accept your offer," the voice finally called. "Yes, I could go to America and solve your Great Depression, but then I would be out of a job; here on my flagpole I shall have a job forever. After all, a man must be concerned with his position in life."

For Shchutskii, instead of the revolution, the NKVD came, and he was arrested early in 1937. They took him away in the night along with all his books and papers. Mrs. Shchutskii and their daughter of a few months were left alone. Poppe himself managed to escape through the forests to Finland. Shchutskii's doctoral dissertation, which we have here in English translation, also escaped. It had been deposited at the Institute library and was buried somewhere in the book-bindery, where it remained until after the death of Stalin.

Although Shchutskii was never brought to trial, Poppe was able to find out that he perished in a prison camp, along with his friend Nevskii and at least one other student. His skull was crushed with a chain. Nevskii, an expert on Japanese as well as Hsi-hsia language, had interested Shchutskii in a study called "anthroposophy."[3] According to Poppe, "these activities were condemned, and this was certainly one reason he was eliminated." Nevskii's wife was also taken by the secret police, leaving a two-year-old daughter. The girl stayed two days in an empty apartment until found by Nikolai I. Konrad, the Russian editor of the present work. Konrad was a younger friend of Shchutskii, Poppe, Nevskii, and the others.[4] Konrad apparently had a keen sense of how to survive, because he

3. It is not known whether Shchutskii's brand of "anthroposophy" is the same as that of Rudolph Steiner, who founded the Anthroposophical Society in 1912. Steiner called his version a "spiritual science" and claimed that man could again regain the faculty of spiritual perception.

4. Nikolai Iosifovish Konrad (1891–1971) was an instructor and then professor of Japanese Language and Literature from 1922 to 1939 at Leningrad University. In 1941, he was made chairman of the same department at the Moscow Institute of Oriental Studies.

eventually found his way into an important position in the Soviet Academy of Sciences. According to Poppe, Konrad was a very compassionate man. One of his first actions after the Stalin era was to publish his old friend's thesis as a book. He also raised Nevskii's daughter as his own child.

Dr. Poppe told us that these purges were accepted as inevitable in Leningrad at the time. "One never knew where the snake would strike next." He feels that "what this young man Solzhenitsyn says in his *Gulag Archipelago* is correct." It is perhaps a poignant ending to a tragic tale that Iulian Shchutskii's work has gained a wider audience with this translation into English.

An Appraisal of Shchutskii's Work

Shchutskii's dissertation was immediately recognized as a major scholarly work, not only for the difficulty and importance of its subject matter, but also for the great amount of new information it contains. In his review in *T'oung-Pao*, Paul Demiéville said of Shchutskii:

Shchutskii did not take long to realize—as all of us do—the necessity for whoever reads the texts, whatever dynasty or subject it may be, to be familiar with and understand as best as possible, the *I Ching*; there is found one of the primary sources of the cardinal points of Chinese thought and of the terminology which is found in most works.[5]

Certainly Professor Demiéville is correct in emphasizing the necessity of being familiar with the *I Ching*, for the *Book of Changes*, as it has come to be known in the West, is part of the very bloodstream of Chinese philosophy. Anyone who wants to study not only traditional Chinese philosophy, but also history and, for that matter, every aspect of Chinese intellectual life, must be conversant with the general cosmological principles of the *I Ching*. Without doubt, Shchutskii's

5. Paul Demiéville, "Review of Kitaiskaya Klassicheskaia Kniga Peremen," *T'oung-Pao* 50 (1963), 266–278.

work is overdue in the West, but with it, much of the difficulty of this unique book will be overcome.

In Part I of his work, Shchutskii calls attention to the many inadequacies of Western scholarship concerning the *Book of Changes*. He calls attention to the Western tendency to approach the book with a set of preconceived constructs about its nature. Thus Lacouperie and Conrady saw the *I Ching* in terms of the European philological tradition—as a dictionary. Shchutskii demonstrates that such a thesis cannot even be stated without involving itself in manifold contradiction.

Shchutskii's critical appraisal of James Legge and Richard Wilhelm reflects his opinion of the views they held on problems in which he had a strong interest, such as the origin and authorship of the text. But he fails to give them credit for their most important contribution, the translation of the text itself. Legge translated the text in accordance with the objective standards of the best available scholarship, but Legge was not particularly interested in the *I Ching*, and one often thinks he would not have translated it at all were it not for the fact that he set out to translate all the Chinese classics.

As with Legge, Richard Wilhelm also used the *Chou I che-chung* edition of the text, but the influence of his teacher, Lao Nai-hsüan (1843–1921), provided an essential difference between his translation and that of James Legge.[6] Legge trans-

6. The biography of Richard Wilhelm's teacher, Lao Nai-hsüan, contains the following: "In November 1913, Lao accepted an invitation from the German Sinologist Richard Wilhelm to preside over the Confucius Society, founded by Wilhelm and a number of former imperial officials in the German-leased territory of Tsingtao. The two men became close friends, and their mutual interest in the *I Ching* (Book of Changes) resulted in a new edition of that text by Lao entitled *Chou I tsun-ch'eng* (the Book of Changes according to the Ch'eng school) and a German rendering of the classic by Wilhelm, the *I Ging. Das Buch der Wandlungen*, published at Jena in 1924." See Howard Boorman, ed., *Biographical Dictionary of Republican China*, II (New York: Columbia Univ. Press, 1968), 282. Legge's relationship with Wang T'ao was not quite the same: Wang T'ao was paid twenty Hong Kong dollars per month to help Legge with his translations of the Chinese classics. See Arthur W. Hummel, ed., *Eminent Chinese of the Ch'ing Period* (rpt. Taiwan, 1970), p. 836.

lated what the text said, while Wilhelm translated what the text meant; that is, Legge was primarily a translator while Wilhelm was more of an interpreter, interested in the overall significance of the text for Chinese intellectual life. Wilhelm was fascinated with the significance of the text for Chinese intellectual tradition, but perhaps even more, he was drawn toward the possible significance of the text as an aspect of world literature. The immense popularity of the Wilhelm translation can only be accounted for by the realization that, for Richard Wilhelm, the *I Ching* was not a lifeless artifact of archaic China, but transcended even China. Richard Wilhelm had an insight that separated him from his predecessors and from Shchutskii as well: the ultimate significance of the *I Ching* is as a guide for one's personal psychic understanding. This is how it was used in old China; that is, the meaning of the book in China was to help one find perspective amid the constant changes of life. Wilhelm saw that it might have that significance also for the West, and therefore in his translation and interpretation he kept the text as faithful to the Chinese understanding as possible. In this way Richard Wilhelm raised the *I Ching* to the status of world literature.[7]

7. Richard Wilhelm was influenced by Lao Nai-hsüan, but he was also encouraged by his friendship with Carl Gustav Jung. The Jung/Wilhelm exchange was one of the more interesting intellectual relationships of the late twenties and deserves a separate study. The effect of this relationship upon Jung was to help crystallize his ideas on mandala and alchemical symbolism and led to the collaborative publication, with Wilhelm, of *Das Geheimnis der Goldenen Blüte*. The effect upon Wilhelm was to give him access, through translations by Jung's student, Cary F. Baynes, to an English readership; first with *The Secret of the Golden Flower* in 1931, and in 1950 with what became the standard English translation of the *I Ching*. Wilhelm was a missionary, not part of the German university community, and in his relationship with Jung he received some measure of recognition when German scholarship was rejecting him. Shchutskii clearly shows how unfair was the criticism of E. Hauer, a representative of the university community. See Richard Wilhelm and C. G. Jung, *The Secret of the Golden Flower: A Chinese Book of Life*. English edition translated by C. F. Baynes (New York and London, 1931; new edition, 1962).

Legge and Wilhelm represent an earlier stage of *I Ching* scholarship. Their intent, although reflecting different assumptions, was to make the book available to Westerners, and in this they were successful. Shchutskii has a different purpose, namely, to get back to the original text, to determine its origin and authorship. Like Legge and Wilhelm before him, Shchutskii opened up new areas of inquiry.

The second chapter of Part I, "Noncommentatory Studies in the Far East," is the strongest section of Shchutskii's work. There is much new material presented on the elaborate and complex questions of lore associated with the *I Ching*, especially in his discussion of Ou-yang Hsiu, Chang Hsüeh-ch'eng, and P'i Hsi-jui. Shchutskii, in the final analysis, does not adopt many conclusions from these writers, but their presentation, together with their argumentation, is not found in Western works on the *Book of Changes*, and on this point alone Shchutskii must be credited with drawing attention to them. Shchutskii outlines some twenty points taken from Ou-yang Hsiu's *Questions of a Youth about the Book of Changes* (*I t'ung-tzu wen* 易童子問), the most important of which is the fact that Ou-yang Hsiu was the first scholar to call the Confucian authorship of the Ten Wings into question.

The primary accomplishment of Chang Hsüeh-ch'eng was to draw attention to an image theory of meaning as recorded in the *Great Treatise* [or *Great Commentary*], the largest and most philosophical essay of the Ten Wings. Shchutskii credits Chang Hsüeh-ch'eng with having reached the conclusion that the images in the line texts of the *I Ching*

are related to the poetical images of the *Shih-ching*, as internal aspects of the external. Even though recognizing the perfection of the images of the *Shih-ching*, he nevertheless thinks that only the images of the *Book of Changes* (proceeding in the final account from the natural images of the world) carry system and harmony in themselves. (p. 86)

Although Shchutskii does not follow Chang Hsüeh-ch'eng's conclusions, he nevertheless holds him in very high regard as a thinker:

We must note that Chang Hsüeh-ch'eng is in general a confirmed Confucianist. But, appreciating such ideas which strongly distinguish him from the rest of the authors who wrote about the *Book of Changes*, we cannot but recognize in him one of those with the most original and interesting ideas who occupied an original place in the development of Chinese philosophy. (p. 87)

Shchutskii devotes some twenty-two pages to a point-by-point discussion of the first eight chapters of *A Comprehensive Discussion of Classical Scholarship (Ching-hsüeh t'ung-lun 經學 通論*) by the late Ch'ing scholar P'i Hsi-jui. As in the case of Chang Hsüeh-ch'eng, Shchutskii does not follow many of P'i Hsi-jui's conclusions, but again he gives him credit for being an original thinker:

Nevertheless, while disagreeing with the basic concepts of our author, we cannot but recognize that his was a colossal study of the *Book of Changes* and that his treatise is full of the most valuable information not yet taken into account in the European study of China. (pp. 108–109)

Thus, although Shchutskii by no means entirely agrees with Chang Hsüeh-ch'eng and P'i Hsi-jui, this translation provides us with all that is now available in English of their studies on the *I Ching*.

Part II of Shchutskii's work consists of his research on eleven separate problems about the *I Ching*. But before we can give a general account of his results, we must correlate Shchutskii's text divisions with the material in Wilhelm/Baynes. The general reader who may know no Chinese can still follow Shchutskii's argument—indeed, that is one of the great strengths of this work. To follow the line of Shchutskii's argumentation, however, one must know where in Wilhelm/Baynes to find the appropriate elements.[8] Thus the basic text for Shchutskii consists of the following parts: the name of the hexagram; the divinatory formulae; the remainder of the

8. Richard Wilhelm, trans., *The I Ching or Book of Changes*, English trans. by Cary F. Baynes, 3rd ed., with a preface by Hellmut Wilhelm, Bollingen Series XIX (Princeton Univ. Press, 1967), hereafter Wilhelm/Baynes.

hexagram texts or *kua-tz'u* 卦辭; and the line texts or *yao-tz'u* 爻辭. In the third edition of Wilhelm/Baynes, the first three of Shchutskii's four-part basic text are included under the general title of "The Judgment." Thus in Hexagram 30, for example, under the Judgment text we have: "The Clinging. Perseverance furthers. It brings success. Care of the cow brings good fortune."

The term "The Clinging," is the name of the hexagram, the first of Shchutskii's four parts. The name of the hexagram or *kua-tz'u* is found in the first position in all of the sixty-four hexagrams, both in the Chinese original and in Wilhelm/Baynes. The so-called Four Qualities, *yüan*, *heng*, *li*, and *cheng* (or *chen*) 元亨利貞, are the second part. These terms in Wilhelm/Baynes are consistently translated: *yüan*—"Supreme"; *heng*—"Success"; *li*—"Furthers"; *cheng*—"Perseverance." Since *li* and *cheng* only occur together (with a few exceptions of adjectives inserted between *li* and *cheng*), they are consistently translated by Wilhelm/Baynes as "perseverance furthers." *Yüan* never appears without *heng* and is translated in Wilhelm/Baynes as "Supreme success." [9] The term *heng*, on the other hand, does appear without *yüan* and with qualifiers other than the name of the hexagram. In those cases it is translated by Wilhelm/Baynes as "success."

Shchutskii's third part of the basic text is the remainder of the hexagram text. This is also called "The Judgment" in Wilhelm/Baynes. This Judgment or hexagram text is, for Shchutskii, older than the fourth part. The fourth part is the line texts or *yao-tz'u*; they are referred to in Wilhem/Baynes as "The Lines." [10]

The other texts, known collectively as the Ten Wings, are

9. There is a single exception to this statement. Hexagram 50, *Ting*, has the term *chi* 吉 ("good fortune") inserted between *yüan* and *heng*. This is translated by Wilhelm/Baynes as "Supreme good fortune. Success."

10. Later research into the *Book of Changes*, principally by Hellmut Wilhelm, has shown that Shchutskii is probably wrong in this estimation. We shall discuss the problem later.

all later commentaries. Although this work is principally concerned with the basic text, there is much new information concerning the Ten Wings in Shchutskii's research. The first of the Ten Wings and the fifth part recognized by Shchutskii is the *T'uan-chuan* 彖傳, and is called the "Commentary on the Decision" in Wilhelm/Baynes. It is a commentary on the hexagram text and provides a wealth of technical terms for a discussion of both the line relationships in the hexagram and the verbal symbolism in the hexagram text. For an example of the technical term "correspondence" in the Commentary on the Decision we can look to Hexagram 13, *T'ung Jên.* Here we have:

> Fellowship with Men. The yielding finds its place, finds the middle, and the Creative corresponds with it: this means fellowship with men.[11]

When we look at Hexagram 13 ䷌ we see immediately that the yielding line referred to is six in the second place, that is, the second from the bottom, broken line. The "correspondence" referred to occurs between this yielding line and the firm or Creative line in the fifth place.[12] The verbal symbol in this case is the term "Fellowship with Men." This verbal symbol is illustrated by the correspondence between the two lines.

The *Ta-hsiang chuan* 大象傳, which is called "The Image" in Wilhelm/Baynes, is the sixth part recognized by Shchutskii. It appears under each Judgment text in Book I and after each Commentary on the Decision in Book III of the Wilhelm/Baynes. This commentary also explains the hexagram texts of Judgment texts, but from the point of view of the component trigrams.

The seventh part of the total text is the *Hsiao-hsiang chuan*

11. Wilhelm/Baynes, p. 452.

12. This is discussed in Wilhelm/Baynes, p. 356. But most of what occurs in Richard Wilhelm's essay, "The Structure of the Hexagrams," is found in the Commentary on the Decision.

小象傳 or Commentary on the Small Image, and is found in
Wilhelm/Baynes only in Book III as a commentary to each
of the lines. It is prefaced by "b)" to show that it is commentatory to the "a)" part above, the line texts themselves.
The *Hsiao-hsiang chuan* is the source of certain explanatory
concepts, the most important of which is the notion of *wei*
位 or "relative position."

The eighth part of the *I Ching* text is the *Hsi-tz'u chuan*
繫辭傳 or *Ta-chuan* 大傳, translated in Wilhelm/Baynes as
The Great Treatise. This is not a commentary as such, but a
collection of separate essays on philosophical topics.

Shchutskii's ninth part is the *Shuo-kua chuan* 說卦傳, translated in Wilhelm/Baynes as "Discussion of the Trigrams."
This is similar to *The Great Treatise* in that it is not a commentary, but a separate collection of essays discussing the *I
Ching* from the point of view of the trigram school of
interpretation current in the late Chou.

The *Hsü-kua chuan* 序卦傳 forms Shchutskii's tenth part of
the text. It is translated by Wilhelm/Baynes as "The Sequence"
and is placed, along with the Miscellaneous Notes, before the
Judgment. The Sequence is a long prose poem, cut up and
attached to the various hexagrams; it is concerned with the
ordering of the hexagrams from one through sixty-four.

Shchutskii's eleventh part is the *Tsa-kua chuan* 杂卦傳 and
is translated by Wilhelm/Baynes as "Miscellaneous Notes." It
is primarily composed of glosses on the names of the hexagrams.

The last of Shchutskii's divisions is the *Wen-yen chuan* 文言
傳, translated in Wilhelm/Baynes as the "Commentary on
the Words of the Text." This is a series of glosses on the words
of the Judgment and line texts for the first two hexagrams.

Having made correlations between Shchutskii's divisions
and the parts of the text as they appear in Wilhelm/Baynes,
we are now in a position to give a general account of Part II
of Shchutskii's work, together with a comment upon its
content.

The first chapter, entitled "Monolithic Nature of the Text, is the longest in Part II and comprises almost half of the rest of the work. Shchutskii is here interested in showing that the present text of the *I Ching* as it has come down to us is not monolithic, but instead, composed of several parts. For Shchutskii, the oldest layer is the Judgment text. As was outlined before, the Judgment text itself is composed of several parts. There is first, the hexagram name itself; second, the terms *yüan*, *heng*, *li*, and *cheng* (or *chen*); and third, the remainder of the Judgment text. We must consider what this means in terms of Wilhelm/Baynes. A particular Judgment text, such as for Hexagram 25, *Wu Wang*, which contains all four terms *yüan-heng li-cheng*, is really composed of three different parts. First is the hexagram name "Innocence" and second, the terms *yüan-heng li-cheng* which Shchutskii calls "mantic formulae." Thus *yüan* is translated by Wilhelm/Baynes as "Supreme"; *heng* is translated "Success"; *li* is translated "Perseverance"; and *cheng* is translated "Furthers."[13] The third part of the Judgment text is the remainder of the Judgment text under each hexagram. Thus, the characters translated in Wilhelm/Baynes as "If someone is not as he should be, he has misfortune, and it does not further him to undertake anything" comprise the second layer of this particular Judgment text and are later additions.

It should be evident by now that Shchutskii's purposes are different from those of Richard Wilhelm. Wilhelm meant to translate the text as it came to be understood by the best Chinese intellectuals of his time. Shchutskii is trying to find out how the book was put together and what the terms meant when they were written. There are twenty-seven centuries between Shchutskii and Wilhelm on the problem of

13. These four mantic formulae comprise the second part of the Judgment text and are found in various combinations which, however, do fall into recognizable patterns. Thus we never find *heng-li* or "Success-Perseverance," but rather *li* and *cheng*. *Yüan* and *heng* may stand alone or may occur together as *yüan-heng*.

yüan-heng li-cheng and it is not surprising that the meaning and significance of the terms had an evolution of their own. Shchutskii's conclusions on the original meanings of the terms are that they are mantic formulae, the real meaning of which has been lost:

> Thus we can draw the conclusion that these terms represent some special layer of the text. I can suggest only the following hypotheses to explain their presence: the sentences made out of the characters *yüan*, *heng*, *li*, and *cheng* are mantic formulae, the meaning of which has been lost. However, their completely amorphous synthesis testifies to the fact that these formulae are much older than the rest of the text. Probably they are remnants of a much earlier system of divination. (p. 143)

Shchutskii next formulates the existence of an earlier system to explain the terms:

> It is much more natural, in my opinion, to imagine the following: the system of divination by a milfoil took shape under the influence of another older system from which the terminology was partially borrowed. Originally this system had only the names of the divination categories (the names of the hexagrams) and formulae constructed of the terms *yüan*, *heng*, *li*, and *cheng*. (p. 144)

But Shchutskii, with his usual careful scholarship, provides us with an early meaning of the terms and then seems to ignore the evidence. In the case of *heng*, Shchutskii quotes Takada Tadasuke to show that the terms originally meant "to sacrifice" and "to partake of an offering" in dealing with gods.[14] The term is used several times in the *Shang-shu*, or *Book of history*, in the sense of "to sacrifice."[15] It is also

---

14. Shchutskii (p. 141) presents a very interesting suggestion that *hsiang* 饗 ("to entertain a guest," or "to partake") is a correlative of *hsiang* 享 ("to sacrifice to a god"). That is, the former is concerned with a ritual action toward a human end while the latter is concerned with that same action directed toward a deity.

15. See James Legge, *The Shoo King (Shu Ching). The Chinese Classics*, vol. 3 (rpt. Hong Kong, n.d.), pp. 210, 215, 230, 295, 379, 398, 412, 417, 441, 446, 449, 466, 467, 470.

used in the same way in some of the line texts of the *I Ching* itself.[16] Shchutskii is well aware of this, but insists, nevertheless, that there was a shift in meaning from some unknown earlier sense to the meaning of "to penetrate." From there it is a short step to the notion of "development," which is how many traditional commentaries gloss the term.[17]

The modern scholar Kao Heng also equates *heng* with *hsiang*

16. *Heng* 亨 is associated with stock formulae of the early Chou ruling house:

"The king introduces him to the Western mountain." Wilhelm/Baynes, p. 475.

"The King offers him Mount Ch'i." Wilhelm/Baynes, p. 622.

"A prince offers it to the Son of Heaven." Wilhelm/Baynes, p. 459. *Hsiang* 享 is also associated with the same, or nearly the same stock formulae:

"Thus the kings of old sacrificed to the Lord and built temples." Wilhelm/ Baynes, p. 691.

"The king presents him before God." Wilhelm/Baynes, p. 599.

But if *heng* and *hsiang* are the same character, they became separate by the time of the *t'uan chuan*, or Commentary on the Decision: "The holy man cooks in order to sacrifice to God the Lord, and he cooks feasts in order to nourish the holy and the worthy." Wilhelm/Baynes, p. 642. Of course, in this last example, the term in question is not *heng*, but *p'eng* ("to cook"). The Ch'ing scholar Wang Fu-chih recognized this and in his *Chou I nei-chuan* 周易內傳 (*ch'uan-shan i shu* 船山遺書) 1.3b combined the glosses on cooking and sacrifices to derive the term *t'ung* 通, which is how the term *heng* is explained in nearly all the commentaries: "In ancient times *heng* 亨 was the same as *p'eng* 烹 ("to cook, to boil") and *hsiang* 享 ("to sacrifice"). In cooking, the vapors penetrate and cook the food. In the *chien* 薦 sacrifice, the *li* and the feelings involved penetrate and commingle. Therefore we take it to have the meaning of *t'ung* 通 or 'to penetrate.'"

17. Shchutskii roundly condemns the Sung school for imposing its systematic philosophy on the terms, but in the end tranlates *yüan, heng, li, cheng* almost the same way. Shchutskii construes *yüan* as "impulse"; *heng* as "completion" or "development"; *li* as "favorable"; and *chen* (or *cheng*) as "steadiness." The only difference between his translations and the sense in which the terms were understood by Chou Tun-i of the Sung, is that Shchutskii shows that the systematic connection of the four terms into a four-stage process cannot be supported by an analysis of the texts. Thus Shchutskii shows, by example, that philosophy cannot precede philology.

in the sense of "to sacrifice." He has this to say about the terms *yüan-heng li-cheng* as they occur in the first hexagram:

> When the ancients instituted a great sacrifice, having divined by milfoil, they obtained this *kua* and therefore recorded it, saying "*yüan-heng*." "*Li-cheng*" is like saying "propitious prognostication." When they divined with the milfoil and obtained this *kua*, and when the affair was beneficial, they therefore said "*li-cheng*." [18]

But yet the question persists: how do we get the notion of "completion" and/or "development" as *heng* is for Shchutskii, or "success" as it is for Wilhelm/Baynes, out of an original meaning of "to sacrifice?" Shchutskii himself offers two possibilities: first, the term *heng* in its original sense is now lost to us. Second, the term *heng* does not mean to sacrifice, but "for a sacrifice to penetrate the deity." Thus in the second solution Shchutskii postulates a continuous meaning for the term; in the first he implies a change from some unknown meaning to its current meaning.

But there seem to be other possibilities. As Shchutskii himself points out, the source for the standard gloss on *heng* is the *Wen-yen chuan* or Commentary on the Words of the Text. Here we have the terms *yüan-heng li-cheng* defined, or perhaps we should say redefined, in accordance with a certain philosophical position. In Wilhelm/Baynes, the translation is, "Succeeding, *heng*, is the coming together of all that is beautiful." [19] What seems to be happening in the *Wen-yen chuan is* the conscious deliberate redefinition of four key terms of the Judgment texts.

18. Kao Heng 高亨 , *A Modern Annotation on the Ancient Classic of the Book of Changes* (*Chou-i ku-ching chin-chu* 周易古經今注) [Shanghai: *K'ai-ming shu tien* 1947], p. 1 under the *ch'ien* hexagram. Bernard Karlgren in *Grammata Serica Recensa* 716a–d says this about the two characters: "*xiang/xiang:/hiang 亨 sacrificial offering (Shi); feast (Tso); enjoy (Tso); *xang/xong/heng 亨 penetrate (Yi); loan for 烹 (Shi). a. and b. are primarily identical, two variants of the same char.; the usage to write a. for *hiang* and b. for *heng* is modern; in T'ang time the two forms were still used *promiscue*."

19. Wilhelm/Baynes, p. 376.

This notion of conscious redefinition is very important both for the history of ideas in general, but also for the *I Ching* in particular. For it is redefinition of the earlier layers of the text that marks the divisions within the text. This is true not only in the obvious case of the difference between the *ching* and the *chuan*, that is, between the classic itself and the Ten Wings. It is also true in the line texts themselves—in the conceptual redefinition of primordial images associated with specific lines.

Certainly Shchutskii was aware of the glosses in the *Wen-yen chuan*, but the process of redefinition evidently did not interest him. He saw the process as the shift from religion to philosophy:

> The most complicated and at the same time the most simple answer did not occur to anyone; that is that the *Book of Changes* came into being as a text around the very ancient practice of divination and subsequently served as ground for philosophizing, which was especially possible since this (the *Book of Changes*), as a little understood and enigmatic archaic text, presents a wide scope for creative philosophical thinking. (p. 55)

Shchutskii evidently did not see a wide cleavage between an earlier divination text and its later philosophical commentaries since he criticizes Western attempts to extend the ideas found in the Ten Wings back into the earlier layers of the text. But on this point we might suggest an alternative explanation. Divination and philosophy do not mix in the West, but Chinese philosophers and intellectuals did not see this as a problem until they started to study Western philosophy. That is, in traditional China there was little, if any, difference between philosophy and religion, if by religion we mean the broad set of ideas that gives coherence to the world. A distinction that would separate divination from philosophy is a Western one. For the Chinese there was a set of classical texts whose explication changed as the times changed, and indeed they changed to meet the needs of the time. The Chinese intellectuals themselves saw the situation in terms of a continuity that built, generation upon generation, to a final climax in the Ch'ing dynasty.[20]

In other parts of the first chapter of Part II, Shchutskii occasionally rises above his own excellent scholarship to some brilliant insights about the *I Ching*. The best and probably most important occurs on p. 54, where he says:

> As in speech, the meaning is not in sounds but in the words and phrases expressed by these sounds, so in the *Book of Changes*, as well, the meaning is not in the images, but in *how* these images as a whole are coordinated in the system. If it were not so, then how would it be possible to make clear that for a thousand years some kind of collection of records of omens has been the starting point for the philosophy of one of the greatest people on earth?

What this passage means is that the images which occur in the line texts derive at least a portion of their meaning from the relative position they have in the whole hexagram. That is, part of the significance of the particular image depends upon the system of the whole book. This has generally been a relief to scholars of the *Book of Changes* since the early meanings of many of the images are lost.[21] Perhaps one reason why the significance of some of them is lost is that they are not all Chou images. In some, such as the story of King Hai of the Shang dynasty, the significance was lost even before the development of the set of commentaries known as the Ten Wings. Yet we must presume that every literate Chinese of the middle Chou period understood the significance of the story of King Hai. For even in the "struc-

20. Shchutskii is clearly generalizing from the Western model provided in 1912 by Cornford. See F. M. Cornford, *From Religion to Philosophy: A Study in the Origins of Western Speculation* (New York: Harper rpt. 1957). The Chinese experience does not quite fit the model.

21. Shchutskii, via Naitō, provides some interesting observations on the patterns of common images in the various hexagrams. Thus there are three hexagrams with images in all six lines; ten with five images; five hexagrams with four; eight hexagrams with three images; and two with two. A total of twenty-eight hexagrams contain repeated images within the line texts.

ture of the image" we see its normative significance: "He loses his sheep in *I*."[22] We do not clothe our images with such normative significance, and although everyone now understands what "Watergate" means, it will no doubt be lost within a hundred years. So it is not surprising that many of the *I Ching* line text images are lost even to the Chinese understanding. Yet much remains, and the system helps us with a set of guideposts. Shchutskii penetrated to the point of seeing that the relational system, however rough, was prior in time to the putting together of the line texts:

> The fact is that according to ancient Chinese ideas, the color spectrum consists of five colors and that yellow occupied the central position among them. Thus in the texts of the second and fifth lines, one often encounters the image with the epithet "yellow." Furthermore, yellow is the "earth color." The fifth line in this hexagram is the main one and occupies the most advantageous position in the upper trigram signifying the external and symbolizing the possibility of external display. The external is represented by a type of clothing. But since here the hexagram deals with the Earth, its position, lower in relation to Heaven, finds its reflection in the fact that the lower part of a Chinese garment, the "skirt," is indicated in the image. The favorable nature of this position makes it possible to speak here not only of "fortune," but even of "eternal fortune." After these explanations perhaps the text no longer seems strange and incomprehensible: "A weak line in the fifth position: a yellow skirt, eternal fortune." That is why the line text has to be thought of as a special (and also in view of its sophistication, a later) text. (pp. 135–136)

The point Shchutskii is making here is that, to a certain extent, the relational position of the lines determines the overall significance and perhaps determines even the character

22. Thus six in the fifth place of Hexagram 34 should read "Loses his sheep in *I*" rather than "Loses the goat with ease." Traditional commentaries had missed this point. See Hellmut Wilhelm, *Heaven, Earth, and Man in the Book of Changes: Seven Eranos Lectures* (Seattle: Univ. of Washington Press, 1977), pp. 215ff. The image which also occurs in Hexagram 56, nine at the top: "Through carelessness he loses his cow" should read, "He loses his cow in *I*." Thus in both cases the term *I* is a place-name.

of the image itself. In the twenties, Shchutskii did not have the language to explain the correlation of images and lines in the hexagram. Today, largely owing to Joseph Needham's synthesis of earlier scholarship, this phenomenon is called "correlative thought." [23] The tendency on the part of the early Chinese to correlate significant aspects of reality with each other, rather than relate them through class inclusion to a concept of substance, forms the basis of what one scholar has called the cosmological gulf that separates East from West. [24]

23. Needham explains correlative thought thus: "A number of modern students—H. Wilhelm, Eberhard, Jablonski, and above all Granet—have named the kind of thinking with which we have here to do, 'coordinative thinking' or 'associative thinking.' This intuitive-associative system has its own causality and its own logic. It is not either superstition or primitive superstition, but a characteristic thought-form of its own. H. Wilhelm contrasts it with the 'subordinative' thinking characteristic of European science, which laid such emphasis on external causation. In coordinative thinking, conceptions are not subsumed under one another, but placed side by side in a *pattern*, and things influence one another not by acts of mechanical causation, but by a kind of 'inductance'.... The key-word in Chinese thought is *Order* and above all *Pattern* (and, if I may whisper it for the first time, Organism). The symbolic correlations or correspondences all formed part of one colossal pattern. Things behaved in particular ways not necessarily because of prior actions or impulsions of other things, but because their position in the ever-moving cyclical universe was such that they were endowed with intrinsic natures which made that behaviour inevitable for them. If they did not behave in those particular ways they would lose their relational positions in the whole (which made them what they were), and turn into something other than themselves. They were thus parts in existential dependence upon the whole world-organism. And they reacted upon one another not so much by mechanical impulsion or causation as by a kind of mysterious resonance." See Joseph Needham, *Science and Civilization in China*, II (Cambridge: Cambridge Univ. Press, 1962), 280–281.

24. Mote expresses it in this way: "History, culture, and man's conceptions of his ideal roles all must be explained in terms of Chinese cosmology, and not—if we really want to understand Chinese civilization—by implicit analogy to ours. It is not too much to suggest that an ill-detected cosmological gulf separates Western civilization, as well as other civilizations including Eastern ones, from Chinese civilization." See Frederick W. Mote, *Intellectual Foundations of China* (New York: Alfred Knopf, 1971), p. 28.

In Part II, chapter 2, "Differentiation by Content," Shchutskii divides the content of the Ten Wings into commentaries, theoretical treatises, and glosses. The true commentaries are the *T'uan-chuan* and *Hsiang-chuan*; the theoretical treatises on the *I Ching* as a whole are the *Ta-chuan* (or *Hsi Tz'u-chuan*), the *Hsü-kua chuan*, and chapters 1 and 2 of the *Shuo-kua-chuan*; the glosses include the *Tsa-kua chuan*, *Wen-yen chuan*, and chapter 3 of the *Shuo-kua chuan*. Shchutskii points out that the authors of the Ten Wings did not distinguish their works by content, but rather the seven texts that have come to be known as the Ten Wings developed somewhat randomly and without internal connection to one another. About the content of the *Shuo-kua chuan*, Shchutskii is certainly correct in maintaining that they are "glosses which aim to explain the significance of the names of the trigrams and hexagrams, and also to inform the diviner of the established mantic associations of various animals, articles, and phenomena with certain trigrams and hexagrams" (p. 161).

One of the chief advances in our knowledge of early Chinese cosmology concerns just how these "established mantic associations" were understood. We now understand the established mantic associations of the *Shuo-kua* text as an aspect of "correlative thought." Such an understanding of the text of the *Shuo-kua chuan* allows us to place it within the context of a general cosmological scheme of explanation current in late Chou philosophical texts.

Since in the previous chapter he has shown that there is no necessary connection between the Ten Wing texts, in chapter 3, "Differentiation by Techniques of Thinking," Shchutskii attempts to outline the conceptual process by which the basic text and Ten Wings did in fact come into existence. His first point is that the basic text (the mantic terms *yüan-heng li-cheng*, the line texts, and the hexagram texts) is not really composed of *terms*, since terms imply precise definition. This layer of the text is composed, rather, of *images* which have the possibility of integrating several Chinese characters *in composita*, as well as great flexibility in correlating various artistic, poetic, or mantic images to one image. Thus the line and hexagram texts developed, not by the construction of accurate terms expressing concepts, but by ideas invested in verbal images.

The next stage came about through the necessity to interpret these symbolic images, which for Shchutskii was the only reason that the ancient commentatory literature came to life. For this stage of interpretation, thinking had to take a step forward in the direction of conceptual elaboration. Conceptual elaboration of images eventually took the direction of ethical judgment; this stage is characterized by the development of the true commentaries, the *Ta-hsiang chuan, Hsiao-hsiang chuan*, and the *T'uan chuan*. But this stage is also characterized as basically unsystematic and thus arose the need for a systematic world view. This is found in the *Great Treatise* and the first three chapters of the *Shuo-kua chuan*. The final stage in Shchutskii's development of the basic text and Ten Wings is the *Hsü-kua chuan* which returns to the original hexagram images and integrates them into a higher order.

This chapter is certainly provocative and demonstrates the boldness on Iulian Shchutskii's part to tackle a very difficult subject. More recent research by Hellmut Wilhelm has tended to confirm Shchutskii's hypotheses on this point, but Dr. Wilhelm's observations show that the conceptual elaboration of the line text images occurs within the line texts themselves.[25] Thus if both Shchutskii and Wilhelm are correct in their suppositions, the Ten Wings are a later "mirror" of processes already started in the line texts themselves.

In chapters 4 and 5 Shchutskii discusses the language of the *Book of Changes*. The results of chapters 3 and 4 must be seen as converging evidence yielding the same conclusions. Shchutskii argues that a very precise "profile" of the grammatical auxiliaries of the basic text can be put together which will

25. Hellmut Wilhelm, "The Interplay of Image and Concept," in *Heaven, Earth, and Man*, p. 211.

allow for the chronological coordination of the divisions of the basic text. For Shchutskii these divisions correlate exactly with the divisions of the thought processes he observes in the text. That is, the three divisions of the basic text (the mantic formulae, line texts, and hexagram texts) are more similar to one another than to any of the texts of the Ten Wings, both in language and types of thought. The conclusions he reaches from this line of argument are that the date of the composition of the basic text is no later than the seventh century B.C. and the date of the Ten Wings can be no earlier than the fifth century B.C.

The fifth chapter in Part II represents the first attempt to build upon and utilize the very important study of early Chinese dialects as reflected in the *Tso-chuan* and *Lun-yü* made by Bernard Karlgren in 1926.[26] Shchutskii applies the same methodology to the *Book of Changes* as did Karlgren to the *Tso-chuan*. He then correlates his results with the linguistic profile of the *Shih-ching* and concludes not only that the language of the *Book of Changes* is rather close to the *Shih-ching*, but that it is most closely associated with "Kuo-feng" section of the *Shih-ching*, tentatively considered by scholars to be the last section to enter the collection.

Chapters 6 and 7 deal with problems of dating the various parts of the *Book of Changes*. On the basis of his own research in chapters 1 through 6, Shchutskii unites the texts of the *Book of Changes* in the following order,

1) First layer of the basic text (its sources are lost in the inadequately documented past).

2) Second layer of the basic text (in language it is a younger contemporary of the "Kuo-feng," or a work of the following generation or generations).

3) The third layer of the basic text, with the exception of interpolations, is close to the second.

4) The most ancient citations in the *Wen-yen chuan*.

26. Bernard Karlgren, "On the Authenticity and Nature of the Tso chuan," *Goteborgs Hogskolas Arskrift* 32, 3 (1926).

5) *Ta-hsiang chuan.*

6) *T'uan-chuan.*

7) *Hsiao-hsiang chuan.*

8) *Hsi-tz'u chuan,* the first three paragraphs of the *Shuo-kua chuan,* and the *Hsü-kua chuan.*

9) *Shuo-kua chuan* beginning with the fourth paragraph, the glosses of the *Wen-yen chuan,* and the *Tsa-kua chuan* (p. 185).

Through an exhaustive analysis of social terminology found in the *Book of Changes,* Shchutskii concludes that the book is not only a document of feudal literature, but a book belonging only to the upper classes. Shchutskii examines sixteen instances of the use of the *Book of Changes* as recorded in the *Tso-chuan* from the years 671 B.C. to 487 B.C. He observes that by the sixth quotation of the sixteen preserved in the *Tso-chuan* there is a rather obvious shift from the use of the *I Ching* as a divinatory manual for the upper classes to a text containing philosophical significance. From this he concludes:

> Only in 602 B.C. was the *Book of Changes* not used for divination; it is referred to as a doctrine containing a certain world view. Further, although it remains a text intended for divination, more and more perceptibly there appears the tendency to use it, with the help of a judgmental faculty, for explaining the world and the phenomena which occur in it. Thus during the sixth and fifth centuries B.C. the *Book of Changes,* while preserving its mantic significance, comes to be understood as a philosophical text. (p. 193)

Following the observation of the Japanese scholar Endō Ryūkichi that the basic text contains no terminology taken from the sea, Shchutskii concludes that the text evolved in an agricultural environment in Western China.

> Thus the basic text of the *Book of Changes* is originally a divinatory and subsequently a philosophical text which took shape from the materials of agricultural folklore in the Chin or Ch'in territories between the eighth and seventh centuries B.C. (p. 195)

Chapters 8 and 9 of Shchutskii's study are concerned with the various commentary schools of the *Book of Changes.* In chapter 8, he outlines the history of these commentatory schools up through the Sung dynasty. The first period is the sixth century B.C. to the first century A.D. which he calls the "classical period." It was during this period that the Ten Wings were written. The second period lasted from the second century A.D. to the fifth century A.D. and was characterized by what Shchutskii calls the "mantic school of commentators." The emphasis in this period was upon divination rather than philosophical speculation, although there were some exceptions to this general trend. In this period the main scholars were Wang Pi, Han K'ang-po, and Cheng Hsüan; they were influenced to some extent by the development of religious Taoism and its concern with alchemical symbolism. The third period of Buddhist scholasticism, from the eighth century to the tenth century, influences the fourth period— the Sung Neo-Confucian school which cannot be separated from the *I Ching*.

Shchutskii concludes chapter 8 with long quotations on *yüan-heng li-cheng* by eight different commentators from the Han to the sixteenth century Buddhist Wan-yi to demonstrate how the *I Ching* was understood differently at different times.

In chapter 9 Shchutskii divides these eight commentators into two distinct types of interpretation: the traditional school composed of K'ung Ying-ta, Ch'eng Yi-ch'uan, and Chu Hsi, and a critical school composed of Ou-yang Hsiu, Tiao Pao, and Itō Tōgai.

Shchutskii also points out that certain commentators seem to favor one or another of the Ten Wings and indeed their commentaries are often written either in the same style or in imitation of one of the Ten Wings. An excellent example of this is Wang Pi's interest in the *Great Treatise*. And since the Sung school was greatly interested in Wang Pi's interpretations, he then becomes a link from the *Great Treatise*, as opposed to other possibilities among the Ten Wings, to the Sung school. On p. 211, Shchutskii provides a chart illustrating other lines of development from the original Ten

Wings through the main *I Ching* commentators down to P'i Hsi-jui.

In chapter 10, "Influence on Chinese Philosophy" Shchutskii argues that the Confucian school did not accept the *Book of Changes* as part of its canon until the Han scholar Chia Yi became interested in it, sometime between 213 and 168 B.C. After that time the Confucian school was much more influenced by the *I Ching* than the Taoist or Buddhist schools. Shchutskii briefly discusses the two main Han dynasty influences of the *I Ching*—the *T'ai-hsüan ching* 太玄經 or *Classic of the Great Mystery* by Yang Hsiung and the *Chou I ts'an-t'ung-ch'i* 周易參同契 or *On the Reuniting of the Three Equals [from the point of view of]* the *Chou Book of Changes* attributed to Wei Po-yang.

Chapter 11, "Problems in Translating the Book, provides more than the chapter title would indicate. Shchutskii discusses not only the many problems in translating the *I Ching* into any Western language, but provides us with a set of presuppositions upon which he built his own translation. He feels that the text should be translated twice: first, a strict philological translation which only mirrors the sinological development of the period in which it is made; second, an interpretive translation should be made from the point of view of the oral tradition and its understanding in China and Japan. From the point of view of the present oral tradition in the Far East, Shchutskii gives rather high marks to Richard Wilhelm:

Consequently, the *Book of Changes* should be translated twice. However, the interpretive translation from the point of view of the present oral tradition has already been completed by Richard Wilhelm. Thus there is no need to repeat his work, in spite of the errors he tolerated. (p. 224)

Shchutskii's own interpretive translation was not, however, made from the point of view of the present oral tradition. He based his interpretation on the work of three scholars: Wang Pi, the Buddhist Wan I, and the Japanese scholar Itō Tōgai.

In this respect he spanned three rather divergent schools, but the result led to a perhaps more general, more all-encompassing, interpretation of the text than one based entirely upon the Sung school. The presuppositions of his interpretive translation are interesting because they reveal how Shchutskii understood the book; they deserve to be quoted at length:

> Each hexagram is a symbol of some life situation which develops in time. Each text to a hexagram is a short characterization of this situation, basically or completely. Each text to a line is a concrete characterization of some stage in the development of the given situation. With this, one must take into account that in the view of the authors' level of thinking and language techniques, such characterizations almost never are expressed in the form of precise ideas. The elements of the *Book of Changes* are elements of imagery. (p. 226)
>
> ... As was pointed out above, the texts to individual lines narrate the sequence of the situation's development. The first position characterizes only the very beginning of the given process, when it still has not appeared with all its typicality. The second position characterizes the apogee of the internal development of the given situation, just as the fifth position is the maximal exposure of it in the outside. The third position characterizes the moment of crisis, the transition from internal to external.
>
> ... The fourth position characterized the beginning of the appearance of the given situation in the outside. Thus it is as little typical as the first. However, it is favorably influenced by the proximity of the fifth position. Thus the aphorisms to the fourth are not as gloomy as the preceding. The fifth position has already been mentioned in connection with the second position. The sixth position is the completion or overdevelopment of the process of the given situation, in which it either loses its typicality or turns into its opposite. (pp. 226–227)

This long quotation is interesting in that it suggests in Shchutskii an unconscious bias toward the trigram method of interpretation. That is, he considers the fifth line more or less a repeat of the second line. In another interpretation, the hexagram interpretation, the first and sixth lines are essentially "outside the time," and lines two through five are a continuum of development culminating in the fifth line. The trigram interpretation relies upon the component trigrams, and sometimes the hidden nuclear trigrams *hu-kua* 互卦 , while the hexagram interpretation relies upon the hexagram as an organic whole. Both interpretations are found in the Ten Wings.

Shchutskii concludes this provocative chapter with what he considers to be seven basic presuppositions of the world view of the *Great Treatise* commentary of the Ten Wings; these also deserve special attention:

(*a*) the world is both change and immutability and, what is more, the natural unity of them; (*b*) at the basis of this lies the polarity which runs through the world, the antipodes of which are as opposed to each other as they are attracted to each other; in their relationship appears the world movement like a rhythm; (*c*) thanks to the rhythm, that which has been established and that which has not yet been established unite into one system, according to which the future already exists in the present as a "sprout" of coming events; (*d*) both the theoretical understanding and the practical realization of this are necessary and, if the activity of a person is thus normal, then he harmoniously takes part in his environment; (*e*) thus is excluded the conflict of internal and external, and they only contribute to the development of each other by the fact that the internal is defined by the external and is creative in the external; (*f*) in this way the personality devotes sufficient attention to itself and to the society around it, and being satisfied with its position, finds the possibility of higher forms of creation, creation of the good and not just the fulfillment of any copybook morality; (*g*) thus, thanks to the sustaining unity of abstraction and concreteness, the full flexibility of the system is achieved. (p. 228)

In his final chapter Shchutskii examines the place of the *Book of Changes* in artistic literature. He translates six poems, including two from the great Sung philosopher Chu Hsi. Shchutskii, with a studied understatement, points out that the lyrics devoted to the *I Ching* are not the best verses in the treasure house of Chinese poetry. But the point remains that the *I Ching* became part of the poetic corpus in the Chinese literary heritage. Shchutskii's translations show, at the very least, that there were philosophers who thought highly enough of the *I Ching* to tolerate bad poetry.

Yet the best part of this chapter is the translation of an important eleventh century essay by Su Hsün, father of Su Tung-p'o, on the *I Ching*. This essay deserves a commentary of its own, but the ideas in it represent what a well-educated Chinese intellectual thought of the *I Ching* in the eleventh century. If we compare the first few chapters of the *Great Treatise* with Su Hsün's essay we can easily see the influence of the *Great Treatise* upon his essay. The difference in time between the two is approximately thirteen centuries. Thus Shchutskii is entirely correct in his earlier observation of the tremendous influence of the *Great Treatise* on every subsequent period of Chinese thought.

And I feel that Shchutskii is correct on a good deal more than just the influence of the *Great Treatise*; many of his conclusions will be accepted. Although there will be criticisms made, I think it is fair to say that none of them could have been made at the time his study was written. The only major point the present writer has against this work is really a criticism of Konrad rather than Shchutskii. Konrad tried to justify Shchutskii's choice of Chang Hsüeh-ch'eng and P'i Hsi-jui by rejecting both the mainstream of Ch'ing scholarship on the *I Ching* and the European translations that came from them:

Knowledge of the extensive Chinese literature on the *I Ching* allowed Shchutskii to avoid the usual path of European translators of the *I Ching* and even of Chinese classical literature in general. Translators of these classics appeared in the eighteenth and nineteenth centuries. The best of the translators prepared their translations in China. This was Ch'ing China, feudal China of the absolute Manchu regime. We know what was the status of classical philology in China at that time. The Manchu government, especially during the K'ang-hsi and Ch'ien-lung reign periods had learned very well the significance of ideology and understood that traditional Confucianism could be a serious ideological support for an absolute regime if Confucian thought was assigned to corresponding channels and surrounded by explanatory literature. This was even more important because within Confucianism was hidden also the ideological opposition which operated with the same concepts, positions, and ideas as that line which took place between these two lines and we also know what measures were taken by the government so that the protective line of Confucianism was always superior. Thus the European sinologues of the eighteenth and nineteenth centuries working in China dealt mainly with the literature which offered an approach to the classics. In this very way they fell under the influence of a certain, in any case limited, line of philosophical thought. (pp. lvii–lviii)

This is perhaps suitable for a Russian audience, but I think it needlessly politicizes the effect of Ch'ing scholarship upon the classics. For even if Konrad is right, which is doubtful, this does not alter the fact that Ch'ing scholars produced much that would have interested Shchutskii on the problems and questions to which he chose to address himself. Our criticism is not with Shchutskii; we are certainly grateful that he did choose Chang Hsüeh-ch'eng and P'i Hsi-jui, if only because these thinkers *did* stand outside the main Ch'ing line of *I Ching* scholarship. Our criticism, rather, is with Konrad who suggests that, because of political reasons, the leading Ch'ing scholars on the *I Ching* were not worthy of consideration.

But who, then, were the main-line Ch'ing scholars of the *I Ching*? Chiang Fan lists Hu Wei, Chang Erh-ch'i, Hui Shih-ch'i, Hui Tung, Chang Hui-yen, Ku Yen-wu, and Huang Tsung-hsi as outstanding scholars of the Han school who contributed works on the *I*.[27] Liang Ch'i-ch'ao concludes that the most important of the Ch'ing *I Ching* scholars were Hui Tung, Chang Hui-yen, and Chiao Hsün.[28] It is the opinion of

27. See Chiang Fan 江藩 , *Han-hsüeh shih-ch'eng chi* 漢學師承記 (rpt. Taiwan, 1974), under the chapter for each scholar named.

28. See Liang Ch'i-ch'ao 梁啓超 , *Chung-kuo chin-san pai-nien hsüeh-shu shih* 中國近三百年學術史 (rpt. Shanghai: *Min chih*, 1916), pp. 286–89. In his *Ch'ing-tai hsüeh-shu kai-lun* 清代學術概論 he selects Hui Tung, Chang Hui-yen, and Yao P'ei-chung. See Liang Ch'i-ch'ao, *Intellectual Trends in the Ch'ing Period*, trans. Immanuel C. Y. Hsü (Cambridge: Harvard Univ. Press, 1959) bibliography, p. iv.

the present writer that if Konrad's account of Ch'ing scholarship on the *I Ching* is allowed to stand, we have a very distorted view of the contributions of the leading *I Ching* scholars of the last dynasty. It is important, therefore, to consider the larger picture of Ch'ing dynasty scholarship on the *I Ching*.

I Ching Scholarship during the Ch'ing Dynasty (1644–1911)

The following pages provide a brief overview of trends and achievements in *I Ching* scholarship in recent centuries that remained beyond the ken of Iulian Shchutskii. The treatment is necessarily selective. A complete bibliography of works on the *I Ching* during the Ch'ing period would involve thousands of entries. We shall therefore limit ourselves to the most important scholars and then consider only their best works.

Huang Tsung-hsi 黃宗羲 (1610–1695) and his brother Huang Tsung-yen 黃宗炎 (1616–1686)[29] were the first of the Ch'ing scholars to question the antiquity of the *Lo-shu* and *Ho-t'u* charts of the Sung philosophers. See also Huang Tsung-hsi, *Essay on I Ching Numerology* (*I hsüeh hsiang-shu lun* 易學象數論) in six *chüan*. Huang Tsung-yen's most important works are *Image Terms in the Book of Changes* (*Chou I hsiang-tz'u* 周易象辭) in twenty-one *chüan* and his *Reappraisal of I Ching Charts* (*T'u-shu pien-huo* 圖書辨惑) in one *chüan*. These two works are included under the title *A Study of the Book of Changes in Times of Anxiety* (*Yu-huan hsüeh I* 憂患學易). In his *Supplementary Notes to an Inquiry on the Book of Changes* (*Hsün-men yü-lun* 尋門餘論) 1.28a, which is a supplement to his major work, *Chou-i hsiang tz'u*, Huang Tsung-yen includes several essays on the etymologies of key characters in the *I Ching* system: "*Kua* 卦 does not mean *kua* 掛, 'to take or place yarrow stalks between the fingers' as maintained by K'ung Ying-ta. Rather *kua* follows *pu* 卜 for its meaning and takes

29. For Huang Tsung-hsi's biography, see Hummel, *Eminent Chinese*, pp. 351, 354.

its sound from *kua* 圭 ." He has also written similar essays on "line texts" (*yao* 爻), "hexagram texts" (*t'uan* 彖), "images" (*hsiang* 象), "good fortune" (*chi* 吉), "bad fortune" (*hsiung* 兇), "regret" (*hui* 悔), "milfoil" (*shih* 筮) and "nothingness" (*wu* 无).

Chang Erh-ch'i 張爾岐 (1612–1678) is chiefly known for his studies of the *Book of Etiquette* (*I-li*) which, in the opinion of Hellmut Wilhelm, "ranks even today as one of the best treatments of that classic." [30] His major *I Ching* work, *Summary Discussions on the Book of Changes* (*Chou I shuo lüeh* 周易 說略) in six *chüan*, is a paraphrase of the *I*. The preface to this book is in part a paraphrase of the *Great Treatise*, but written in the style of Mencius. Chang's work is important to historians of religion. He was interested in the metaphysical relationship between *li*, ceremony, and the world order. He also has an interesting theory of human relations showing how an accumulation of words and thoughts can influence situations.

Ku Yen-wu 顧炎武 (1613–1682) is seen as the founder of the "*Han-hsüeh*" school of the Ch'ing. Fang Chao-ying has this to say about him:

In their search for new evidence the Ch'ing classicists discovered that scholars of the Han dynasty had studied the ancient texts successfully without benefit of *Li-hsüeh* and that, having fewer metaphysical preconceptions, they had no need to "resort to vague generalizations to cover up their intellectual poverty." A study of the views of Han scholars, being "not far from antiquity," presumably had a firmer grasp on the ancient texts. Because of this emphasis on Han commentaries the school which arose under Ku Yen-wu's influence came later to be known as the "School of Han Learning" (*Han-hsüeh p'ai* 漢學派) and the type of scholarship which it espoused came to be designated *Han-hsüeh*, to differentiate it from the *Sung-hsüeh* mentioned above. [31]

Ku Yen-wu is noted mostly for his *Phonological Study of the Book of Changes* (*I yin* 易音), which was included in the *Huang*

30. *Ibid.*, p. 35.
31. *Ibid.*, p. 423.

Ch'ing ching-chieh. In his *Notes in a Daily Acquisition of Knowledge* (*Jih-chih lu* 日知錄), are essays on the *San-i* 三易 , that is, the *Lien-shan, Kuei-tsang,* and *Chou-i.* Ku argues that the *Lien-shan* and *Kuei-tsang* have nothing to do with the *I*—any more than one could suppose that simply because a book like *Mo-tzu* mentions a *ch'un-chiu* from *Chou, Sung, Yen,* and *Ch'i,* that they were in fact the *Ch'un-ch'iu* of *Lu.* One of his essays argues that Wen Wang did not double the trigrams. Ku also discusses why Confucius never talked about the *I Ching.* Most of his essays discuss passages from the Ten Wings, especially the *Great Treatise.*

Wang Fu-chih 王夫之 (1619–1692)[32] is probably the most powerful writer on the *I Ching* in the entire Ch'ing period. He was not a member of the *Han-hsüeh* group, but was deeply influenced by Chang Tsai of the Sung. Hellmut Wilhelm says this about Wang Fu-chih's cosmological system:

> His premise is an ordered continuum of existence, which is governed by laws and is all-embracing. This continuum "lacks appearance"— that is, it is not immediately accessible to sense perception. But through the dynamism inherent in existence, images are differentiated out of the continuum; they are, in a sense, individuations of this continuum. On the one hand, these images—that is, the sixty-four situations of the *Book of Changes*—can be perceived and experienced; on the other hand, as embodiments of the law and thereby governed by it, they are open to theoretical speculation. With this they enter into the field of numbers and may be numerically structured and ordered as objects of theory governed by law.[33]

Wang Fu-chih's *Prolegomena to an Esoteric Commentary on the Book of Changes* (*Chou I nei-chuan fa-li* 周易內傳發例) in one *chüan,* is a series of speculative essays on various *I Ching* topics. In all some twenty-four separate topics are discussed, including the following: "Prognosticating for the present while searching for the *wei-yen* 微言 'profoundly subtle' words of Fu (Hsi) and

32. *Ibid.,* p. 817.
33. Hellmut Wilhelm, *Heaven, Earth and Man,* p. 11.

Wen (Wang)"; "The *I* is an oracle book and the doing of this did not wait for the words of Wang Pi!"; "On the one *Tao* in the divinations bequeathed by the *I Ching* to the ten-thousand generations"; "On the constancy of good fortune which comes from being in the appropriate place and the bad fortune which comes from being in the wrong place"; "On the *I* as a subject for scholarship"; "Difficult things to understand about the *I*"; "The unity of the six classics comes from their orthodox determination by Chu Hsi"; "On the method of separating the milfoil."

Wang Fu-chih's *Explication of the Great Image Commentary* (*Chou I ta-hsiang chieh* 周易大象解) is perhaps the best commentary on this text. His most important work is probably *A Critical Explication of the Book of Changes* (*Chou I pai-shu* 周易稗疏). *An Esoteric Commentary on the Book of Changes* (*Chou I nei-chuan* 周易內傳) and his *Exoteric Commentary on the Book of Changes* (*Chou I wai-chuan* 周易外傳) in six and seven *chüan* respectively, are both important works.

Hui Tung 惠棟 (1697–1758) has written several important works on the *I Ching*.[34] *The Essence of the Book of Changes* (*I ta-i* 易大義) in one *chüan* is a speculative essay on the general significance of the *I*. It is essentially an attempt to relate the *I Ching* to the Confucian school through the metaphors and concepts of the *Chung-yung*. *A Discourse on the Book of Changes* (*Chou I shu* 周易述) in twenty-three *chüan*, a work not completed by Hui Tung before his death, consists of a commentary to the basic text and Ten Wings. The last section of the book, entitled "Profound Terms in the *I*" (*I wei-yen* 易微言), contains Hui Tung's explanation of the forty-one technical terms of the *I Ching* literature. In this work[35] Hui Tung explains *heng* by quoting the phrase as it occurs in the *t'uan* commentary for Hexagram 63, "The hard and soft are *cheng* 正 "correct" while the six positions *tang* 當 "match."[36] In using this method

34. Hummel, p. 357.
35. *Huang Ch'ing ching chieh* ed. 330.la.
36. Wilhelm/Baynes, p. 710.

to explain the term *heng* he is following the Han master Fei Chih by using the *chuan* to explain the classic. In this explanatory technique, which Shchutskii explicitly rejects, the *ching*, or basic text, is explained in terms of metaphors used in the *chuan*, or Ten Wing commentaries. Thus Fei Chih and Hui Tung presuppose a continuity between the classic and its commentatory literature such that the ideas which are finally spelled out in the later commentaries are implicit in the earlier classic.

His other works include *Exemplary Essays on the Book of Changes* (*I li* 易例) in two *chüan* and *Han Studies on the Book of Changes* (*I Han-hsüeh* 易漢學) in eight *chüan*. *I Han-hsüeh* is an important attempt at writing a history of Han dynasty *I Ching* scholarship and has influenced Kao Huai-min and Suzuki Yoshijirō.

Chang Hui-yen 張惠言 (1761–1802) is one of the major *Han-hsüeh* scholars.[37] His *Interpretation of the I Ching Studies of Yü Fan* (ca. A.D. 164–233 [*Chou I Yü-shih i* 周易虞氏義]) in nine *chüan*, is a reconstruction of Yü Fan's theories on the *I Ching*. He has done a similar study of Hsün Shuang (A.D. 128–190) and the so-called Nine Masters of the Han (*Hsün-shih chiu-chia i* 荀氏九家義) in one *chüan*. This work contains twelve essays on different terms in Han dynasty *I Ching* theories. Chang Hui-yen's other works include: *The Essentials of the I Ching Studies of Cheng Hsüan* (A.D. 127–200 [*Chou I Cheng-shih i* 周易鄭氏義]) in two *chüan*—an explication of Cheng Hsüan's theories on the *I Ching*. In his *Additional Observations on I Ching Interpretation* (*I i pieh-lu* 易義別錄) Chang Hui-yen pulls together all there is to be known about fourteen Han *I Ching* masters. This important work contains a collection of Meng Hsi's surviving fragments on the basic text and Ten Wings followed by a reconstruction of his theory of *kua-ch'i* 卦氣 . There is also a similar treatment for Yao Hsin 姚信 in addition to a short preliminary essay of nineteen lines.

---

37. Hummel, p. 42.

Yü Fan's Remarks on the Book of Changes (*Yü-shih I yen* 虞氏 易言) and *Yü Fan's I Ching Cedules* (*Yü shih I hou*虞氏易侯) are commentaries on Yü Fan's collected fragments up through Hexagram 50, and a series of short essays on topics from the hexagrams. Chang's *Item by Item Explication of the I Ching Diagrams* (*I t'u t'iao-pien* 易圖條辨) is a reconstruction of all that is known about the *ho-t'u* and *lo-shu* and related charts. This is the best work on the subject up to his time. In his *Human Import of Yü Fan's I Ching Studies* (*Yü-shih I shih*虞氏易事) in two *chüan*, Chang Hui-yen presents a series of longer essays on the fragments contained in the *Yü-shih I yen*. He seems to enlarge on the political topics in this work.

Chiao Hsün 焦循 (1763–1820) was the first Ch'ing scholar to apply the principles of mathematics to the *Book of Changes*.[38] Three of his main works are included in the *Huang Ch'ing ching-chieh*: *A Reading Commentary on the I Ching* (*I chang-chü* 易章句) in twelve *chüan*; *A Brief Study of I Ching Diagrams* (*I t'u lüeh* 易圖略) in eight *chüan* and *Comprehensive Explanations on the I Ching* (*I t'ung-shih* 易通釋) in twenty *chüan*. The *I t'ung-shih* is an enormous work containing over 191 separate essays in the first fifteen *chüan*. The first *chüan* of this book is devoted to *yüan-heng li-cheng*. He points out that *heng* occurs forty times in the hexagram texts and three times in the line texts and discusses each occurrence.

Other *I Ching* scholars of the Ch'ing who merit more attention than this brief survey can give are Mao Ch'i-ling (1623–1716)[39] and his thirty *chüan Chung-shih's Studies on the Book of Changes* (*Chung-shih I* 仲氏易); Hu Wei (1633–1714)[40] and his *Clear Explications of I Ching Diagrams* (*I t'u ming-pien* 易圖明辨); Li Kuang-ti (1642–1718)[41] the editor of the imperial edition *Chou I che-chung* 周易折中 (*A Synthesis of I Ching Interpretations*) of 1715—the text used by both Legge

38. *Ibid.*, p. 144.
39. *Ibid.*, p. 563.
40. *Ibid.*, p. 335.
41. *Ibid.*, p. 473.

and Richard Wilhelm; Hui Shih-chi 惠士奇 (1671–1741),[42] father of Hui Tung and his *Discussions on the I* (*I shuo* 易說) in six *chüan*.

But why did Shchutskii neglect so much of the *I Ching* scholarship of the last three hundred years? Shchutskii selected his commentators on the basis of the views they held upon a single question: the question of Confucian authorship of the *I Ching*. But we have seen earlier that Shchutskii rejects nearly all the conclusions of his commentators. The value of his commentators, then, is to provide the material for the questions in which he was interested. Secondary questions, such as the meaning of *yüan-heng li-cheng*, questions on the lore associated with the *Lien-shan* and *Kuei-tsang* texts, and the notion of an image theory of meaning all come to Shchutskii's attention through the essays of his commentators, primarily Chang Hsüeh-ch'eng and P'i Hsi-jui. But in the essays examined above, there is more basic information on the subjects in which Shchutskii was interested, plus many more critical questions of which Shchutskii seems totally unaware, than in the essays of the commentators he did use, selected because of their critical nature. Thus Ku Yen-wu's essays on the *Lien-shan* and *Kuei-tsang* would have interested Shchutskii, if for no other reason than that there is more basic information in them on this question than Shchutskii otherwise had access to, even from the best of his commentators. Wang Fu-chih's speculations upon an image theory of meaning, in the opinion of the present writer, are far more penetrating than those of Chang Hsüeh-ch'eng. And the views of Wang Fu-chih, Hui Tung, and Chiao Hsün on the problem of *yüan-heng li-cheng*, at the very least, contain much more basic information than the essays of P'i Hsi-jui on the same subject. Thus Shchutskii would have been very interested in the essays and speculations of the main *I Ching* scholars of the past three hundred years if only because they would have provided him with more lore asso-

---

42. *Ibid.*, p. 356.

ciated with the *I Ching*, even if he was forced to reject the
significance these scholars saw in that lore. Also the essays by
the main *I Ching* scholars of the past three hundred years would
have demonstrated to Shchutskii just how vast is this lore and,
despite Shchutskii's own thorough scholarship amounting to
two volumes and seven hundred pages, how much he merely
scratched the surface.

It is very important for an evaluation of Shchutskii that he
seems (see p. 22) to agree with Konrad that Chinese scholarship
of the past three hundred years, with the possible exception of
two or three scholars, was the product of a decadent age and
thus not worth consideration. It is difficult to say, especially in
light of Poppe's insistence upon Shchutskii's political indifference, whether Shchutskii actually held this view or whether
Konrad was merely trying to rationalize Shchutskii's choice of
commentators. The political interpretation, for that matter,
might have ultimately issued either from Alekseev or from
political necessities of the Leningrad group of Soviet sinology
to maintain their own continuity. For his part Shchutskii
makes a very strong distinction between historical fact and
myth and criticizes Richard Wilhelm for confusing the two.
It seems more likely, in the view of the present writer, that
Shchutskii chose the commentators he did on the basis that
they were supposedly closer to historical fact (and less interested
in the mythic dimensions surrounding the *I Ching*) rather than
on the basis of political considerations.

Works on the I Ching since the Ch'ing

Shchutskii's is one of those few works of merit since the
Ch'ing, but there are other post-Ch'ing scholars not discussed
by Shchutskii who deserve to be studied. We could certainly
suggest Liu Pai-min 劉百閔 ' *A Comprehensive Interpretation of
the Book of Changes* (*Chou I shih-li t'ung-i* 周易事理通義 [Tai-
pei: Hsüeh pu chüan chai, 1965]). This is probably the best of
the modern commentaries on the basic text and Ten Wings.

To support his interpretations Liu quotes Chou and Han philosophical literature with enormous erudition. His work is especially helpful to students of the *Great Treatise* Commentary
of the Ten Wings.

Continuing in the tradition of the great *I Han-hsüeh* of Hui
Tung are Suzuki Yoshijirō 鈴木由次郎, *Research on Han
Dynasty Studies of the Book of Changes* (*Kaneki kenkyū* 漢易研究
[Tokyo: Meitoku Shuppansha, 1963]), with English summary,
and Kao Huai-min 高懷民, *A History of I Ching Studies in the
Han Dynasty* (*Liang-Han i-hsüeh shih* 兩漢易學史 [Taipei:
Tung-wu ta-hsüeh chu-tso chiang-chu wei-yüan hui, 1970]). Also
see Kao's recent *Hsien Ch'in i-hsüeh shih* 先秦易學史. (Taipei:
*Tung-wu ta-hsüeh, chung-kuo hsüeh-shu chu-tso chiang-chu wei-
yüan hui*, 1975). Suzuki's book is a good deal more detailed,
primarily because of two large sections on the *Forest of I Ching
Interpretations by Chiao Yen-shou* (*Chiao-shih i-lin* 焦氏易林)
and the *Chou I ts'an t'ung ch'i* 周易參同契. The appearance of
these excellent works now provide most of the information
necessary to produce a history of Han dynasty *I Ching* studies
in English.[43]

For a philological study of the hexagram and line texts see
Kao Heng 高亨, *A Modern Annotation on the Ancient Classic of
the Book of Changes* (*Chou I ku-ching chin-chu* 周易古經今注
[Shanghai: *K'ai-ming shu-tien*, 1947]), p. 230. Kao Heng is
trying to get back to the original meaning of the basic text.[44]
A smaller study of the same nature, but an excellent work, is
Gerhard Schmitt, "*Sprüche der Wandlungen*" *auf ihrem geistes-
geschichtlichen Hintergrund*. Deutsche Akademie der Wissen-
schaften, Berlin: Institut für Orientforschung, no. 76 (Berlin:

43. For an excellent example of the use of Han *I Ching* material see Ch'en
Ch'i-yün 陳啓雲, "A Confucian Magnate's Idea of Political Violence: Hsün
Shuang's (A.D. 128–190) Interpretation of the *Book of Changes*," *T'oung-Pao*,
series 2, vol. 54 (1968), pp. 73–115.

44. Nathan Sivin, in his review of John Blofeld's translation of the *I Ching*,
provides a very interesting "tentative Reconstruction of Primitive Sense" of
Hexagram 36. He draws upon Kao Heng, Li Ching-ch'ih, and Arthur Waley.
See Nathan Sivin, *HJAS* 26 (1966), 290–98.

Akademie Verlag, 1970). An interesting study would translate some of Kao Heng's and Gerhard Schmitt's reconstructions and compare the results with Wilhelm/Baynes.

One of the most valuable pieces of Chinese scholarship on the *I Ching* since the Ch'ing dynasty is Ku Chieh-kang 顧頡剛 , ed., *Discussion on Ancient History and Philosophy (Ku shih pien* 古史辨 , vol. III [Peiping: *P'u-she*, 1931]). Ch'ien Mu 錢穆 and Li Ching ch'ih 李鏡池 have written essays in the *Ku-shih pien* maintaining that the Ten Wings were not written by Confucius. Ch'ien Mu has ten arguments, some of which were noticed by Shchutskii, others of which were not. Thus Ch'ien Mu cites the same *Tso-chuan* passage as does Shchutskii to show that the divination formulae *yüan-heng li-cheng*, as found in the *Wen-yen chuan*, existed before Confucius. Ku Chieh-kang has written an important essay on five pre-Chou historical citations found in the line texts of the *I Ching*. In the case of the King Hai story, the significance of Ku Chieh-kang's essay is particularly important. Since this story was not known to the commentators used by Legge and R. Wilhelm, they translated the passage according to the ordinary meanings of the characters.

Following in his father's tradition, Hellmut Wilhelm has produced much of what our generation knows about the *Book of Changes*.[45] His major works are two sets of *Vorträge*, or lectures. The first set of lectures, delivered in German to friends and scholars in Peking during World War II, was translated into English by Cary Baynes in 1960.[46] Since that time the

45. Demieville has this to say about Hellmut Wilhelm:

Shchutskii could not have known the works of the presently best Occidental specialist of the *I Ching*, Hellmut Wilhelm; they surely would have interested him. Notably, he would have found a critical analysis of the "oracles" of the *I Ching* which are mentioned in the *Tso chuan* and the *Kuo yü*. Those of the *Tso chuan* (16 instances from 671–487 B.C.) are studied by Shchutskii. One can less explain why he doesn't mention, on the same subject, the later study by Li Ching-ch'ih, dated 1930, and published in 1931 in the *Ku shih pien*, Vol. III. (pp. 266–278)

46. Hellmut Wilhelm, *Die Wandlung: Acht Vortrage zum I-Ging* (Peking:

xlv

"Eight Lectures," as they have come to be known, have been read in conjunction with his father's translation. They are, in a very real sense, the place where one starts.[47]

Hellmut Wilhelm's second set of seven *Vorträge* was given in the famous Eranos Meetings established by Olga Fröbe-Kapteyn (1881–1962) in 1933. The set of seven lectures was given in German (except the last lecture, which was in English) over the years from 1951 to 1967. Each lecture lasted two hours, with an hour of questions. Unlike the audience for the lectures in Peking, the audience at the Eranos Meetings knew the *Book of Changes* very well and the interplay of audience and lecturer often produced a better final version than the one that was to have been read.[48]

Of the seven Eranos Lectures the most important for Shchutskii's interests are the first lecture, "The Concept of Time"; the second, "The Creative Principle"; and the last, "The Interplay of Image and Concept." In these lectures Wilhelm develops evidence for a set of conclusions which differ from Shchutskii's. In particular, the line texts are older than the hexagram texts. This is because the lines are seen to contain essentially three parts: an image, a concept, and a diviner's formulae, while the hexagram texts, with only two exceptions, contain only concepts—concepts which are shown to be later in development. Dr. Wilhelm develops the methodology for his approach from the Ten Wings, notably the *Ta-chuan* (*Great Treatise* [or *commentary*]).[49] There exist in that com-

---

Henri Vetch, 1944). English translation of this by Cary F. Baynes, *Change: Eight Lectures on the I Ching*, Bollingen Series LXII (New York: Pantheon Books, 1960. Paperback, New York: Harper Torchbooks, 1964; Princeton/Bollingen Paperback, 1973).

47. For Hellmut Wilhelm's bibliography, see his *Book of Changes in the Western Tradition: A Selective Bibliography*, *Parerga* 2 (Seattle: Univ. of Washington Press, 1975), p. 29.

48. These lectures have been translated and reprinted as Hellmut Wilhelm, *Heaven, Earth and Man*.

49. On the *Ta-chuan*, see Gerald W. Swanson, "The Great Treatise: Commentary to the *Book of Changes*." Diss. Univ. of Washington, 1974.

mentary in particular several confusing references to the notion of images and their creation by the legendary sages. These references were then organized into a coherent scheme and then compared with the line texts. From this he was able not only to reconstruct a hypothetical evolution of the line texts, but also to provide some insights into the development of consciousness itself, much as Erich Neumann had done with Western materials, but with different results and different conclusions.

Shchutskii realized that the lines developed through a stratified matrix of six stages and was able, from that, to determine the significance of a few of the difficult images. But the Eranos lectures demonstrate the overwhelming complexity of the line texts themselves, and these later developments have made Shchutskii's translation of the *Book of Changes* out of date.

In conclusion, the *Book of Changes* given to the West by Richard and Hellmut Wilhelm, C. G. Jung, and Cary Baynes is the best description of the *I Ching* as a phenomenon within Chinese culture.[50] The Wilhelm/Jung tradition in Western scholarship is concerned not only with the scholarly traditions, but also with the more important ultimate significance of the text as an aspect of world literature. And to what extent was Shchutskii concerned with the meaning of the text as an aspect of Chinese civilization? He comes closest in his own interpretive translation where he combines the understanding of Buddhist and Japanese commentaries. But Shchutskii's contribution is really his wealth of critical essays on the lore associated with the *I Ching*. We can only hope that with the material presented in this volume as an introduction to the standard English translation of the *Book of Changes*, in addition to the material provided by the Ch'ing scholars and the work done since

50. Also working in this tradition is Rudolf Ritsema, "Notes for Differentiating some Terms in the *I Ching*," *Spring*, 1970, pp. 111–25; "The Corrupted, A Study of the 18th Hexagram in the *I Ching*," *Spring*, 1972, pp. 90–109; and "The Pit and the Brilliance; A Study of the 29th and 30th Hexagrams of the *I Ching*," *Spring*, 1973, pp. 142–70.

Shchutskii, Western scholars who really hope to study Chinese thought can, through the *Book of Changes*, bridge the cosmological gulf that separates China and the West.

Gerald W. Swanson

Underhill Center, Vermont

Introduction to the Russian Edition

The present work was written by Iulian Konstantinovich Shchutskii between 1928 and 1935 and was defended by him in the Institute of Oriental Studies of the USSR Academy of Sciences as a dissertation for the degree of Doctor of Philology. The official examiners were acting members of the Academy of Sciences Vasilii Mikhailovich Alekseev and corresponding member of the Academy Nikolai Iosifovich Konrad. After the defense, the Academic Council unanimously accepted the dissertation for the doctorate.

Subsequently, the author rewrote his dissertation for publication and it was handed over to the Academy of Sciences Publishing House. However, it was not published during the author's lifetime, though a copy fully prepared and signed by the author was preserved. This last work, edited by Shchutskii, is now published in Russian with some deletions, about which more will be said below. Preparation of the work for publication was conducted by N. A. Petrov, a collaborator of the Leningrad section of the Institute of Peoples of Asia of the USSR Academy of Sciences, and N. I. Konrad was appointed editor of the volume.

Iu. K. Shchutskii came to his work on the *I Ching* in a complex way. Undertaking the study of ancient, and later also medieval, Chinese literature, Shchutskii devoted considerable attention to documents which reflected the development of philosophical thought. The Confucian line of this thought from the very beginning brought him face to face with the *I Ching*, since as early as Han times it was not only included in the Confucian canon but also occupied first place in it. When Shchutskii began the study of the Sung period in the history of Chinese philosophy, it appeared that mastery of the *I Ching* was absolutely necessary since without an understanding of this ancient document it would be impossible to investigate not only such works of paramount importance of the Sung school as Chou Tun-i's *T'ai-chi t'u-shuo*, Ch'eng I-ch'uan's *Chou I chuan*, and Chu Hsi's *Chou I pen-i*, but also the system of Sung school philosophy in general.

Shchutskii paid even greater attention to the Taoist line of Chinese philosophical thought. Evidence of his work on the Taoist classics are his translations of Lao-tzu and a significant part of the works of Lieh-tzu and Chuang-tzu. Here, Shchutskii dared to go beyond the cherished borders at which many students of Taoism in Europe stopped: he went into the study of medieval Taoism. His translation of Ke Hung (Pao P'u-tzu), which is unfortunately lost, is evidence of his work in this area. Proceeding in this direction, Shchutskii came to the *T'ai-hsüan-ching* and again found himself before the *I Ching*: it was clear that the *T'ai-hsüan-ching*, for all its originality was nevertheless a special variant of the same trend of theoretical thought, the first appearance of which we find in the ancient *I Ching*.

At this time, Shchutskii turned to the study of Buddhism. He was brought to the study of Buddhist philosophy first of all by the Sung thinkers (since as is well known, Buddhist philosophy exerted a very serious influence on the development of the Sung philosophical school), by all their irreconcilable attitudes to the doctrine of Buddhism. In addition, in tracing the history of philosophical thought of the Chinese middle ages (Third–Ninth centuries), Shchutskii could not but see the process of intensive diffusion of Buddhism in China, the strengthening of its position as a dogma, and the development of its philosophical line; he could not but take into account the enormous significance for philosophical thought in China of the translations into Chinese of Buddhist philosophical literature, translations which carried with them the entire canon of philosophical concepts which were understood

1

through the medium of the Chinese language. He saw how on Chinese soil Buddhist philosophy came into contact with the philosophical thought of Confucianism and Taoism and how in Wan I's treatise it came close to the *I Ching* itself.

Thus, for Shchutskii all roads led to the *I Ching* and he began to consider a special study and translation of this document. We, Shchutskii's colleagues in the study of China, unanimously supported him. We suggested that he direct the implacable logic of his own academic development to the *I Ching* and in addition, all of us—those who worked on Chinese literature and those who studied historical documents —constantly ran into the *I Ching* in citations, in certain concepts and images, and in echoes of the thought of the *I Ching*. It was always clear that it was impossible to correctly understand anything in the *I Ching* in isolation, that is, outside its whole system; that the understanding of any part cut off from the whole could introduce errors in the understanding of that place in the document we were studying in which the *I Ching* appeared in some way or other. Someone had to make a study of the *I Ching*, and we thought Shchutskii best prepared for it. Under such conditions, Shchutskii made the decision to start in on the *I Ching*.

It turned out, however, that on the road to understanding the *I Ching*, stood the *I Ching* itself. The *I Ching*, like the P'eng bird flew on its Ten Wings over the more than two-thousand-year history of Chinese philosophical thought. These Wings grew on the *I Ching* even in deep antiquity and were so firmly attached to it that subsequent generations could not separate them from the corpus itself. The corpus, that is, the basic text (*ching*) itself consisted, as is known, of sixty-four hexagrams and the texts ("aphorisms," as Shchutskii calls them) attached to each of them; the Wings appeared—even according to the orthodox tradition—later and are in their way Appendices to the basic text, developing the ideas stated in it and supplementing it in some way. Through these appendices, mainly through the first of them, the *Hsi-tz'u chuan*, was later seen generally the entire *I Ching*. When it is said that the history of philosophical thought in China begins with the *I Ching*, this refers mainly to the *Hsi-tz'u chuan*. The first sentence of the *Hsi-tz'u chuan*, "The Yin and the Yang are called the Way," became the point of departure of perhaps the most powerful line in the history of Chinese philosophy.

Of course, this statement, expressed in words in the *Hsi-tz'u chuan*, has its correspondence in the basic text, too—in its graphic part, where it is expressed in different combinations and alternations of solid and broken lines. However, the statement "The Yin and the Yang are called the Way" is already the final understanding of these combinations, is already the formulation of a particular law of existence, derived from the graphic symbol. Leaving aside the question of whether or not the graphic symbol was interpreted correctly, nevertheless, this was the interpretation: i.e., something connected with the graph. And though the significance of these formulae made it real wings on which the basic text was so highly elevated, nevertheless, this is related to the history of the development of the conceptions which were derived from the *I Ching* and not to the basic text itself. It was for this reason that Shchutskii began by decisively putting aside the Wings and studying the basic text, i.e., the *I Ching*.

In this way he posed great difficulties for himself. Everyone who has studied the *I Ching* knows very well that the road to this document of ancient philosophical thought was sought primarily through the Wings. Outside the context of the Wings, the primordial part of the document, even if it turned out to be somehow basic, is really only for the mantic practice, and to understand the *I Ching* in the world of mantic phenomena of high antiquity was very difficult even in the presence of the enormous literature which has taken shape around this aspect of the *I Ching*.

Shchutskii decided first of all to investigate the text which accompanied each hexagram. As is known, it is composed of three elements: the name given to the hexagram, the "texts" (*tz'u*), which explain each line of the hexagram and the "texts" which interpret the hexagram as a whole. To these three elements is sometimes added a fourth which comes immediately after the name of the hexagram: in total these elements consist of the so-called Four Qualities (*ssu-te*). Regarding the Four Qualities as accepted in *I Ching* studies as well as directly connected with the graphic foundation of the *I Ching* and with their appeal to the commentatory literature, he tried to understand them.

Shchutskii noticed the presence of several layers which differed from one another in images of thought, in language, and content, which allowed him to suggest the hypothesis of three layers of a basic text which arose at different times. This hypothesis does not reiterate in another form the usual position of the *I Ching* tradition which refers to the different "authors" who successively created the basic text of the *I Ching*, which is an obvious recognition of the different times of parts of this text. As authors of the "texts" which are related to individual lines and the "texts" which are related to the hexagram as a whole, tradition names different persons among historical or legendary persons of high antiquity; Shchutskii, however, distinguished the layers by language and content. This allowed him to show the presence in the basic text of divinatory formulae, signs, sayings, expressions in the language of imagery and two other layers which are composed of judgments expressed in the language of concepts.

It was in accordance with such an understanding of the basic text that Shchutskii tried to translate it into Russian. He translated each layer separately, figuring that the methods of translation in each layer should reflect the peculiarities of language and thought of each layer. Thus he has three texts in the translation: a translation of the first layer; a translation of the second layer with the inclusion (in brackets) of the first; a translation of the third layer with the inclusion (in brackets) of the first two. Of course, a similar breaking up of the text of the basic part of the *I Ching* should still be comprehensively verified by scholarship, but the understanding of the "layered-ness" of the basic text suggested by Shchutskii and well validated by him, reveals not only the simple historically different times of separate parts of this text that are admitted by tradition but, more importantly, the reflection in such different times of developments in language and thought.

In any case, through Shchutskii's translation we feel the profound popular character of the basic text of the *I Ching*, its inseparability from folklore with its sharp power of observation, keen appraisals, allegorical nature, and wit. In the picturesqueness of the *I Ching* one can to a certain extent judge the poetic, figurative thinking of the ancient Chinese and the entire original text begins to seem to be a unique document of popular poetry. Such is the fascinating conclusion uttered by Shchutskii on the character of the original basis, purely mantic for some, deeply philosophical for others, but for all, the always mysterious ancient Chinese document which enjoyed the important title *Book of Changes*.

It should be mentioned that the notion of the presence of folklore elements in the *I Ching* was already arrived at by one of the Western sinologues, A. Waley. Shchutskii mentions Waley's article in which this idea was stated. But the road which Shchutskii traveled was completely different: the main thing is that he indicated the place of these elements and defined their limits and characterized their role.

However difficult this one problem—to investigate the complex composition of the texts which accompany the hexagrams—before Shchutskii stood yet another, more difficult problem: he had to understand the connections between the hexagrams.

As is known, the hexagrams were not arranged in a random order. Each hexagram was called upon to designate a definite situation, one not static, but dynamic: the composition of the hexagrams indicates this, pointing to the transition from one line to another. The transition designates movement within a situation; the situation is depicted as something developing, and leading to something. And this indication is enlarged upon in the correlation of the hexagrams: each hexagram moves away from the preceding and approaches the succeeding. Thus the sixty-four hexagrams which are arranged in a definite order, present an integral picture—also, not static but dynamic. While the dynamics of the individual hexagrams indicate the course of development of a situation, the dynamcis of the sixty-four hexagrams indicate the transition from one situation to another. Since the *I Ching* is the *Book of Changes*, i.e., deals with life in its unending, on-going changes, the picture of the sixty-four hexagrams in their sequence with the connections of each link with the links preceding and succeeding should reveal the dynamics of life.

This is what Shchutskii attempted to explain. He tried to do this with the help of what he called "interpretive translation."

The notion of interpretive translation was proposed by V. M. Alekseev, Shchutskii's teacher. Working on a translation of *Categories of Poetry*, the well-known poetry treatise by Szu K'ung-t'u, Alekseev was forced to accompany the literal translation with an "interpretive" one, i.e., an explication of the statements of the content of the first translation in the words of the translator. Shchutskii, having created a literal, or as he called it "philological," translation of the text, felt that without a special explanation of the thought of what he had translated it would appear incomprehensible. He therefore decided to reinforce the philological translation with an interpretive one.

The task of interpretive translation turned out to be broader for Shchutskii than for Alekseev. Shchutskii not only had to make comprehensible the text appended to each hexagram, but also to reveal the connections between the hexagrams, i.e., to present the "basic text" of the *I Ching* as some sort of entire work. Shchutskii tried to solve this complex problem in the following way.

He wanted to reveal the contents of the *I Ching* not in his own words but in the images and ideas given in the "texts" appended to each hexagram, thus revealing the sequence and connections of each of the hexagrams and their order in a general chain.

He wanted everything that he himself had to say in explanation of both the images and ideas of the *I Ching* as well as their connections to be confined within the world of the *I Ching*, and very distinctly organized around it.

This thought removed the author's work from the realm of commentary, even of the very highest sort; it placed before the author a creative problem. An "interpretive translation" is also a creative reproduction of the concepts of the *I Ching*.

In the interpretive translation before us there are thus two texts: the text of the *Book of Changes* itself and Shchutskii's own text. The first text, of course, is taken from translation. How did this second text come to be? Well, as indicated above, Shchutskii wanted in his text to build on the images and ideas of *I Ching* studies. Hence, the author faced a problem: to create an "*I Ching* fulcrum" for himself.

In solving this most difficult problem, Shchutskii naturally turned to the enormous literature which had grown up around the *I Ching* over two thousand years. This literature forms a dense wall which bars access to the citadel—to the very document, but there are gates in it through which one might make his way to this citadel. It is impossible to doubt that a key to these gates should exist: many outstanding minds, the greatest thinkers of China and Japan have pondered over the *I Ching*; some of them have the unquestionable right to occupy a place in the first rank of the great thinkers of mankind.

It is extremely interesting to see where Shchutskii began to search for the key to the *I Ching*. As is obvious from his work and well known to those who in their time followed his scholarly path, he diligently studied the *I Ching* literature: first of all, of course, that which appeared in the homeland of the *I Ching*, i.e., the Chinese, and after that the one which is a branch of the Chinese—the Japanese. He did not limit himself only to those parts of it which were written in Chinese but also devoted attention to those works about the *I Ching* which Japanese investigators wrote in their own language. By this alone Shchutskii immediately advanced ahead of a number of European sinologues who had studied the *I Ching*, for even the best of them thought it possible to avoid Japanese sinology. Shchutskii turned to this sinology, not only to the old, which was created in accordance with Chinese tradition, but also to the new, which combines elements of the old tradition with the methods of contemporary scholarly research.

This was the first characteristic of Shchutskii as an investigator of the *I Ching*. There was also a second, no less essential, characteristic.

Knowledge of the extensive Chinese literature on the *I Ching* allowed Shchutskii to avoid the usual path of European translators of the *I Ching* and even of Chinese classical literature in general. Translations of these classics appeared in the eighteenth and nineteenth centuries. The best of the translators prepared their translations in China. This was Ch'ing China, feudal China of the absolute Manchu regime. We know the state of classical philology in China at that time. The Manchu government, especially during the K'ang-hsi and Ch'ien-lung reign periods had learned very well the significance of ideology and understood that traditional Confucianism could be a serious ideological support for an absolute regime if Confucian thought was directed into the appropriate channels and supported by explanatory literature. This was even more important because within Confucianism was concealed also the ideological opposition which operated with the same concepts, positions, and ideas as that line which the government took as a weapon. We know of the struggle which took place between these two lines and we also know what measures were taken by the government so that the conservative line of Confucianism was always superior. Thus the European sinologues of the eighteenth and nineteenth centuries working in China dealt mainly with the literature which offered an approach to the classics. In this very way they fell under the influence of a certain, in any case limited, line of philosophical thought. Shchutskii took an entirely different road. Of course, he knew the Ch'ing commentatory literature, but his main attention was attracted to two works: the articles of Chang Hsüeh-ch'eng (1738–1801) and the monograph of P'i Hsi-jui (1850–1908). These were works of an investigative nature written in the mode of China's critical school of classical philology during the Ch'ing. The fact that in our day they have been reprinted in the Peoples Republic of China testifies to their scholarly value. Shchutskii had the honor of being the first of the European sinologues to understand the scholarly importance of the works of these Chinese scholars.

Shchutskii was attracted to these works mainly for their illumination of the origin and structure of the *I Ching*. In understanding the sense of the basic part of the *I Ching* he was helped by totally different researchers: Wang Pi (226–249), Wan I (1598–1654), and Itō Tōgai (1670–1736).

This choice deserves special attention. As is known, Wang Pi sought the key to an understanding of the *I Ching* in Taoist philosophical thought; Wan I attempted to interpret the ideas and concepts of the *I Ching* with the help of the concepts and ideas of Buddhist philosophy; Itō Tōgai approached the *I Ching* from the point of view of Confucianism.

For those who observed the path by which Shchutskii himself came to the *I Ching*, the choice of these authors is understandable: as said above, the study of Confucianism, Taoism, and Buddhism led him to the *I Ching*. All that is demanded is an explanation of why, of all the Confucian authors, Shchutskii selected the Japanese Itō Tōgai. Why did he not dwell, for example, on such works as Ch'eng I-ch'uan's famous treatise or the important researches of Chu Hsi? The explanation apparently lies in his realization that to be guided in his work on the *I Ching* by the treatises of these two great thinkers of old China would have meant immersing himself in the ideas of the Sung philosophical school. In the interpretation of the *I Ching* by Ch'eng I-ch'uan and Chu Hsi, the *I Ching* belonged, first of all, to this school: it was one of the bases of its system. It is quite possible—and from the point of view of the history of philosophy in China—really necessary to subject to attentive investigation the *Chou I chuan* of the younger Ch'eng I-ch'uan and the *Chou I pen-i* of Chu Hsi, but this would have been an investigation of the philosophy of the Sung school. In getting to know these celebrated works Shchutskii apparently understood this and decided to select from the Confucian works on the *I Ching* those which would attempt to approach the *I Ching* as much as possible in its proper form. Such a work he saw in Tōgai's treatise.

Shchutskii's appeal to Tōgai can be understood. Tōgai, like his famous father Itō Jinsai, belongs to the so-called School of Ancient Studies (Kogaku-ha), i.e., to that trend of Confucian thought in Japan in the seventeenth–eighteenth centuries which contrasted itself to the Chu Hsi-ist trend encouraged by the Tokugawa government, in other words the Sung philosophical school. The criticism of the School of Ancient Studies proceeded from the conviction that the philosophy of the Sung school had departed greatly from ancient Confucianism and the mission of adherents of "Confucian truth" consisted in disclosure of the old, i.e., in the ideas of that type of thinker and of genuine Confucianism. In this sense they called their line the "School of Ancient Studies."

In the light of history we can see in this school the critical tendency of classical philology of the era of feudal absolutism. We are greatly obligated to this trend in the scholarly study of ancient documents—their authenticity as a whole, the degree and limits of authenticity of individual parts or places and equally for the disclosing of the original content of many concepts and ideas. Such a critical trend arose in Ch'ing China in classical philology, and it also appeared in Tokugawa Japan, in which—for the same historical reasons—classicism also flourished then. Shchutskii dwelt on the Japanese representative of the critical trend of classicism. In the Japanese variant of this trend he paid great attention to what interested him—the question of the ideational content of ancient documents.

However right Shchutskii was in this assessment of the critical line of Chinese classicism in Japan, one can show only comparative study of this classicism in China and Japan. Such a study has not been carried out. One can only say that for an understanding of the historical essence, content, and object of classical philology in China it is necessary to take into account also Chinese philology in Japan, which for all its local peculiarities at bottom reproduced the same trend of research.

Thus Shchutskii, in his desire to disclose the content of the *I Ching* so that everything would be clear, that all elements of the whole were connected with each other and jointly paint a dynamic picture of phenomena which depend on each other, turned to very different versions of treatises on the *I Ching*. But this does not mean that his interpretation represents the combination of thoughts from different sources, some sort of combination of Taoism, Buddhism, and Confucianism. To read his interpretive translation is to be convinced that this is not so: Shchutskii interpreted the connections of the hexagrams in his own way. The reliance of his interpretation on the sources he cited was reflected only by the fact that he did not allow anything which was not admitted by thinkers selected by him, who represented three tendencies of philosophical thought, tendencies which were very different, but which developed in a specific sphere, i.e., the real history of a real people who were the creators of a profoundly unique culture. Shchutskii did not allow himself to tread the path of irresponsible invention, like the announcement that the *I Ching* is a Sino-Bactrian dictionary; at the same time he did not follow uncritically what was said of the *I Ching* by one or another Chinese thinker. Having reasoned out the conceptions of the greatest of them and having compared these conceptions with the *I Ching* material, Shchutskii worked out his understanding of this document.

The "interpretive translation" was done on this basis. In

this way he obtained a special form: the words and phrases of the *I Ching* itself, printed in italics were introduced into the authorial text; in other words, the entire basic text of the *I Ching* was introduced into the translation. So far as the authorial text represents a detailed and coherent statement of the content of the *I Ching*, the extracted "aphorisms" with each hexagram, in their totality, are also a coherent text.

This part of Shchutskii's work is more difficult for the reader. For its understanding two conditions are necessary: first, a proper knowledge of the *I Ching*, even if limited to the works of Wang Pi, Wan I, and Itō Tōgai; second, a thoughtful regard for the conceptions of Shchutskii himself, to a considerable degree based on elements which come from these three *I Ching* scholars, but which as a whole were interpreted by Shchutskii in a new way. It should also be remembered that the author himself wanted to speak of the *I Ching* and his understanding of it in a language close to that of *I Ching* studies. One can accept or not accept such methods of the author's work. But it is impossible not to admit that in order to do such an interpretive translation it was necessary not only to ponder the *Book of Changes*, but also to feel it.

Learned connoisseurs of the *I Ching* may not agree with much in Shchutskii's interpretation. It is quite possible to understand a number of things in the *I Ching* differently. Even individual concepts of the *I Ching* were interpreted differently by investigators, but the understanding of the *I Ching* as a whole depends on the understanding of individual concepts. But not to consider Shchutskii's interpretation from now on is impossible. The range of investigative work, the understanding of the essence of the problem, the well-thought-out argumentation, the exceptional knowledge of the *I Ching* literature both old and new—all these qualities of Shchutskii's work firmly introduce it into the canon of *I Ching* studies. Furthermore, it has a special and very significant value: the author included his translations of some materials concerning the *I Ching*, namely, the well-known treatise by Ou-yang

Hsiu, Su Hsün's judgments on the *I Ching*, Itō Zensho's "Preface" to Itō Tōgai's researches and also poems by a number of Chinese authors devoted to the *I Ching*. There is also a long excerpt from Yang Hsiung's *T'ai-hsüan-ching*.

It was mentioned above that Shchutskii's work is published, with some deletions which were made by the editor. In the editorial process, many repetitions, prolixities, digressions, and notes which did not have any direct relation to the theme were removed. The chapter "The Problem of the Reflection of the Social Structure in the Basic Text of the *Book of Changes*" was out of date and only some materials were preserved from it: the list of terms in the *I Ching* denoting persons as members of the family and society (four pages), and the list of all the places in the *Tso-chuan* which refer to divination by the *I Ching* (two and a half pages). In addition, in this chapter is defined the time to which, in Shchutskii's opinion, this document can be dated: eighth–seventh centuries B.C. An entire chapter "The Problem of the Contemporary Role of the *Book of Changes* in China and Japan" (four pages) was deleted since the situation described in these pages is quite different today from what it was in the early thirties when the work was written. Also deleted was the chapter "The Problem of the Facilities of the Sinological Laboratory Necessary for Translation of the *Book of Changes*" (four pages), in which the author gives a list of literature and reference works which in his opinion were necessary for work on a translation of the *I Ching*. The picture of the special literature and reference works is completely different today, thirty years after Shchutskii began his work. Instead of this list, we have drawn upon N. A. Petrov's bibliography of the most important works on the *I Ching* which appeared in the forties and fifties in China. Thus only a rather inconsequential part has been removed from the manuscript.

The editor considered it necessary to add some notes to Shchutskii's work. Some of them are intended to explain to the reader what the author left unexplained; others supplement what is said in the work; finally, in some cases the editor thought it necessary to inform the reader of the possibility of other interpretations of some of the phenomena touched on by the author.

In Shchutskii's work there are elements of the past, the present, and the future. The past, i.e., signs of that time when he wrote his work, affects the conception of feudalism accepted by the author: for him the time of the *I Ching's* creation, i.e., eighth–seventh centuries B.C. is the feudal epoch. Such a conception was rather widespread in historical scholarship in the thirties. Another sign of the past in Shchutskii's work is his use of arguments of language and thought which were connected with the idea of their phasic nature in determining the multi-layered nature of the basic text. In the thirties this was considered most important in linguistics.

In encountering the echoes of these conceptions, the reader should take into account the time when the work was written. But the reader should also take into account that the question of the time when feudalism began in China is still the subject of argument. It is true for the majority of Chinese historians and also for our specialists in Chinese history, that the eighth–seventh centuries B.C. were the epoch of slave-owning; it should be remembered that this point of view was established literally in recent years. Moreover, even now there are proponents of the concept of feudalism even for these centuries. As far as the ideas of the phasic nature of language and thought are concerned, it must be said directly: for Shchutskii it is purely external. In fact, the author uses arguments from language in the spirit of Karlgren and not Marr.

The "present" in Shchutskii's work is his historical method. Even from the most superficial reading of the work it is evident that first and most important for the author is his liberation from the view of the document as some sort of age-old whole. He not only pushes aside decisively the Ten Wings as a later addition to the basic text, but even in this basic text noted three layers of different times. Another manifestation of the

lxiii

author's historical method which should be recognized is his striving in his interpretation of the document not to impose on it anything which is external. ˙

The "future" in Shchutskii's work is the scale of his sinological erudition. He is the first of us, who, along with a knowledge of Chinese special literature and also European sinological literature, showed a knowledge of Japanese sinology, which in its significance for the study of the Chinese classics doubtlessly immediately follows the Chinese. Here is opened the path to an escape from the orbit of specific discipline which is called "sinology" and the bridge to the sphere of general discipline of history—for historians of China; for specialists in Chinese literature and linguistics; for students of the Chinese language.

N. I. Konrad

Biographical Sketch

Iulian Konstantinovich Shchutskii was born in 1897 in Sverd-lovsk (the former Ekaterinburg) into the family of a forester. Having received his secondary education in Petrograd, Shchut-skii entered the economics division of the Polytechnic Institute. However, his interests were far from the disciplines taught there. This apparently bespeaks the influence of his mother, a teacher of music, French, and German, who instilled in him an unusual interest in foreign languages. By the end of his life Shchutskii knew and taught several Eastern languages: Chinese (both Peking and Canton dialects), Japanese, Manchu, An-namese; knew German, French, English and Polish; and was acquainted with Dutch, Sanskrit, and Latin. In 1917 he left the Polytechnic Institute in order to enter the Practical Oriental Academy. After a year, Shchutskii transferred to the university, from which he graduated in 1922 in the sinological faculty of General Studies.

Under the guidance of the expert on Chinese language and literature V. M. Alekseev, Shchutskii mastered the knowledge necessary for the study of sinology so successfully that after finishing at the university he was retained in the Scientific Research Institute. During these years (1922–1923) Shchutskii published his first translations of Chinese poetry of the T'ang period.

In 1924 a special qualifying commission made it possible for Shchutskii to become an Assistant Professor, teaching various sinological courses in the university (later the Leningrad Insti-tute of History, Philosophy and Linguistics). The same year he began to teach in the Leningrad Institute of Modern Oriental Languages (later the Leningrad Oriental Institute), giving courses on the history of Chinese philosophy and on the Chinese and Japanese languages. For the first time in the history of Russian and Soviet oriental studies, Shchutskii introduced instruction in Cantonese and Vietnamese, having written a textbook for the latter, published in 1933.

Shchutskii's academic interests were broad, covering the areas of linguistics and literature. Having begun his scholarly activities in the Asiatic Museum of the Academy of Sciences in 1920, he subsequently went through all the stages from Research Worker III to Curator of the museum. After the reorganization of the Asiatic Museum into the Institute of Oriental Studies in 1930 he became a research specialist. He participated in an ad hoc commission on the romanization of the Chinese writing system under the All-Union Central Committee for a New Alphabet.

In 1928 Shchutskii as a young scholar was sent to Japan by the Academy of Sciences of the USSR to acquire Japanese and Chinese books and to become familiar with the scholarly work of Japanese sinologists.

In 1935 a Special Commission of the Central Research Committee of the Union conferred on him the title of professor and in 1937 he defended his doctoral dissertation, which is the monograph translated here.

Shchutskii wrote about 30 scholarly works.

N. A. Petrov

PART I

Introduction to Part I

This introduction is directed to the nonsinologist. It is necessary as a kind of guide to the work presented below. It should familiarize the reader with the problems, without consideration of which the *Book of Changes* itself will not be understood, nor will it be understood why the author undertook the translation and analysis of a document which, at first glance, means little to the contemporary reader. In addition, it is here that we should introduce and explain the basic terminology which will constantly be used below and which is indispensable in a specialized study of the document.

We undertook this work because in studying the materials on the history of Chinese philosophy we constantly found it necessary to preface the analysis of each philosophical school with preliminary analysis of the *Book of Changes*—a fundamental starting point of discussion of almost all philosophers of ancient China.

The *Book of Changes* is first among the classical books of Confucianism and in bibliographical surveys of Chinese literature as well. This is understandable since bibliology and bibliography in feudal China were established by people who had received traditional Confucian education. Bibliographers of old China firmly believed in the tradition (not of antiquity but quite old) that traced the formation of the *Book of Changes* to such an extreme antiquity that no other classical book could

Note: The authorship of the notes is identified by an abbreviation following each note. "S." means Shchutskii's original note; "K.," the supplementary notes by N. I. Konrad, who edited the MS for the Russian publication; "Tr.," supplementary and explanatory notes provided by the translators and Hellmut Wilhelm.

3

compete with it in chronological priority, though actually it is by no means the oldest of the documents of written Chinese, a fact established by Chinese philology itself.

However, independently from tradition and independently from Confucianism the *Book of Changes* has every right to claim first place in Chinese classical literature since its significance in the development of the spiritual culture of China is so great. It showed its influence in widely varied fields: in philosophy, in mathematics, in politics, in strategy, in the theory of painting and music, and in art itself, from the famous example of the ancient painting *The Eight Steeds* 八駿[1] to the inscription of a spell on a coin amulet or ornament on a contemporary ashtray.

Sine ira et studio ["Dispassionately," lit., "without anger and also not without pleasure, satisfaction, emotion" – Tr.] we must consider the *Book of Changes* unquestionably the first among classical books and the most difficult both to understand and to translate. It has always enjoyed the reputation of being a vague and mysterious text, surrounded by a vast literature from commentators of sometimes widely different opinions. Despite the massiveness of this literature of two thousand years, the understanding of some parts of the *Book of Changes* still presents nearly insurmountable difficulties, so unfamiliar and strange to us are the images in which its conceptions are expressed. Therefore, the reader should not complain to the author about places in the translation of the document which upon first reading do not seem understandable. One can only console oneself with the fact that even in the Far East the original *Book of Changes* is not understood as easily as other Chinese classical books.

In order to help the reader as much as possible, we dwell here on the plan of our work, on a superficial description of the contents of the *Book of Changes*, and on its most important technical terminology.

1. "The Eight Steeds" 八駿 were horses of Emperor Mu of Chou (1001–940 B.C.) glorified by historical legends. K.

4

Our work is divided into three parts: in the first part are set forth the fundamental data obtained from studies of this document made in Europe, China, and Japan. The second part is a concise statement of the data we obtained in the investigation of thirteen fundamental questions related to the *Book of Changes*. The third part is devoted to the translation of the book.[2]

The text of the *Book of Changes* is not uniform either from the standpoint of the parts of which it is composed or from the standpoint of the very characters in which it is written. In addition to common characters, it also includes special signs which consist of two types of lines or *hsiao*. One type is a solid horizontal line called *yang* "light", *kang* "rigid", or more often, according to the symbolics of numbers, *chiu* (nine). The other type is a horizontal line divided in the middle and called *yin* (shadow), *jou* (pliable), or more often, according to the symbolics of numbers, *liu* (six). In each sign there are six such lines which are arranged in varied combinations, for instance ☰ ☷ ☶, etc. According to the theory of the *Book of Changes* all processes of the world are the interchanges of situations which emerge from the interaction and struggle of the forces of light and darkness, rigidity and pliability, and each of these situations is expressed symbolically by one of these signs, of which there are sixty-four in the *Book of Changes*. They are regarded as the symbols of reality and are called *kua* (symbols) in Chinese. In European sinology they are called hexagrams. Contrary to the practice of the Chinese written language, the hexagrams are written from bottom to top and thus the first line of a hexagram is at the bottom. Consequently, the bottom line, called the "starting line," is regarded as the first line; the second line is the second line from the bottom; and the third line is the third line from the bottom, etc. The uppermost line is called, not the sixth, but the upper line ("*shang*"). The lines symbolize the stages of development of various situations ex-

---

2. In this publication the first two parts are presented. Tr.

pressed in the hexagram. Places which the lines occupy between the lowest, the starting line, and the sixth, the upper line, are named *wei* ("positions"). The odd positions (starting, third, and fifth) are considered positions of light—*yang*; the even positions (the second, fourth, and upper) are positions of darkness—*yin*. Naturally, only in half of the cases the light lines appear in light positions and the dark lines in the dark positions. These cases are called the "appropriateness" of the lines; the forces of light or darkness "find their own place" in them. Generally, this is considered a favorable disposition of the forces, but not always regarded as the best. In this way we obtain the following diagram.

Positions	Names	Predispositions
6	Upper	Darkness
5	Fifth	Light
4	Fourth	Darkness
3	Third	Light
2	Second	Darkness
1	Starting	Light

Thus the hexagram with perfect "appropriateness" of the lines is the sixty-third ☷, and the hexagram with perfect "non-appropriateness" of the lines is the sixty-fourth ☷.

In the most ancient commentaries to the *Book of Changes* it is already mentioned that eight symbols, the so-called trigrams, had originally been established out of three lines. They received specific names and were connected with a specific range of concepts. Here we give their configuration and their basic names, attributes, and images.

Sign	Name	Attribute	Image
☰	*ch'ien* ("creation")	firmness	heaven
☷	*k'un* ("fulfillment")	self-devotion	earth
☳	*chen* ("excitement")	mobility	thunder

6

☵	*k'an* ("immersion")	danger	water
☶	*ken* ("stay")	stability	mountain
☴	*sun* ("refinement")	penetration	wind (tree)
☲	*li* ("cohesion")	clarity	fire
☱	*tui* ("dissolution")	joy	reservoir[3]

From these concepts alone it is possible to picture how the process of emergence, existence, and disappearance was regarded in the theory of the *Book of Changes*. The creative impulse, immersing itself in the *meon*[4]—*fulfillment*, acts above all as the *excitement* of the latter. Its complete *immersion* ensues further in the *meon*, which leads to creation of the created, to its *stay*. But since the world is a process, a struggle of oppositions, the creative impulse gradually recedes and a *refinement* of creating forces occurs. Later, owing to inertia, there remains briefly only their *cohesion*, which leads finally to the disintegration of the whole situation which has been created, to its *dissolution*.

Each hexagram can be considered a combination of two trigrams. Their mutual relationship characterizes the given hexagram. In the theory of the *Book of Changes* the lower trigram is customarily regarded as referring to internal life, to what is coming, to what is being created, and the upper trigram

3. This is an extremely interesting translation for the image of *tui*, usually rendered as "lake." More recent semantic studies by the late Erwin Reifler arrive at a similar conclusion. It will also be noted that the terms in this list have been translated by S. differently in other parts of the text. Tr.

4. *Meon* is a Greek word meaning "nonbeing." According to George Ivask, N. Minsky (pseud. of Nikolai Mikhailovich Vilenkin, 1855–1937) developed a theory which he called "meonic philosophy" in his book *The Religion of the Future*, 1905. This philosophy, which combined the ideas of Nietzche and oriental mysticism, affirmed that the absolute is something negative—"nonbeing." Ivask suggests that the term might mean "nirvana" here. Since Minsky's "meonism" was widely discussed in the early 1900s it is certain that Shchutskii was familiar with the philosophy and the term *meon*, which would account for its use here. As Shchutskii quotes Chou Tun-i here, it might be permissible to understand it as 物 ("the phenomenal world"), a term used by Chou in this context. Tr.

to the external world, to what is receding, to what is dissolving; i.e.:

≡ } External, receding, dissolving
≡ } Internal, coming, being created

In addition, the hexagram sometimes can also be regarded as consisting of three pairs of lines. According to the theory of the *Book of Changes* three cosmic potentials act in the world —heaven, man, earth.

= } heaven
= } man
= } earth

There is also a symbolism elaborated in the divinatory practices of the *I Ching* experts.

Position	Meaning		
	In Society	In the Human Body	In the Body of Animals
6	Perfect person	Head	Head
5	King	Shoulders	Front legs
4	Court official	Torso	Front part of body
3	Prefect	Thighs	Back part of body
2	Low official	Shins	Back legs
1	Commoner	Feet	Tail

There were also other ways to examine the structures of the hexagram, but their complete enumeration here would be superfluous. Therefore, we shall limit ourselves to the following statements.

Analogous positions in the upper and lower trigrams have the closest relationship to each other. Thus the first position is analogous to the fourth, the second to the fifth, and the third to the sixth.

Furthermore, it was supposed that light gravitated toward darkness and darkness toward light. Therefore, in the hexagrams also, solid lines correspond to divided lines. If corresponding positions (1–4, 2–5, 3–6) are occupied by *different* lines, then it is considered that there exists a "correspondence" between them; if they are occupied by the same line, then there is "no correspondence" among them.

In the analysis of hexagrams special attention is given to the second and the fifth positions. Each of them (in both the lower and the upper trigram) is central, i.e., they are the ones in which the qualities of the trigrams are manifested in the most perfect and balanced form.

In addition, in the analysis of the hexagrams it is customary to consider that the light lines or dark lines acquire greater significance if they are in the minority. Thus in the hexagram ☰ the only dark line (second) "controls" the rest of the lines and is for them the center of gravity.

The second part of the text of the *Book of Changes* is written in ordinary Chinese characters and represents interpretation of the hexagrams as a whole, and the relationships of their component trigrams and individual lines. Strictly speaking, it is the text of the *Book of Changes*. It is not uniform, belongs to different authors, and was written in various periods.

In this text we first of all distinguish the basic text and the commentaries attached to it which long ago became somewhat interwoven with the basic text so that voluminous commentatory literature subsequently developed not only around the basic text, but also around the commentaries included in it.

The basic text consists of the following twelve parts.

I. Name of the hexagram *kua-ming*; the names of its constituent trigrams were added later.

II. A divinitory formula, expressed by four terms (qualities), the so-called *szu-te*; these terms are: *yüan* ("beginning"), *heng* ("penetration, development"), *li* ("favorableness, determination"), and *chen* ("steadiness, existence"). All of these terms may be present, or only some of them, or they may be altogether absent.

III. Texts to the whole hexagrams, *kua-tz'u*,[5] which may be more or less developed. Sometimes the Four Qualities or one of the four basic mantic prophesies (good fortune, misfortune, remorse, regret), which apparently are a later insertion in the text, are included. Also included are explanatory words like "there will be no error," "there will be no praise," "there is nothing favorable," etc.

IV. Texts to individual lines, *yao-tz'u*; in language and type they are very close to text III and include the same items. All the rest of the texts (V–XII) are ancient commentaries which were compiled considerably later than the basic text.

V. Commentaries to text III, *T'uan-chuan*. In this commentary the hexagram is examined from the point of its constituent trigrams, lines, etc., and on this basis text III is explained.

VI. The large image commentaries, *Ta-hsiang chuan*, where the hexagram is examined from the point of view of the images of its component trigrams and an indication of ethical order is given. Like all of the *Book of Changes*, V and VI of the text are *mechanically* divided into the first part and the second part between the thirtieth and thirty-first hexagrams.

VII. The small image commentary, *Hsiao-hsiang chuan*. It is completely different from the previous commentary both in its intent and in its language; it consists of commentatory postscripts to the sayings of text IV. Explanations concern mostly the technique of divination and are based on the structure of the hexagrams. They do not have any relation to the philosophical concept of the *Book of Changes*. The origin of this text is comparatively late.

VIII. A commentatory essay to the texts, *Hsi-tz'u chuan* or *Ta-chuan* (The Great commentary). It is a kind of treatise in which are set forth the basic philosophical concepts of the *Book*

---

5. The Judgment texts of the Wilhelm/Baynes version. Tr.

of Changes (ontology, cosmology, gnosiology, and ethics), the technique of divination according to the *Book*, and a kind of history of Chinese culture in extreme antiquity. It was included in the composition of the document comparatively late, but undoubtedly is most interesting for the history of Chinese philosophy. It is also mechanically divided into two parts.

IX. Interpretation of trigrams, *Shuo-kua-chuan*. The text consists of two unequal parts. The first part—significantly shorter—is similar to text VIII in character, language, and subject, but wound up in text IX, presumably because of the mistake of copyists. The second and longer part includes individual characteristics of the trigrams, their classification, and corresponding objects of the world according to the categories of trigrams. In its character, the text of this part is completely different from the first part and is strongly reminiscent of the mantic speculations of the early Han commentators.

X. Interpretation of the order of hexagrams, *Hsü-kua-chuan*. The text greatly differs from all the rest of the texts of the *Book of Changes*. The sequence of the arrangement of hexagrams in the *Book* is developed and argued. This text deserves more attention than is usually given to it. Only Ch'eng I-ch'uan (eleventh century)[6] elaborated on it more consistently and converted it into brief introductions for each hexagram. This text is extremely valuable for the history of the ways of thinking in China.

XI. Various opinions about hexagrams, *Tsa-kua-chuan*. This is something like a continuation or, more precisely, some remnants of the second part of text IX. It is not of great value.

XII. Glosses, *Wen-yen-chuan* in Chinese, in which are given explanations of the terms of the texts of the first two hexagrams. This is a very mixed text, full of repetitions, which is apparently composed of ancient quotations of the oral mantic tradition together with later interpretations of terms. Essentially this text gets lost in a sea of analogous commentatory

6. I.e., Ch'eng I (1033–1107). Tr.

glosses and would have remained unnoticed if an old but unfounded rumor had not connected it with the name of Confucius.

In various editions of the *Book of Changes* these texts are arranged differently, but in general two systems of arrangement of the texts are maintained. The first one is the older system in which the texts I, II, III, and IV do not come one after another, but are arranged in this way: the first hexagram, the text I, II, III, and IV relating to it, and then text XII relating to it; after this the second hexagram, text I, II, III, IV, and XII relating to it; then the third hexagram with the same successive texts (except for XII), etc. After the texts of the sixty-fourth hexagram, the texts V, VI, and VII, VIII, IX, X, and XI come one after another. The second way of arrangement of the texts is a much later system which differs from the first system only in that texts V, VI, and VII are divided according to the hexagrams; then texts V and VI come directly after text IV, but text VII is divided under the corresponding individual line texts of text IV. This system appeared in the commentatory literature as early as the third century A.D. This difference in arrangement of the texts indicates that from the ancient period the nonuniformity of the text was recognized even in commentatory schools. Texts I, II, III, and IV are valuable as documents, and texts V, VI, VIII, and X as more advanced commentaries. The rest of the texts contribute little to the understanding of the *Book of Changes* and in many cases are inferior to commentaries. In the present work main attention is focused on the basic text and only minor attention is paid to the commentaries V, VI, VIII, and X.

CHAPTER I

The Study of the Book of Changes *in Europe*

It is hardly necessary to point out that the study of the Chinese literary heritage is impossible without a basic investigation of the so-called classical, or canonical, books. They remained for centuries the basis of any education, not only in China, but also in Japan, Korea, Vietnam, and such countries as the dynasties of Liao, Chin, Hsi-hsia, and so on,[1] which had adopted Chinese culture. Though the canonical books have ceased to be the basis of education at the present time, they still continue to be taught in institutions of higher education.

The *Book of Changes* (*I Ching* or *Chou I*) occupies first place among these Chinese classical books. We may call it the first book in the Chinese library.[2] On the basis of these in-

1. In speaking of the Liao and Chin dynasties the author has in mind the Khitans and the Jurjens who occupied the territory of later Manchuria and Northwestern Mongolïa and extended their power for a while to a part of Northwestern China. Liao (916–1124) is the name of the Khitan state, and Chin (1115–1264) is the Jurjen's state. Hsi-hsia is the name of the dynasty formed on the northwestern border of China by the Tanguts. The Khitan, the Jurjens, and the Tanguts, who were located in direct proximity to China, took much from Chinese civilization. K.

2. These statements by the author need explanation. It is true that the *I Ching* is the first book in the catalogues of Chinese libraries, but only in those libraries that maintain the officially recognized bibliographical system. This system was established in the last quarter of the eighteenth century, when books were collected all over the country and the imperial library was formed. The collection was named *Ssu-k'u ch'üan-shu* (Collection of books of four depositories), and in its catalogue, which was published with comprehensive annotations, all the books were arranged in a definite order. In first place were the classics of Confucianism, including the *I Ching*. The system of this bibliography reflects, first of all, the idea of literature which was held by the ruling class of

troductory remarks, one can imagine how necessary it is for
sinology to study this document of ancient Chinese literature.

However, this study is as difficult as it is necessary. Thus,
one of the early translators of the *Book of Changes*, James
Legge, reminisced: "I wrote out a translation of the Yi King,
embracing both the Text and the Appendixes, in 1854 and
1855; and have to acknowledge that when the manuscript
was completed, I knew very little about the scope and method
of the book." It is important to note that James Legge was
not the first European scholar to work on this "secretive
classical book." It is true that though his successors were, so
to speak, bolder in their hypotheses (above all I have in mind
the most fantastic one held by the sinologist Terrien de
Lacouperie), they were not bold enough, as Legge was, to
confess their ignorance in the first sentences with such frank-
ness.

Of course, the first scholars had difficulties in understanding
our document, for they could not avail themselves of such
well-equipped reference books and later researches and articles
of the sinological laboratories which are available to the
sinologists of our time. However, even today, despite these
laboratories, in many respects one must begin his work from
scratch, for reference books and many specialized works are
still far from perfect.

Let us take the dictionary *Tz'u-yüan*,[3] for instance, which

feudal China—at that time mainly the official-bureaucratic strata of this class
—and secondly, the desire of the ruling circles to establish Confucianism in a
definite, officially approved version as the foundation of the state ideology. K.

3. In referring to the famous contemporary dictionary, *Tz'u-yüan* (1st ed.,
1915), which is also a kind of encyclopedia, the author wants to show what
information a contemporary popular reader of Chinese can obtain about the
I Ching by consulting detailed reference books. For a correct understanding of
the information that the *Tz'u-yüan* or any other similar reference book provides, as well as most of the works on the *I Ching*, it must be remembered
that mention of Fu Hsi, King Wen, the Duke of Chou, and Confucius as the
authors of the *I Ching* does not mean that they are recognized as the real
creators of this document. The traditional legend about their participation in

is one of the most widely used Chinese dictionaries and reference books considered to give the most general information. There we read the following about the *Chou I:*

Chou I—name of a book. Composed by King Wen, the Duke of Chou, and Confucius. Based on the eight trigrams which were invented by Fu Hsi, the authors created the sixty-four hexagrams and three hundred eighty-four lines by superimposing the trigrams on one another. When books were burned under the Ch'in dynasty, the *Chou I*, being a divinatory book, survived. Therefore, among all classical books it is the one which is in the most perfect shape. Those who call it *Chou I* think that this name indicates the all-dimensional and universal character of the system of this book [a play on one of the meanings of the word *chou* which means "all-comprising" or "cycle" – S.]. Others assume that the name Chou comes from the name of the direction to the south of the mountain Ch'i, mentioned in a verse, "The plain of Chou looked beautiful and rich." (See *Shih-ching*, Ta-ya I, 3, 3.) This name would have been given to this book in order to distinguish it from the *I* of the *Yin*. The commentary of Cheng Hsüan is now lost. Commentaries exist by Wang Pi of the Wei dynasty. K'ung Ying-ta of the T'ang wrote a sub-commentary to it. This is now called the *Chu-lü-pen*. At the time of the T'ang dynasty the collected commentaries by Li Ting-tso came into existence. Under the Sung the *I-chuan* of Ch'eng-tzu and the *Pen-i* of Chu-tzu appeared.

That is all the information about the *Chou I* one can obtain from the dictionary *Tz'u-yüan*! Information from other ref-

---

the composition of the *I Ching* is so interwoven with the very document that they became inseparable from it. Tradition similarly identifies the Christian Gospels with Mathew, Mark, Luke, and John. These names are cited in every general reference book on the Gospels, independently of the problem of how scholarship determines the authors of evangelical texts.

The entry in the *Tz'u-yüan* does not fail to mention two interpretations of the name *Chou I*; these interpretations actually exist and it is necessary to include them in a reference book, but again completely independently of the problem of which one of them is right or wrong. In the *Tz'u-yüan* a list of works concerning the *I Ching* is also given with good reason and the collections referred to are, indeed, the most important for the literature of the *I Ching* in its basic line. K.

erence books of the same character is more or less the same. In all of them the legend that the *Book of Changes* was written by King Wen, the Duke of Chou, and Confucius is commonly repeated, despite the fact that the authorship of Confucius was already questioned in China about a thousand years ago.

In the East two schools of understanding and study of the *Book of Changes* have been competing. One is based on tradition and the other on critical philology. This competition has lasted for about a thousand years, and in the modern period also the traditional school has been more firmly established in the works of many contemporary scholars in China, Japan, and Western countries.

On the basis of sources known to us[4] it is possible to assume that the first information of the *Book of Changes* in Europe appeared in the preface to a book published in Paris in 1681: *Confuzius Sinarum philosophus, seu scientia Sinensis latine exposita studio et opera Patrum Societatis Jesu iussu Ludovici Magni e bibliotheca regia in lucem produit P. Couplet.* It was not until 1736 that the first translation into Latin of the *Book of Changes* was done by a Jesuit missionary, Regis, who in turn based his translation on earlier but not dated works of other missionaries, such as the translator Joseph de Mailla and the interpreter Pierre-Vincent du Tartre. The translation was done with the assistance of the Manchurian version of the *Book of Changes*. Regis' work is merely the extension, by means of his own remarks, of the works of his predecessors.[5]

Even before the translation of the *Book of Changes* appeared, fragmentary information about this book inspired interest in

4. Information obtained from the review of E. Hauer, "I Ging. Das Buch der Wandlungen," pp. 242–247. S.

5. See Legge's preface to his translation of the *Book of Changes*. The translation by Regis was published under the title: *Y-King, Antiquissimus Sinarum liber*, quem ex latina interpretatione P. Regis aliorumque ex S.J.P.P. edidit Julíus Mohl (Stuttgart & Tübingen, vol. I, 1834; vol. II, 1839). S.

it in Europe. Thus in 1753 a book by Haupt on the *I Ching* was published.[6]

It is worth noticing that in this book Leibniz is mentioned as a scholar of the *Book of Changes* who established his own theory of its interpretation. This problem is concisely and well set forth in Hauer's review mentioned above, and all we have to do is to quote from it.

From this book we know that some other than Leibniz himself in Germany was the first to work on the *I Ching*. [He quotes a passage from Haupt:] "He found in the figures of the emperor [Fu Hsi – S.] an Arithmeticam Dyadicam, or a system of counting by two numbers, and in accordance with this he interpreted the whole book so that it became possible to conceive of something reasonable in relation to its lines and figures. He did not wait long to inform the Chinese of his new explanation. Finally, he wrote to a missionary, P. Bouvet, who was in China at that time. Though we know that this priest accepted this explanation and expressed his satisfaction in his answering letter to Baron von Leibniz, we still do not know how the Chinese scholars reacted to this discovery.

Haupt examines Leibniz' hypotheses in §§ 28–41 of his work and further goes on to examine two other explanations which were both published in 1745. A certain F. A. Knittel had found out that

Emperor Fohi presented in his book only arithmetic relations, the difference of which is half (§ 42–46), and a certain Johann Heinrich Hasenbalg confirmed that "this emperor wanted to bring out all possible forms of deductions in his art of combinations. According to this new hypothesis the so-called *Book of Changes* must be a chapter of the *Logic* of Emperor Fohi, and the rest of which was presumably lost" (§ 47–51). Johan Thomas Haupt was quite shrewd (ist ganz schlau gewesen). He disproves his predecessors and proclaims in § 52

6. Königlich-Preussische Kirchen und Schulen Inspector Johan Thomas Haupt . . . , *Neue und vollständige Auslegung des von dem Stifter und ersten Kaiser des Chinesischen Reichs Fohi hinterlassenen Buches Ye-Kim genann* (Rostock & Wismar: Bey Berger & Boedner, 1795). S.

his own solution of the enigma: "What is the content of the book Ye-kim?" I answer: "It contains the same and nothing else but all factors of a Cubocubus or, to express myself in the manner of the Arabian mathematicians, of a Zensicubus whose root consists of two parts, (radicis binomiae) and wherein the Cubicubi of these two parts and all factors thereof are listed two by two in juxtaposition to each other, so that one half of the factors of one factor (together) with the half of the factors which are in opposite position to the first factor be equal to all the other halves of factors in both factors." In this way the so-called Ye-kim is a genuine remnant of a system of counting, invented by Emperor Fohi.[7]

For those who are familiar with the primary sources and with the development of interpretations of this document in China, the artificiality of the views cited above by the first European scholars of the document is entirely obvious. One can hardly dispute that the person Fu Hsi whom these scholars took on trust was only legendary. But if the problem of "authorship" of Fu Hsi falls apart by itself, the theory of the logical and mathematical significance of the *Book of Changes* requires some consideration in order to refute it conclusively.

---

7. This passage is a translation of one paragraph (p. 242) of Hauer's review mentioned in n. 4 above. Shchutskii's notes at this point are somewhat confusing. Following the quotation from Haupt, Shchutskii inserts the note, "Erich Hauer, 'I Ging. Das Buch der Wandlungen. Aus dem Chinesischen verdeutscht und erläutert von Richard Wilhelm,' p. 242." This seems a little premature since Shchutskii translates the rest of the paragraph from Hauer's review until he encounters another quotation from Haupt cited in the same review. This second passage Shchutskii leaves in German with the comment, "Hereafter, I shall maintain the language of the original, for I do not regard myself as a translator [*sic*] nor competent in mathematics." The German text of this passage, which follows "I answer" is: "Es enthält dasselbe nichts anderes als alle Facta eines Cubocubus, oder mich nach der Art der Arabischen Mathematiklehrer auszudrücken, eines Zensicubus, dessen Wurzel aus zwei Teilen bestehet (radicis binomiae) und worin die Cubicubi der Teile und alle Facta desselben je zwei und zwei dargestalt gegen einander geordnet sind, dass die Helfte der Factorum des einen Facti mit der Helfte der Factorum des andern dem ersten gegenüberstehenden Facti den übrigen Helften der Factorum in beiden Factis einander gleich ist." Tr.

Let us take first the view of the *Book of Changes* as a treatise of logic.

It is well known to everyone who is thoroughly familiar with the history of Chinese philosophy that ancient philosophers did not leave behind any treatises on logic. It is known that formal logic which is systematically set forth did not appear in China until the spread of Buddhism, with the translations of Indian logical treatises. It is true that in the modern period in Europe (Maspero) as well as in China (Liang Ch'i-ch'ao) attempts were made to find a treatise on logic in the chapters of *Mo-ching* and *Mo-ching-shuo* in the books of Mo-tzu. However, these attempts are based on a reconstruction of the text in which the presumed lacunae are filled with such quantities of reconstructed phrases that the authenticity of the text remains to some degree doubtful. Let us suppose that Mo-tzu is a logician. But even though, under his disciples, his school competed with the schools of the Confucians and Taoists, yet in the following generations it did not find any successors, while Confucians and Taoists further developed for a few centuries and became represented in widely varied currents. Buddhist logic, as is known, did not have to compete with "the logic of Mo-tzu." If one takes this into account, how can one maintain that logic was already elaborated in the time of the legendary Fu Hsi?[8]

8. The book *Mo-ching*, to which the author refers here, is traced by common tradition to Mo Ti, one of the thinkers of ancient China, and is regarded as his work or at least an exposition of his teaching. There is very little information about Mo Ti himself and his lifespan is considered to be approximately 478–397 B.C. Some sections of his book (經上, 經下, 經說上, 經說下, 小取, 大取) contain elements of logic and dialectic (in the ancient Greek sense of this word, that is, method of reasoning.) Scholars find that original definitions given in these sections correspond to such notions of European logic as judgment, conception, deduction, and there are differentiations among affirmative, negative, and hypothetical judgments; between conceptions of the general and the particular, and in deductions between attempts and conclusion; the presence of middle terms is noticed, and modus and figures are examined. Of course, the text known to us is not uniform as far as the time of composition of its

19

The mathematical interpretation of the *Book of Changes*, though it originated from such a thinker as Leibniz, also can be refuted by almost the same arguments. But the fact is that these complicated mathematical notions of which the advocates of the mathematical interpretations speak could not have had any place in China in the period of the creation of this document, that is, in the eighth and seventh centuries B.C. This theory, nevertheless, can be impressive, for (1) the embryo of the theory of numbers and primitive observations concerning the equality of different prime numbers (the so-called magic squares) were since antiquity connected by legend with the myth concerning the origin of the *Book of Changes*; (2) the cabalism of numbers was elaborated in one of the commentatory schools which had developed the maxims of the *Hsi-tz'u chuan* concerning divination; and lastly (3) in the sixty-four hexagrams, which are figures composed of solid or broken lines arranged in six strata, one cannot but notice a mathematical series of permutations representing the sixth power of two.

However, these foundations for the mathematical interpretation are unconvincing. The first two fall apart, for they are not based on any historical document, but on a legend and the apocrypha; also the third, since mathematical regularity can be observed equally in wordly phenomena which do not have direct relationship to mathematics, though they can be studied by mathematical methods. Thus, even if we accept that in the hexagrams of the *Book of Changes* mathematical regularity of numbers of permutations in the sixth power of two is recognizable, we categorically deny that the essence of our document is hidden in this conformity or that it represents the document's forgotten (?)[9] content. It is true that these

---

individual chapters or the origin of these chapters is concerned, but there remains no doubt that what can be considered later supplements actually date to antiquity. A number of scholars and sinologists in China and Japan (Koyanagi Shikitaro) have done research on these sections of the *Mo-ching* from the standpoint of logic and with complete relevancy. K.

9. The question mark is Shchutskii's. Tr.

theories cannot be denied their cleverness, but they are based
on a superficial familiarity with the document.

For completing the picture of this period of the study of
the *Book of Changes* in Europe it is necessary to mention only
Schumacher, about whom Alfred Forke[10] writes: "According
to I. P. Schumacher (Wolfenbüttel, 1763) the Yiking contains
a history of the Chinese, an opinion which also seemed to
have appealed to P. Regis, the first translator."[11] To these
words Forke adds a footnote: "However, Hexagrams 11, 54,
62, 63 contain some historical notes which related to the years
1191 and 1320 B.C. (Edkins); however, there is still a long
way to go from this point to history."[12] Of course, the mention of names of historical figures or geographical places does
not immediately make the *Book of Changes* historiographical,
but it should not be forgotten that in the second part of *Hsi-
tz'u-chuan* the entire "history of culture" of ancient China is
expounded. Undoubtedly this could serve as evidence for the
opinion that the *Book of Changes* is an historical document.[13]
We can, of course, doubt the documentary value of the
evidence of *Hsi-tz'u chuan*. However, one must admit that
this part was written in such fine and witty language that it
can no doubt be impressive. The famous Japanese philosopher
of the seventeenth century, Kumazawa Banzan 熊澤蕃山,[14]

10. See A. Forke, *Geschichte der alten chinesischen Philosophie* p. 11. S.

11. We have translated the German text which Shchutskii cites in the
original: "Nach I. P. Schumacher (Wolfenbüttel, 1763) enthält das Yiking
eine Geschichte der Chineses, eine Ansicht, welcher auch der P. Regis, der
erste übersetzer zuzuneigen scheint." Tr.

12. Shchutskii notes: "Forke refers here to J. Edkins, 'The Yi King with
Notes on the 64 *kwa*,' *China Review*, XII (1883–1884)." We have again trans-
lated the German text which Shchutskii cites in the original: "Allerdings
enthalten die Hexagramme 11, 54, 62, 63 einige Notizen, die sich auf die
Jahre 1191 und 1320 v. Chr. beziehen (Edkins), aber von da bis zu einer
Geschichte ist doch noch ein weiter Schritt." Tr.

13. It can be pointed out that this Appendix to the *Book of Changes* is sometimes considered an historical document, even in China. For instance, the
Shih-chi is based on materials of the *Hsi-tz'u chuan*. S.

14. See Kumazawa Banzan, *Shūgi washo* 集義和書. This book is provided
with an index where, under 易 (*eki*), one can find all corresponding places. S.

for instance, and almost three centuries after him, a German scholar, Richard Wilhelm,[15] who is the best of all European translators of the *Book of Changes*, surrendered to its influence. One can, of course, argue with Wilhelm on his understanding of the particular place of the second part of *Hsi–tz'u-chuan*, but we shall deal with the problem in detail later. Here it is enough to mention that Schumacher's opinion is based, not on the four places[16] in the text of the *Book of Changes*,[17] but mainly on the whole passage of the *Hsi–tz'u chuan*. Therefore, we cannot subscribe to this theory, either, for it is based on an uncritical confusion of the basic text with the commentary *Hsi–tz'u chuan*. In addition, this point of view tolerates the use of legendary material as historical document.

The philosophico-ethical speculation based on incorrect understanding of the text which Piper[18] constructed in 1849 does not have any significance.

The first period of the study of the *Book of Changes* in Europe, which lasted more than one hundred and fifty years and is characterized by insufficient knowledge of the text and by the formation of various fantastic theories, was limited to these men. At the present time all these works have lost their scholarly significance and can be mentioned only in relation to the history of the study of the book in Europe.

The second period is characterized by the appearance of complete translations of the document. In a comparatively short period of time (twenty-one years) five translations appeared.[19] Their quality will be discussed below; here we

15. See R. Wilhelm, *Geschichte der chinesischen Kultur*. S.

16. Incidentally, the authenticity of these places is controversial, as Chinese and Japanese critical literature (Wang Ying-lin and Naito) often mentions this problem, which will be discussed at greater length below. S.

17. That is, in the old layer of the text. Tr.

18. See Forke, p. 11, n. 5. S.

19. T. McClatchie, *A Translation of the Confucian Yi-king*; J. Legge, *The Yi King*; P.L.–F. Philastre, *Tscheou Yi*, Ch. de Harlez, *Le Yih-king. Texte primitif, rétabli, traduit et commenté*; Ch. de Harlez, *Le Yi-King, traduit d'après les interprètes chinois avec la version mandchoue*. I cite the last translation from the review

shall investigate the views of the translators of our document on the problems connected with it. Since there are other sinologists who did not do their own translations, but expressed their opinions about it based on these translations (or only partly based on the original), it is appropriate to examine their opinions as well.

McClatchie's translation came out in 1876. It is unnecessary to repeat the nature of this incomplete translation, for it has been discussed often with sufficient clarity. Legge wrote: "I have followed Canon McClatchie's translation from paragraph to paragraph and from sentence to sentence, but found nothing which I could employ with advantage in my own" [Legge original – Tr.]. Unfounded statements characterize the "style of the work" of McClatchie and it would be unnecessary to mention this were it not for the "originality" which impresses some sinologists[20] even now. His fantastic views are rather laconically introduced in Forke's above-mentioned book (pp. 11–12): "For McClatchie the *I Ching* is a cosmogony based on the dualism of *yin* and *yang*. Connected with it is his discovery of a phallic cult in ancient China which he substantiates with one quote from Appendix III." Forke continues [in a note to the above, – Tr.]:

We are informed that the *I Ching* originated, as did all the other pagan religious books and sacred writings, at the time of the division of the sons of Noah—Shem, Ham, and Japheth, or at least from the reports about these times. The ancestors of all pagans, as Moses says, must have been gathered at one place where they wrote down the despoiled religious forms and took them along when they dispersed. The *I Ching* was saved from the Great Flood by "the Great Father" of the present-day human race. It (the *I Ching*) gives us the materialism of ancient Babylonia and the eight deities: Father, Son, and six children—the

---

by Hauer mentioned above. S. [Zottoli's Latin translation of 1880 is not mentioned here, but below on p. 39. It appeared in the third volume of his *Cursus Litteraturae Sinicae*. Tr.]

20. The myth of phallic worship as the basis of the *Book of Changes* was partially adopted by Conrady and Erkes. See "Yih-king Studien," p. 417. S.

Dii majorum gentium (McClatchie, "Symbol of the Yih-king," pp. 152ff.). According to the *I Ching* the first and second hexagrams— Ch'ien and K'un—are Shang-ti (God), the phallus, the god of paganism, the hermaphrodite, or the all-embracing monad of the pagan world. *Ch'ien* is the male and *K'un* the female sexual organ. They are both united in one ring or phallus—in T'ai-i, from which all creatures originate. Legge shouts: "Ah, shame!" [Legge, *The Yi-King or Book of Changes*, p. 396 – Tr.] Shang-ti is identified with the Baal of the Chaldeans. The Dragon is *membrum virile* and at the same time the symbol of Shang-ti. The Bible and the *I Ching*, Babylonia and China, mythology and comparative history of religion, antiquity and the modern world form a queer jumble in McClatchie. He does not adduce a trace of evidence for his statements. The Chinese themselves do not have the slightest idea of a phallic cult (cf. McClatchie, "Phallic Worship," pp. 257ff).[21]

After such characterizations one can hardly mention McClatchie's work as other than a pseudoscientific delirium.

Terrien de Lacouperie[22] is no less reckless but with some theoretical success. The basic ideas of Lacouperie can be summarized as follows. The *Book of Changes* is a collection of genuinely ancient materials, the understanding of which was subsequently lost and thus it was used as a divinatory text. At bottom, the book is of non-Chinese origin. It was brought to China in 2282 B.C. by the "people of Bak origin" under the leadership of Prince Hu-Nak-kunte (Yu Huang-ti).[23] In the West, whence they came to China, they must have familiarized themselves with the cuneiform writings of the Middle East. They still first had to struggle with descendants of Sargon (Shen-nung). These "people of Bak" were familiar with Babylonian dictionaries, and the *Book of Changes* is only an imitation of the latter. Lacouperie proceeds from the correct observation that in many hexagrams the line texts repeat

21. J. Legge, *The Yi King*, p. 390. S.

22. A. Terrien de Lacouperie, *The Oldest Book of the Chinese*, vol. 1: S.

23. See Lacouperie, p. 106. The "Bak families" are Lacouperie's identification of the Chinese Po-hsing 百姓 and he equates "Hu Nak-kunte of Sunana" with one Yu Na Hwang-ti, presumably the Yu of the Great Flood. Tr.

the name of the hexagram, but this name is not always re-peated six times in all the six lines.[24]

This observation could have been fruitful, but departing from it, Lacouperie starts to do savage violence to the text. He eliminates what bothers him from the text without fol-lowing any system. He either eliminates or maintains the same word depending on what he must prove. He completely dismisses the commentatory tradition. The basic text is not quoted completely, but only the most ancient layer (again it is a correct observation on the multilayered nature of the text, but with the wrong conclusions). After such a "treatment" of the text, more correctly of only the most ancient layer, Lacouperie goes on to the conclusion that what we have is a dictionary in which a sort of handbook of state management is set forth under the sixty-four words. Furthermore, sub-jecting the signs of the *Book of Changes* to an entirely inadmis-sible "treatment," examining them from various aspects, he "proves" that one of the dead languages of the Near East lies at the basis of the text. Of course, it is correct that the text consists of various layers, that not in all hexagrams is the name repeated six times, that in the text quite often one encounters poems, the meter of which is often broken by interspersed divinatory additions like "good fortune," "misfortune," "no error," etc. However, one can hardly agree that the book is of "Bactrian" origin and at the same time is the book of the Chinese themselves.

One should remember that this theory is based on extremely shaky "evidence," on the declaration that the simple term *po-hsing* (bak-sing) 百姓 , which means a hundred (many, all) families—peasants—people, is construed as "people from the origin of Bak" that is, Bactrians. Believing this to be the "Bactrians," on the basis of accidental consonance of semanti-cally unrelated terms, Lacouperie concludes that the *Book* is from the Near East and for this reason places it in the Pro-

24. Such correct conclusions can be drawn from this; see Naito's opinion on the *Book of Changes*, below. S.

crustean bed of his own arbitrariness. Moreover, let us suppose for a moment that is really is a dictionary, if not Bactrian-Chinese, at any rate X-Chinese. But in that case the "theory" of Lacouperie does not stand up to criticism either, for as Forke notes on good grounds, "Lacouperie does not show why a dictionary was needed which consisted of only the sixty-four signs, and how incoherent stories happened to be included in it."[25] It would be possible to assume that we have only a fragment. However, this assumption should also be discarded[26] if one is to take into consideration that the number of hexagrams, as the number of permutations in the sixth power of two, can only equal sixty-four. Therefore, in the sixty-four hexagrams we have an internally complete whole. Is it not clear that Lacouperie's "theory" falls to the ground?

However, this theory impressed Legge in his time. Although he rejected it as a whole, he still showed some interest in it, considering that if it threw some light on the written language of China on the basis of discoveries made in the sphere of dead languages of Akkad and others, then it should not be dismissed. But on the same page[27] he strongly doubts the understanding of the text by the author of this "theory." Nevertheless, seven years after the appearance of Legge's translation in print, de Harlez again turned his attention to the "lexical theory" of Lacouperie. He developed this theory, admiring Lacouperie's (p. 6), and while denying the Akkadian origin of the *Book of Changes* (p. 9), he adopted the view of the *Book of Changes* as a dictionary with such conviction that he constructs his entire technique of translation on this basis (pp. 11–12). He writes:

The original *Yi-ching* consisted of sixty-four divisions or chapters, each of which had one idea as its object, *one word* [italics ours – S.] which was expressed by a hexagram and by a character of [the Chinese]

25. See Forke, p. 13. S.
26. "Yih-king Studien," p. 413. S.
27. See J. Legge, *Yi King*, p. XIX. S.

language. This word was accompanied by a general explanation and moral reflections. To this word were added other explanations of details, examples, quotations showing the cases of usage of a word, sometimes a whole passage, or a small poem.[28]

It is remarkable that this view was adopted by Conrady, despite the fact that, criticizing Lacouperie, he himself speaks against the lexical theory. In the opinion of de Harlez, the *Book of Changes* subsequently became entirely overgrown with a series of aphorisms, in which one often encounters a grain of original wisdom. It is true, as Forke correctly notes, that "owing to his rather tendentious translation with a strong involvement of commentators, he succeeds in bringing into the text more than it contains in reality."[29] Based on such premises and such a translation, de Harlez comes to the conclusion that the *Book of Changes* is in essence a notebook of some political figure,[30] which another political figure turned into a divinatory text.[31] In actuality what happened was exactly the opposite: the divinatory text, after a treatment of many centuries in commentatory schools, was employed by politicians in China and Japan.

Two works which belonged to this period have been mentioned above: these are the works of Philastre and Legge. The former is, despite its substantial size (two big volumes), not worthy of attention concerning theory. The introduction to the work is very short, repeating only the traditional viewpoints which we have already mentioned sufficiently. It is enough to mention only that Philastre was the first to decide to pay the necessary attention to the Chinese commentatory literature. He obviously attached great significance to it; this can be seen from the fact that throughout the whole translation

28. Ch. de Harlez, *Le Yih-king. Texte primitif, rétabli, traduit et commenté,"* p. 12. S.

29. See Forke, p. 13. S.

30. *Ibid.* S.

31. A similar view is adopted by Conrady's school: H. Haas, E. Erkes. S.

he adds to each phrase the recapitulation of the commentaries of Ch'eng I, Chu Hsi, and other philosophers whose names he more often than not fails to identify. At the basis of his work there obviously lies the compiled commentary *Chou I che-chung* 周易折中 ,[32] which is very popular also among the other translators (Legge, Wilhelm). Of course, this publication can be acknowledged as quite authoritative. Certainly the desire to take adequately into account the findings of the Chinese tradition is praiseworthy. But this correct purpose notwithstanding, Philastre's work should be regarded as unsuccessful. The reason for the failure is the insufficiency of the author's sinological technique. Philastre is a bad translator. He is too subjective to write an account of the commentaries which really reflect the Chinese tradition. In corroboration of our judgment we can again cite Forke. In the above-mentioned book we read (p. 13, n. 2): "From Philastre's translation we cannot obtain a correct picture, since both commentaries [which Philastre recapitulates–S.] are more independent development [of ideas] than explanation of the *Yi-ching*." Obviously Philastre's work has only historical significance, as a work by the first European who understood that it was better to take into consideration Chinese scholarship than to create one's own fantastic theory on the little-researched text.

In contrast to Philastre's work, Legge's has a long preface and introduction (pp. xiii–xxi and 1–55) and numerous footnotes scattered through the translation. Temporarily leaving aside the problem of Legge as a translator, we must dwell on his work in more detail than that of his predecessors for in

---

32. *Chou I che-chung* is a large (22 chüan) collection of commentaries on the *I Ching* and was compiled in 1715 by order of the K'ang-hsi Emperor by a group of experts on ancient written documents headed by Li Kuang-ti 李光地 . By publishing such a collection, the ruling circles of the time, who were struggling with all kinds of free-thinking, endeavored to lead the study of the *I Ching* into a definite channel. This collection, which enjoyed extremely wide dissemination, became the chief textbook for the study of the *I Ching* by European sinologists in the nineteenth century. K.

bourgeois sinology, his work played a most important role. It continues to have significance even now, as can be seen from the fact that H. Maspero refers the reader to Legge's translation as follows: "There are many translations of the *I Ching*, but they are all very bad; for such a work, by its nature, seems almost untranslatable. I refer to Legge's translation 'The Yi-king.'"[33] We are far from the opinion that Legge's work is the best that has ever been done in European sinology. However, one cannot but recognize that it was the fruit of long assiduous labor. Legge started his work a long time ago; as early as 1854 and 1855 he finished his first translation of the entire document, having only Regis as his predecessor. After the final editing his translation saw the light only in 1882, that is, after twenty-seven years! One of the reasons for such a delay in publication was an unhappy incident: "The translation was soaked in 1870 for more than a month in the water of the Red Sea. By dint of careful manipulation, it was recovered so as to be still legible, but it was not until 1874 that I began to be able to give the book the prolonged attention necessary to make it reveal its secrets" (p. xiii). Despite a series of deficiencies, the translation is nonetheless the best for the period. In the extensive preface, Legge shows his knowledge of the material through the primary sources.

However unsatisfactory it may seem, one cannot deny his knowledge for this period, for Legge was more brilliant than any of his predecessors and contemporaries when he mentions, for instance, one of the Appendices (if one is to follow his terminology) to the *Book of Changes*: that is, the so-called *Wen-yen chuan*. It is known that, according to naive tradition, this text was attributed to Confucius. But Legge correctly refers to one place in the text of the *Tso-chuan*, where it mentions divination by the *Book of Changes* which took place fourteen years before the birth of Confucius. With perfect soundness Legge doubts that Confucius was the author of this

33. H. Maspero, *La Chine antique*, IV, 444. S.

Appendix, denying in passing his authorship also with regard to the rest of the Appendices (pp. 30ff). Much earlier (p. 4), speaking about the *Chou-li*, where there is a story on divination by the *Book of Changes*, Legge correctly doubts the genuine antiquity of this document. The description of the relation of Confucius to the *Book of Changes*, which was given by Ssu-ma Ch'ien, was known to Legge and he also knew that the information about this relationship in Ssu-ma Ch'ien is not completely accurate. Also the catalogue of Liu Hsin 劉歆 [34] was familiar to him, as was the extent of the commentatory literature. One can assume that Legge obtained this information, as well as the other, mainly from *Chou I che-chung*, which we have already mentioned.

Legge was remarkably conscious of his own superiority when he wrote that if European scholars of the book constantly encountered failures, it was because they were not sufficiently familiar with the document itself and with the literature about it. Thus, in this introduction, Legge had to contrast his knowledge with the incorrect opinions of his time. The introduction is divided into three large chapters. The first chapter investigates problems concerning unity of the text, date of the document, authorship, and its relationship to Confucius (pp. 1–9).

The second chapter (pp. 9–26)—the weakest one—is mainly devoted to a description of the document. In it Legge is entirely under the influence of Chinese tradition, and says almost nothing new in view of the fact that all this had long been known in China. The basic source for this chapter is the

---

34. The catalogue of Liu Hsin to which the author refers is the *Ch'i-lüeh* 七略. The writing of the book was begun by Liu Hsiang 劉向 (80–8 B.C.) and completed by his son Liu Hsin, who lived from the end of the first century B.C. to the beginning of the first century A.D. In this catalogue are registered all the documents of ancient writings which were known in this period. Liu Hsin, who had divided these documents into seven parts, established bibliographical classification and became the founder of bibliography as a branch of philology in China. K.

Appendices (particularly the *Hsi-tz'u-chuan* and *Shuo-kua-chuan*) and Chu Hsi's treatises, attached to the *Chou I che-chung*.

The third chapter (pp. 26–55) is devoted to the Appendices. In this chapter, Legge entirely repudiates the tradition of the authorship of Confucius, but he himself does not attempt to clarify a possible author or discuss the origin of the texts. He also casts aside the problem of their language. A large part of this chapter is devoted to the description of the content of the Appendices.

Obviously, the first chapter is most interesting. Therefore, it is appropriate to examine it in more detail here. Legge starts with the problem of the relationship of Confucius to the *Book of Changes*. That it was known to Confucius, Legge argues on the basis of the famous quotation from the *Lun-yü* (VII, 16): "If some years were added to my life, I would give fifty to the study of the *I* and might then escape falling into great errors." Legge points out that Confucius was at that time seventy years old and is surprised at his wish to add fifty more years. Leaving his bewilderment unsolved, Legge considers that this quotation proves only the fact that the *Book of Changes* was in the hands of Confucius. He reinforces this thesis by referring to the place in the biography of Confucius in Ssu-ma Ch'ien's *Historical Records*,[35] where it is mentioned that in his old age Confucius studied the *Book of Changes* so ardently that leather straps which bound up the slips in his copy were broken three times. Citing Confucius' words quoted by Ssu-ma Ch'ien: "Give me several years [more][36] and I should be master of the I." Legge writes: "I maintain that Confucius ardently studied the *Book of Changes*. It is seen from the materials of the *Lun-yü* that Confucius paid great attention to the reading of *Shih-ching* and the study of *Li-chi*, though in them not a word is given about his study of the

---

35. Concerning the incorrectness of this place, see E. Chavannes, *Les mémoires historiques de Se-Ma Ts'ien*, v, 400. S.

36. Here Legge apparently lost his bewilderment mentioned above. S.

Book of Changes."[37] Legge does not doubt Confucius' familiarity with the *Book of Changes*, but assumes that Confucius
does not seem to have paid special attention to the *Book* in
the first period of his life, learning with his disciples only the
Shih-ching and the *Li-chi*, and that only toward the end of his
life did he appreciate the value of the *Book of Changes* (pp. 1–2).

Legge's theory characterized the problem very well for his
own time, but it is not enough for our time, for without
corresponding criticism we cannot take these quotations on
trust. Confirming Confucius' familiarity with the *Book of
Changes*, Legge nevertheless categorically denies his contribution to this document or any to any part of it as an author,
and did so with complete validity. Therefore, Legge was
extremely cautious in speaking about "some kind of *Yi-ching*"
("a *Yi*"), which existed at the time of Confucius. But the
problem of whether or not Confucius had in his hand the
document as known to us is still not solved. As if he did not
recognize a slight contradiction, Legge says on the following
page (p. 2) that the *Book of Changes*, which survived the
burning under Ch'in Shih-huang-ti better than any other of
the classical books, can be regarded as an authentic document.
Raising himself occasionally above the level of the still rudi-
mentary philological criticism, Legge betrays himself with
regard to the problem of King Wen and the Duke of Chou
as the founders of the text of the *Book of Changes*. Thus,
speaking in the second chapter of doubling of primordial
trigrams and of their transformation into hexagrams, Legge
agrees with Chu Hsi that the legendary Fu Hsi doubled the
trigrams: "I will not venture to controvert his (Chu Hsi's)
opinion about the multiplication of figures (trigrams), but I
must think that their names as we know them now were
from King Wen" (pp. 13–14). Is this agreement on the
authorship of Fu Hsi not in contradiction with his later
statement (p. 40), "Let me observe that divination was prac-

37. The literal Legge quote (in quotation marks) cannot be found by us. Tr.

ticed in China from a very early time. I will not say 5,200 years ago in the days of Fu Hsi, for I cannot repress doubts of his historical personality"?

Once again Legge contradicts himself when he attributes to King Wen the consolidation of the cycle of the sixty-four hexagrams, and when he raises the question of why the figures developed only as far as sixty-four hexagrams and no further —up to one hundred twenty-eight hexagrams, etc. Incidentally, Legge finds the explanation for this only in the fact that since it is difficult enough to operate with even the sixty-four symbols, intellectual speculations with a larger number of symbols would present more difficulties. Whether or not this may be the case, Legge is right at least to the degree that the answer to this problem has not been found in sinology. More than that, the problem was not even raised (p. 14). It can be assumed, therefore, that after his twenty years' study, Legge truly had time to familiarize himself thoroughly, at least with the commentatory literature. In any case, its presence and scope were known to him at least through the publication of *Chou I che-chung* and through the information from Liu Hsin's catalogue (pp. 2–3).

Legge also knew well enough the other classical books, particularly the *Ch'un-ch'iu* and the commentary to it, the *Tso-chuan*. This text mentions the *Book of Changes* many times, and therefore is of special interest to us. On the basis of the facts of the *Tso-chuan*, Legge proves the relative antiquity of divination by the *Book*. He says (pp. 4–5) that the dates of divination go back to the period between 672 and 564 B.C. and that, since the *Tso-chuan* begins only with the year 722 B.C., one can assume there were already earlier divinations by the *Book of Changes*. In any case, it is obvious that the document had existed long before Confucius. Therefore, the legend of the authorship of Confucius should be rejected. However, two other books—still earlier versions of the *I Ching*, the so-called *Lien-shan* and *Kuei-tsang*, are already mentioned in the *Chou-li*. Citing the *Chou-li*, Legge is fully aware that this (the *Chou-li*) is not a sufficiently authentic text. However, Legge is not completely informed of commentary theories with regard to these two versions. He only knows that nothing was preserved from them (p. 4). We shall see below how information on these pre-*I Ching Book of Changes* was interpreted in China.

Maintaining that the *I Ching* came down to us in complete form, Legge, of course, takes a false step but a smaller one than the one taken by McClatchie, who regarded the *Book of Changes* as the most ancient document in Chinese literature. Legge writes (p. 7) that in the *Shu-ching* and the *Shih-ching* there are texts that are much older than the *Book of Changes*. According to Legge, the *Book* may take only third place in Chinese literature. Nevertheless, he notes, the value of the document is especially great, if one takes into consideration the fact that it is preserved in no worse shape than the ancient documents of Israel, Greece, Rome, and India (p. 3). However, if this can be said about the ancient part of the *Book of Changes*, it does not apply to its later parts which are called in China "Ten Wings" 十翼 (Legge calls them "Appendices.") As is known, Ssu-ma Ch'ien ascribed their compilation to Confucius. Legge is entirely right when he separates the Appendices from the basic text (p. 2): "They are published along with the older text which is based on still older linear figures [hexagrams–S.] ... these two portions should, however, be carefully distinguished."

The necessity of such distinction of the text becomes particularly clear under the following consideration: If one had to think that the Appendices date to the period of Confucius and the basic text to the period of King Wen, there is a 660 years' interval between them! If one is to doubt such antiquity of the Appendices, as Legge rightly does, then the interval grows wider. Legge proves that the Appendices were written after Confucius, but that some of them were included in the basic text, and that this led the early scholars astray, compelling them to consider these Appendices very old (p. 8).

It is difficult to pinpoint their compilers, but possible to assume that they were written between 450 and 350 B.C. (p. 3). Following tradition, Legge dates the basic text to the time of King Wen and the Duke of Chou. According to Legge's opinion, the first, smaller part of the basic text was written by King Wen, as Ssu-ma Ch'ien says, in 1143 or 1142 B.C., but the second, larger part was written by the Duke of Chou who died in 1105 B.C. (p. 6).

This is basically everything essential that can be drawn from Legge's work. This is a trustworthy work devoid of mistakes as long as the author reproduces the Chinese theories and does not attempt any dazzling discoveries in Lacouperie's style. That it is possible to elaborate upon the Chinese data will be seen when we come to deal with the account of P'i Hsi-jui's work.

To complete the picture of the second period of study of the *Book of Changes* in Europe we should mention an incomplete and somewhat undistinguished Latin translation by Zottoli and also the opinions of two other scholars. About them Forke writes: "Extremely harsh opinions were expounded on the work [the *Book of Changes* – S.] in the form as we have it before us. Davies calls the basic theses of *Yi-ching* childish and Gützlaff declares that it is absolutely nonsensical."[38]

In general, the views on the *Book of Changes* before the third period of its study in Europe can fundamentally be reduced to three types, as Hauer does.[39]

The first (Grube, Giles, and Wieger) regards the *Book of Changes* only as the divinatory text, which for precisely this reason escaped the fate of the other Confucian books at the time of their burning in 213 B.C. Grube writes:

There cannot be any doubt that the *Book of Changes* is one of the most ancient Chinese documents and as such it also cannot be denied that it is the most obscure and most difficult product in all Chinese litera-

38. Forke, p. 13. S.
39. See the review by Hauer mentioned above (n. 4), pp. 244 ff. S.

ture. But, however interesting it might be as the unquestionably oldest handbook of divination, it can claim only an insignificant literary value.[40]

Giles also maintains the same view and occasionally ironically mentions in passing Legge, who [according to Giles – Tr.] assumed that he finally found a key to the understanding of the *Book of Changes*, but without brilliant success.[41] The most "sensible" is Wieger, who writes:

The eight trigrams constitute the basis of the system. They are composed of solid and broken lines. There is no further secret. It consists of all sorts of combinations of the two elements in the trigrams and that is all. These trigrams are often attributed to the legendary character Fu Hsi. This story was invented in order to inspire more respect for the book. At any rate, King Wen of Chou was the inventor of the sixty-four hexagrams, each formed by a combination of two trigrams out of the possible eight. I call attention precisely to this point which is the key to the secret. The hexagrams are not the trigrams fused together, but two trigrams vertically superimposed on each other in which the second (upper) trigram is considered to rest on the first (lower). There exist changes in the hexagram[42] from the lower trigram to the upper; hence the name *Yi* ("change") which the entire system bears. The diviner interprets the nature and meaning of this change and applies it to a proposed question.[43]

This point of view is partially correct, for in the *Tso-chuan* many cases of divination by the *Book of Changes* are already noted, and the significance of the divinatory book is maintained after that till our times. However, it is only half correct, for it completely ignores the fact that for more than twenty-

40. See Grube, *Geschichte der chinesischen Litteratur* (Leipzig, 1909), p. 34. Tr.

41. H. Giles, *History of Chinese Literature*, p. 23. S.

42. This remark is enough to give us the right to reproach Wieger for his insufficient knowledge of the matter. According to the generally accepted theory, the "Changes" take place from hexagram to hexagram, not within one hexagram, in which only the development of the situation in time takes place. This matter will be discussed in more detail in the chapter on the composition of the *Book of Changes*. S.

43. L. Wieger, *Histoire des croyances religieuses*, p. 79. S.

1. *In Studies in Europe*

five centuries the *Book of Changes* has inspired great Chinese thinkers.

The proponents of the second point of view, taking the basic text beyond the divinatory focus, pay their main attention to the Appendices, particularly to *Hsi-tz'u chuan*, and endeavor to find in them an ancient Chinese document on natural philosophy. De Harlez and de Groot, for example, treat it thus. The latter found in the *Hsi-tz'u chuan* a source of Taoism and constructed on this basis his doctrine of "Universalism."[44] However, neither can this point of view be accepted with satisfaction. It not only ignores the basic text and proceeds from the *Hsi-tz'u chuan*, which was created for the basic text itself, but it also ignores all the numerous passages dealing with mantics, hexagrams, etc. in the *Hsi-tz'u chuan*. It is constructed on only a part of this treatise or, more correctly, on some quotations from it, and at that particularly on only such quotations which help the author to construct his theory of Universalism.

According to the third point of view, the *Book of Changes* is a dictionary. This view started with the version created by Lacouperie and persists up till now (Conrady and Erkes). It is impossible to subscribe to this theory either, for how can one explain that a book which was a simple dictionary for centuries was suddenly transformed into a divinatory book and that later the most learned philosophers of the country declared it the starting point of all philosophizing?

Richard Wilhelm's translation[45] is, of course, the greatest event in the third period of the study of the *Book of Changes* in Europe. There is no doubt that the author understood how his work differed from the works of his predecessors, when he characterizes the most serious one of all as follows:[46]

44. See further the review by Hauer mentioned above (n. 4), pp. 244–245. S.

45. R. Wilhelm, *I Ging. Das Buch der Wandlungen*. S.

46. See *Wilhelm, ibid.*, II, 194n. S. (The English translation by Cary F. Baynes has been used here. Tr.)

James Legge stresses the opinion that a real understanding of the *I Ching* becomes possible only when the commentary material is separated from the text, . . . and then supplies with it the commentaries of the Sung period [A.D. 960–1279]. Legge does not say why he holds the Sung period to be more closely related to the original text than Confucius [551–479 B.C.] What he does is to follow with meticulous literalness the edition called *Chou I Chê Chung*, belonging to the K'ang-hsi period [1662–1722], which I also have used. The rendering is very inferior to Legge's other translations. For example, he does not take the trouble to translate the names of the hexagrams—a task of course not easy but by so much the more necessary. In other respects also, definite misconceptions occur. [Wilhelm/Baynes, p. 257n. 2 – Tr.]

This opinion rests fundamentally upon Wilhelm's philological credulity, which allows him, as we well know, to doubt tradition under pressure only of the most forceful arguments. Thus it is typical for Wilhelm to believe that the basic text was written by King Wen and the Duke of Chou and that even if the Ten Wings do not owe their origin to Confucius himself, then they at least originated from his closest disciples. Wilhelm's work must be clearly divided into two aspects: his research and his commentated translation. Although the latter is done so well (though not without mistakes) that it is simply impossible to compare it with the translations of his predecessors, unfortunately this cannot be said about his analytical part.

In the preface to the first book Wilhelm mentions the origin of his work. From what he says it becomes clear that all his understanding was directed to the translation, not to the research analysis. This translation pays closest attention to the tradition of *I Ching* experts in China. One of them was Wilhelm's teacher Lao Nai-hsüan 勞乃宣,[47] an old dogmatist related to the descendants of Confucius (p. xlv). As a translator Wilhelm is distinguished by his exceptional conscientiousness. The entire text was translated from Chinese into German, and then the German translation was translated back into

47. Chinese transcription of the name mentioned by Erkes. S.

Chinese; and the German translation was accepted only when the Chinese version was satisfactory (apparently to Lao Nai-hsüan ? – S.). Undoubtedly this enabled the translator to understand the text well and to understand it with its positive interpretation, based on recognition of its significance and importance. Consequently, in making a general evaluation of the document, Wilhelm writes: "The *Book of Changes—I Ching* in Chinese—is unquestionably one of the most important books in the world's literature. Its origin goes back to mythical antiquity, and it has occupied the attention of the most eminent scholars of China down to the present day." [Wilhelm/Baynes, p. xlvii – Tr.]

The attention paid to Chinese literature is characteristic of Wilhelm. He understands its significance and clearly prefers it to the European interpretations based on diletante understanding of Chinese culture and on the attempts to explain it with the assistance of observations made on culturally backward people ("barbarians," in Wilhelm's terminology). Having made this remark about MacClatchie (p. xlix, n. 5), the author goes on to discuss the *Book of Changes*. First, he talks about it as a divinatory book. In his opinion, the basic symbols of the book, solid and broken lines—are "yes" and "no" in the most primitive oracle. Subsequently they became complicated by a combination of solid and broken lines in which there already existed a trace of observation not of the objects of the world, but rather of their movement and change (p. l).

Wilhelm assumes that the hexagrams do not represent objects themselves as much as their functions.[48] Thus, if a functional movement is expressed by the symbols of the book, then the study of the technique of representation of this movement by the transformation of one hexagram into the other turns out to be most essential. Wilhelm pays considerable

48. As is known, Maspero emphasized very soundly that in the *Book of Changes* there is no difference between the objects and their symbols. Wilhelm here modernizes the *Book of Changes*. S.

attention to this problem (pp. l–liii). When an attempt was made to explain rationally that at an earlier stage thinking was achieved only in the practice of divination, then the first text appeared (Wilhelm has in mind *Kua-tz'u* and *Hsiao-tz'u*). When to the divinitory signs was attached a lucid text which indicated how a man who consults the *Book of Changes* in order to participate consciously in the perfection of his fate should act, then an important forward step was made in enhancing the assessment of man's role as a participant in the world process (p. liii).

However, this enhancement of the assessment of man's role cannot leave aside the problem of his moral responsibility. Precisely this existence of a moral feature in divination by the *Book of Changes* distinguished it in a fundamental way from all the other kinds of divination in which, as one assumes, only a fatal turn of events is indicated when a man cannot change anything and therefore cannot be regarded as an ethical subject (p. liii). The feature of accidence on which the technique of divination is based, has as its purpose only the inducement to a participation of the unconscious (p. liv). But it does not exclude in future the problem of moral obligations, the existence of which gradually turned this document into the starting point of philosophizing not only in China but also in the countries under the influence of Chinese culture.

After this general characterization of the *Book of Changes* Wilhelm goes on to discuss the problem of its historicity. In this sphere particularly there appears a vulnerable spot for our author. Thus, without the slightest evidence, he says that Lao-tzu and Confucius saw the *Book of Changes*, and that this had tremendous influence upon the world view of these thinkers[49] (pp. liv). Wilhelm finds the leitmotif of the *Book*— the doctrine of changeability—also in Confucius (*Lun-yü*, XI, 16): "Everything flows like it [the river – S.] without a stop,

49. Perhaps in such a semipopular book as his, Wilhelm consciously avoided philological argument, but should he not have given even in such a book at least the results of the critical researches? S.

day and night." [50] A transition to the notion of immutability in change is naturally recognized from such an observation. This immutability is the "Meaning" [51] in Lao-tzu. In the *Book of Changes* it is the "Supreme Ultimate"—T'ai-chi 太極 [52] (p. lv). The notions occupying the place of intermediary between the immutable and the changing are "Darkness and Light." Wilhelm considers the attempt to find a reflection of phallic worship in them a misunderstanding. One of the meanings—Male and Female origin—is merely a later introduction by speculative philosophers (p. lvi). Seeing the basic notion of the *Book of Changes* in the "Supreme Ultimate" Wilhelm discovers in it the idea which inspired Confucius as well as Lao-tzu, both extreme idealists in our author's view: for them the entire visible world is only the reflection of the preternatural. Therefore, the signs of the *Book of Changes* are also for Wilhelm only the images of not the objects, but of the processes (pp. lvi–lvii).

In general, Wilhelm says nothing new about the history of the text. He points out that Fu Hsi is only an allegorical figure and not a real being, but he does not doubt for a moment that King Wen and the Duke of Chou were actually the authors of the text. Rejecting the authorship of Confucius with regard to all Ten Wings, Wilhelm nevertheless considers him, without any evidence, the author of a major part of the *T'uan-chuan*. Though he does not ascribe the rest of the Appendices to Confucius himself, he in any case attributes them to his closest disciples. He therefore considers it possible and correct to interpret the *Book of Changes* with the assistance of the Appendices. Moreover, he commits a mistake which makes

50. Complete translation of the passage is: "The Teacher, standing by the river, said: 'Everything goes out like this! Without stopping day and night. . . .'" K.

51. The famous term of Lao-tzu (Tao) is translated thus. S.

52. We must remember that in the basic text there is no reference to the "Supreme Ultimate." This notion appeared only in *Hsi-tz'u-chuan* and composes its characteristic distinct nature in relationship to the basic text. S.

his work only conditionally acceptable. The anachronistic introduction of conceptions of the *Hsi-tz'u-chuan* into the basic text deprives the latter of its inherent character. However strange it may seem, Wilhelm contradicts himself. He accuses Legge of having attempted to interpret the book with the assistance of Sung commentaries, but he himself does exactly what the Sung *I Ching* experts did! Not only for this school, but also for Wilhelm the concentration of interest mainly on the *Hsi-tz'u chuan* is characteristic. The following fact will show where this led Wilhelm.

Among many works by Wilhelm, there is *A Short History of Chinese Civilization*.[53] This book, remarkable in many respects, is interesting to us from a special point of view. Essentially, what we have here is a general history of Chinese culture which must be written on the basis of documents, monuments of material culture, and historically reliable evidence. However, in this work Wilhelm accepts without reservation the passages mentioned above from the second part of the *Hsi-tz'u chuan* as the reliable source for the essay of the most ancient period of the history of culture in China. He writes:

In the Appendix [the *Hsi-tz'u chuan* – S.] to the *Book of Changes* it is set forth how cultural achievements gradually reached the people. It is difficult to say how old this outline of the history of culture is. But only two things are interesting in it: first, somewhere in antiquity they gradually changed from hunting and fishing to agriculture; cattle-breeding is not recognized in agreement with other indications; secondly, cultural institutions came from the basic cosmic situations understood religiously[54] as they are set forth in the hexagrams of the *Book of Changes*; i.e., the religious foundation of culture is emphasized. (p. 49)

Further Wilhelm brings up corresponding quotations from *Hsi-tz'u chuan*, alternating them with his own explanations.

53. Wilhelm, *Geschichte der chinesischen Kultur*. S.

54. This interpretation is entirely Wilhelm's, for the Chinese material does not substantiate it. S.

In view of the fact that special precision is necessary for a discussion of Wilhelm's work, let us quote from the original:

> He [Fu Hsi – S.] made knotted cords and used them for netting and fishtrapping to be used in hunting and fishing. He must have taken this from the Chinese character *li* ("adherence").
> This character *li* means the (oceanic?) sun-bird. It means at the same time attachment, like the flames which are attached to the wood which it burns. The net is therefore not necessarily a practical invention, but a sacral object which was later profaned.[55]

Since Wilhelm is convinced that cultural institutions are "profanations of sacred objects," there is no question for him that a sacred sign *li* (the thirtieth hexagram) preceded the invention of the net. Therefore, undoubtedly his *wohl* must be understood in the meaning of Russian *konechno* ("of course").[56] Moreover, from the entire context it is clear that Wilhelm places an emphasis on this *konechno*, and that the theory of "profanation of sacred objects" is based on this *konechno*. We have already mentioned that Wilhelm has a predecessor, Kumazawa Banzan, a Japanese Confucianist of the seventeenth century, in using this text for the interpretation of the cultural history of China. However, Kumazawa did not go so far. Of course, Wilhelm did not use Kumazawa's treatise, for he nowhere refers to his Japanese predecessor. We read in this author:

[Fu Hsi] deigned to teach [people] how to get a kind of fiber of hemp

---

55. We have once again taken the liberty of translating the German original which he cites. The text is: "... Er machte geknotete Stricke und benützte sie zu Netzen und Reusen für die Jagd und den Fischfang. Das entnahm er *wohl* [italics ours – S.] dem Zeichen Li (das Haftende).

Dieses Zeichen Li bedeutet den (ozeanischen?) Sonnenvogel. Es bedeutet gleichzeitig das Haften, wie das Feuer an dem Holz haftet, das es verbrennt. Das netz ist also nicht in erster Linie eine praktische Erfindung, sondern Ein sakral gebrauchter Gegenstand, der nachher profaniert wird." Wilhelm, *op. cit.* (n. 53), p. 49. Tr.

56. Actually, the German word "wohl" does not mean "of course" but "possibly," "perhaps." Tr.

and, making thread and rope, how to weave a net from them and catch birds and beasts with them in mountains and hills, and fish in rivers and seas. This he deigned to do in the image of hexagram "*li.*" "*Li*" is to fasten. "*Li*" is an eye [hole]—a play on words; eye-hole – S.] and its power to retain. This has the meaning that two holes of the net, setting the one on the other, hold the object at a particular place.[57]

It is not hard to notice that this can be understood differently than Wilhelm does. What is more surprising is his explanation that he used for his translation of the publication *Chou I che-chung* itself, in which is cited Hu Yüan's commentary devoted to the word *kai*, which Wilhelm translates in the meaning *konechno*. Here is the complete text of Hu Yüan's explanation.[58]

'蓋' 者疑辭也。言：聖人創立其事，不必觀此卦而成之。蓋聖人作事立器，自然符於合此之卦象也，非準擬此卦而後成之。故曰：蓋取。
周易折中，卷十五，上。

The word *kai* is a particle of doubt. It says that the sage, in creating the given institution, created it without necessarily contemplating the given hexagram. The fact is that the sage created the [cultural] institutions and established the implements so that, naturally, they were in complete agreement with the image of the given hexagram, but not in order to create them after the given hexagram was taken in the role of prototype. Thus it is said: "as if [he] took [them] . . . .

On the basis of this commentary it is clear that the corresponding quotation, as well as the following ones which are analogous to it, should be translated: "[Fu Hsi] created ropes with knots and made [from them] nets and snares for hunting and for fishing. As if [he] took [them] [that is, these things] from the hexagram '*li*.'" It is necessary to keep in mind that from the point of view of the authors of the *Hsi-tz'u chuan*, the system of the *Book of Changes* adequately reflects the regularity of the world. Therefore, from their point of view, to create something which is in accordance with a symbol of the *Book of Changes* means to create a thing which is completely

57. Kumazawa Banzan, *Shūgi washo*, pp. 168ff. S.
58. Wood-block edition, 1715. Our punctuation. S.

suited to the norms of the world; and on the contrary, to create something which is suited to world necessities means precisely to use a symbol as a prototype. The given document does not talk about "profanation of sacred objects." This is Wilhelm's personal interpretation, which perhaps makes the text more interesting to read, but distorts, sometimes significantly, the image of the *Book of Changes* that took shape from the familiarity with the text and the history of its understanding in China and in Japan for about 2,500 years. Therefore, it is not surprising that Forke says: "Wilhelm's translation needs to be used with caution, for he allows in his explanation many contemporary ideas which are foreign to the Chinese, and he lets go too freely the rein of his fantasy."[59]

However, despite all this, Wilhelm's translation cannot fail to be recognized as the best that has ever been done in Europe in the study of the *Book of Changes*. Therefore, the extremely critical review by Hauer[60] which, as is true, did not remain without sufficient reply on the part of Wilhelm, seems more than strange. This review is not devoid of valuable information and also represents one of the stages of the study of the *Book of Changes* in Europe. Therefore, we must dwell on one problem which is essential for evaluating Hauer's work.

It often happens that both sides in a dispute employ arguments that seem to them sufficiently convincing for their purpose, but it turns out that the entire dispute would proceed differently if greater attention were paid to the critical evaluation of the documents on which the argumentation of both sides is based.[61]

The dispute around Wilhelm's translation, *Das Buch der Wandlungen*, as he calls the *I Ching* in German, developed

---

59. Forke, pp. 13–14, n. 2. S.

60. In its informational part this review is interesting as a summary of the European works on the *Book of Changes*. The "critical" second part does not include a serious criticism. S.

61. Actually, I have in mind a Manchu translation of the *Book of Changes*. (Collection of the Institute of Oriental Studies, AD, no. 402.) S.

precisely in this direction. As is known, Wilhelm was not a "regular" sinologist and worked outside the tradition of German philological scholarship. He based his translation, first, on the oral tradition which was taught him by his teacher, Lao Nai-hsüan, for whom the *Book of Changes* is above all "the sacred text," suspicion of which, as of tradition in general, was not tolerated; and secondly, on the later eclectic commentary *Chou I che-chung*, which, despite all its eclecticism, basically comes from Chu Hsi's commentary *Chou I pen-i*. In Hauer's opinion, Wilhelm should have used as the basis of his translation the commentary *Jih-chiang I-ching* 日講易經, which is preserved both in Chinese and Manchu versions (it is possible that both versions were composed simultaneously and are not mutual translations, which increases the significance of the Manchurian text). The Manchu version, according to the opinion of the opponent, could have helped the translator in the selection of words, in the grammatical analyses of phrases of the text, etc. Basically it boils down to the fact that the opponent knew the Manchu language whereas the translator did not; and the easiest way for the opponent was to attack on this ground. Wilhelm protested soundly by arguing that the attacks by his opponent are meaningless, since, whether Manchurian or Chinese commentary, it is still just one of the commentaries. It seems to me that Wilhelm used the commentaries of the *Chou I che-chung* as the basis of his translation, because the latter is more widely accepted and understood. Neither the translator nor the opponent verified the accounts by their content and by the degree of criticism of this commentary as well as the Manchurian commentary *Inenggidari giyangnaha I-Dzing-ni jurgan*, nor did either of them clarify the place of these commentaries in the commentatory literature. But the examination of these problems leads to the following conclusions:

1) In the period of the Manchu dynasty in China there were two traditions around the *Book of Changes*: one was the tradition officially approved by governmental circles and the other

was the opposing one, permitting itself to doubt the reliability of the "good old days," not afraid of undermining the authority of Confucius himself. Often the works of the second trend awaited their coming to light longer than the lifetime of their authors. For instance, the commentary *I-cho* 易酌, belonging to Tiao Pao 刁包[62] (eighteenth century) was published only after the author's death. Basically Tiao Pao proceeded from the interpretations of Ch'eng-tzu (eleventh–twelfth centuries) and Chu-tzu (twelfth century) but he differs on some points from them and in any case he did not accept their belief in the "sage" authors of the *Book of Changes*; namely, Confucius and the "sage emperors" of extreme antiquity. Suspicion of this authorship originates from Ou-yang Hsiu (eleventh century), whose criticism was developed at a later period in China by Tiao Pao and P'i Hsi-jui (second half of the nineteenth century and beginning of the twentieth century) and in Japan by Itō Tōgai (seventeenth–eighteenth centuries).

2) These two trends find their reflection in the Manchu translations and interpretations. Thus, *Han-i araha inenggidari giyangnaha I-Dzing-ni jurgan-be suhe bithe*, which was specially recommended to Wilhelm by Hauer as a more highly accomplished study of the *I Ching* in China, is undoubtedly the product of Chu Hsi's school, which enjoyed the significance of official recognition in the Ch'ing period. His treatise on the Four Qualities of the Creative Principle (*Ch'ien*—first hexagram) comes entirely from Chu Hsi, and this, as Hauer correctly notes, sets the tone for all further interpretation. These Four Qualities—four words—Chu Hsi interpreted as follows: *yüan* —great; *heng*—to penetrate; *li*—proper, suitable; *chen*—right, immovable. In the Manchu text we read: "kiyan, amba, hafu, acabun, akdun." According to the dictionary by I. Zakharov, which translates Manchu terms extremely accurately, *kiyan* is simply a transcription of the Chinese *Ch'ien* (adaptation of which the authors of this version of the *I Ching* constantly

---

62. This name is miswritten in Shchutskii's bibliography. Tr.

misused); *amba*—great, big, massive; *hafu*—throughout, wholly, through; *acabun*—combination, conformity, obligation, use; *akdun*—right, hopeful, firm in word. Besides, this commentary basically repeats the legend that "Fu Hsi drew the trigrams and King Wen added the texts to them . . . ," etc., and it goes so far as to maintain Confucius' authorship of the Ten Wings; in other words, it repeats Chu Hsi. Another Manchu translation available to me, *Han-i araha ubaliyambuha Jijungge nomun*, though it pays attention to Chu Hsi, nevertheless does not always give Chu Hsi's interpretation of these terms. We find this quotation in the following form: "Kulun-ikengge, hafungga, acangga, jekdungge." Hauer's quotation is exactly the same, but he does not give an exact translation of it: "Die Himmelsattivität (ist) schöpferisch, durchdringend, zweckmässig (und) sicher" ["The activity of Heaven (is) creative, penetrating, purposeful (and) sure" – tr.]. If one is to speak not on the basis of the Chinese commentatory literature, but only on the basis of the Manchu translation, this should have been translated as follows: "The eternal heaven is primary, thorough (that is, all-penetrating), harmonious, and firm." It is obvious that for more authoritativeness Hauer quotes from the more widely known commentary and translation *Han-i araha inenggidari giyangnaha I-Dzing-ni jurgan-be suhe bithe* . . . while actually using *Han-i araha ubaliyambuha Jijungge nomun* —and only its translation, not its commentary. It is hardly to be regarded as an honest method of critique! Besides, while reproaching Wilhelm for his incorrect translations, Hauer himself is not free from them.

3) Neither the translator nor the reviewer notices the distinction between the two schools (regardless of whether they were Chinese or Manchu). But precisely this difference and the evaluation of these schools should have been made the basis of the selection of one or the other commentary.

4) Giving a preference to the critical school, we must nevertheless give a positive evaluation to Wilhelm, but not to Hauer. Wilhelm not only paid attention to the commentatory litera-

ture known to him, but also thought it out, raising himself up to the philosophical understanding of the *Book of Changes*, whereas for Hauer, the *Book of Changes* is merely a senseless oracle of street fortune-tellers. He cannot understand why it is so highly valuable in China.

5) The translation of the *Book of Changes* must be based on the commentaries of the critical school no matter in which language they may be written. In particular, the Manchu version (namely, *Han-i araha ubaliyambuha Jijungge nomun*) can be of greater service for translation.

Let us now turn to the other recent work, namely the piece by A. Conrady, which was published by E. Erkes after the death of the author.[63] Erkes declares on the very first page: "Conrady did not pay attention to the later interpretations and took the text of the *I Ching* as it was in order to gain information on the original meaning and on the basic significance of the *Book of Changes* with assistance of critical analysis and comparison of individual parts of the text." That could not be better! However, "these analyses brought him to the following thoroughly substantiated conclusions that the *I Ching* is none other than an old dictionary." Thus we have here a resurrection of the old theory on the base of new argumentation.

But whatever the arguments might be, we have already seen that they do not stand up to serious criticism, and it would be useless to repeat the criticism here. It is sufficient to remember that the individual chapters (hexagrams) of the *Book of Changes* form a complete unit, and that this is demonstrated by mathematical necessity; but a dictionary, we repeat, which consists of only sixty-four words, would hardly be used even on the most primitive level of culture, and at the time of the *Book of Changes* the cultural level was not that low. It is sufficient to turn even to earlier texts (*Shih-ching* and the oldest part of *Shu-ching*) or to the texts which are closer to the time of the *I Ching* (authentic chapters of *Kuan-tzu*), in order to understand

63. "Yi-king Studien," pp. 490–468. S.

that even at that time a dictionary of sixty-four words would have been meaningless. Faith in such a theory seems especially strange, because on page 413 Conrady criticizes (and rather sharply) Lacouperie for his "lexical" theory, but after this (p. 415) he himself maintains that the *Book of Changes* is a dictionary. It is true that Conrady directs his main attack at Lacouperie and de Harlez for their desire to relate the *Book of Changes* to Babylonia. There is no doubt that the lexical theory of Conrady is different from the lexical theory of Lacouperie, and Conrady himself gives complete consideration to this. He summarizes the results of his analysis as follows:

1) The *I Ching* is actually a kind of dictionary as Lacouperie maintains, but of considerably later date, namely, Chou times (for it is also called *Chou I*) since:

2) its glossary displays intellectual views which in any case apparently correspond to the moral-political viewpoints of the time of Chou, although this was not on such a wide scale as de Harlez wishes, and

3) hexagrams are an ancient writing system which does not have to go back to extreme antiquity, but is perhaps a kind of local writing of West China—the ancient region of the Chou or of their ruling predecessors there—the Chiang.

Conrady proves the last point by the fact that if supplementary lines are added to the hexagrams, he succeeds in some cases in turning a distorted hexagram into a picture distantly depicting some particular object. He succeeds in this only with regard to four (!) hexagrams out of the sixty-four. There can hardly be a law which is deduced on the basis of 6.25 percent of the entire material. For the "evidence" of his theory Conrady uses a traditional Chinese method: he turns the trigram ☵ (*k'an*) by 90° and points to its similarity in this position to the sign "water" in its written form (p. 419). Even if it proved to be true, one can question why the other seven trigrams do not display the slightest similarity to the signs of some kind of forms of Chinese handwriting. It must be said that the method of twisting a sign is unacceptable as evidence. Indeed, it does not occur to anyone to prove that the Chinese numerals originated from the same source as the "Arabic" numerals on the mere basis that Chinese *i* ("1"), if twisted by 90°, looks like our numeral 1 and Chinese *ch'i* ("7"), if the character is twisted 180°, looks like our numeral 7. How fantastic is Conrady's wish to discover phallic symbols in some hexagrams! In the criticism of McClatchie's work we have already seen that the symbols of the *Book of Changes* cannot acceptably be interpreted in such a manner. And here this should be remembered, only because Conrady's theory (though it is essentially a rehash of McClatchie's) apparently proved to be strongly influential on his successors.

Thus, for instance, B. Schindler in the first volume of his work devoted to the priesthood in ancient China, tracing the term *yin* (darkness) to the character *yün* 云 and adducing its archaic form, finds it possible to discover in it . . . a representation of the female genitalia. We prefer to adhere to the carefully and thoroughly documented analysis of Chinese characters done by T. Takada 高田忠周,[64] who convinces us that the character *yin* does not mean anything but "cloud". Besides, its archaic form survived almost without change in ornaments representing clouds in Chinese art. But even if we leave unattended these unsuccessful conjectures and turn to the evaluation of Conrady's analysis in essence, then the entire account of his work does not inspire any great optimism. It is true that if one is to talk about the criticism of the text made by Conrady, then one cannot but recognize that it was done with exceptional scrupulousness. Conrady does not let a single rhyme or a single (even conjectural) quotation escape his sight. All references are made with the most correct citation of place. Only the historically reliable material is quoted. In a word, it is the most accurate work available. This is especially important from our judgment of Conrady's work.

However, together with such precise analysis of detail,

---

64. See Takada Tadasuke, *Koryūhen* 古籀篇 , *sub verbo*. S.

Conrady allows unfounded conclusions about the whole. His entire work (with the exception of the general theses on the first fourteen pages) is a detailed analysis of the text, which is directed toward a proof that the *Book of Changes* was originally only a kind of interpretative, monolingual dictionary, which (we do not understand why) began to change into a divinatory text.[65] All this analysis and all the "proof" of Conrady's lexical theory is constructed on the analysis of the text of only four hexagrams (first, twenty-second, twenty-ninth, and forty-ninth). And even this material is studied only from the narrow philological aspect, and then only superficially, without suffi-cient consideration of the technical terminology of the *I Ching* scholars. Thus, for example, it is not clear to Conrady what the technical designation *ch'ien chih kou* 乾之姤 ("the creative changes into contraposition") means, that is, the situation reflected in the hexagram Contraposition.[66] Not suspecting that this is the usual and the only possible method of the stereotyped designation of transformation of one hexagram into another one (and in these transformations is the entire essense of the theory of the *Book of Changes*), Conrady con-structs an artificial theory of special designations of individual lines of hexagrams by the names of other hexagrams. It is true that such a method existed in Japan, not at the time of com-position of the *Book of Changes*, but in Tokugawa times, that is, in the seventeenth and eighteenth centuries. The mistake committed by Conrady lies in the fact that he understood the sign *chih* in the more common meaning of indicator of the genitive, but it must be understood as a verb "to go into. . . . "

65. If the latter were possible, then why were the dictionaries *Erh-ya* and *Shuo-wen* not transformed into divinitory books? Or why not divine by the *K'ang-hsi tz'u-tien*, whose tens of thousands of characters give more material than the sixty-four hexagrams! S.

66. The 44th hexagram in Wilhelm/Baynes, p. 170, is "Coming to Meet." Shchutskii's Russian term for this hexagram is *peréchenie* which is an abstract noun derived from *peréchen*, meaning "a cross-beam, girder, or transverse timber." This suggests the separation of two points which are at the same time linked in some fashion. Here we translate *peréchenie* as "Contraposition."

This is not the only annoying misunderstanding in Conrady's work.

But our purpose is not to write a review. We need only understand what this work itself represents among the other European studies of the *Book of Changes*. Despite his fine analysis, Conrady proved to be completely incapable of either a wide and far-reaching grasp of the material or of its correct interpretation as a whole. Therefore, he could not find a satisfactory view on the subject, but only philologically shared a theory which had been stated before him and which, unfortunately, was not the best. This quality of his work is especially important to keep in mind, for his philological technique can be very impressive to sinologists, and his theory can convince many unfamiliar with the material in detail.

After this chapter was completed I had a chance to become acquainted with Waley's article.[67] It is impossible to reject the wit and the originality of this work. However, it does not solve the problem in all its complications, and is only an attempt to understand the basic text of the *Book of Changes* as the amalgam of two heterogeneous elements: (1) folklore proverbs about omens and (2) magic formulae. Considerably greater attention is paid to the first, but the evidence is constructed on completely original translations of a great many places, while maintaining a constant method: one of the words of the quoted text must be understood as *omen*. Thus sometimes a free use of the typical syntax of the *Book of Changes* (for example, p. 127 § 5), sometimes of vocabulary (p. 125, on occasion of the word *fu* 孚), sometimes of documentation (for example, p. 124, arbitrary change of the word *tun* into *t'un* 遯 , 豚) appears, as this is more convenient for the hypotheses of the author. The date of the composition of the book is determined so tentatively between 1,000 and 600 B.C. that there is nothing new in this. The philosophical treatment and purport of the text could have begun, in the author's opinion, around the fourth

67. A. Waley, "The Book of Changes," *The* [*Bulletin of the*] *Museum of Far Eastern Antiquities*, no. 5 (Ostasiatiska Samlingarna) 121–142. S.

century B.C. The author rejects Confucius' familiarity with the *Book of Changes*.

At the end of the article two questions are raised: (1) why is the *I Ching* called the *Book of Changes*? and (2) what conditions the arrangement of the material in it? The author confesses he cannot answer the first question. The second question he answers with reference to an accidentally established plan. Of course, we cannot be fully satisfied with Waley's work. A valuable remark on the closeness of the *Book of Changes* to the *Shih-ching* is unfortunately not well-reasoned. The partially correct thesis that there are popular proverbs in the text is exaggerated to an incredible degree, as if the entire text consisted of proverbs about omens. Thus the systematic character and the organic development of the text went unnoticed by Waley. Unfortunately, while proceeding from the correct principle of separating all the Appendices from the basic text, he simultaneously commits the mistake of ignoring such a systematic treatise as *Hsü-kua-chuan*.

For our research only one assumption in Waley's article proves to be useful: that is, that the authors of the text of the *Book of Changes* used folklore materials of their time. But qualitatively this material played only a most insignificant role; it was used only as figurative material. As in speech, the meaning is not in sounds but in the words and phrases expressed by these sounds, so in the *Book of Changes*, as well, the meaning is not in the images, but in *how* these images as a whole are coordinated in the system. If it were not so, then how would it be possible to make clear that for a thousand years some kind of collection of records of omens has been the starting point for the philosophy of one of the greatest people on earth?

The list of the European works on the *Book of Changes* ends here. Other information about the *I Ching* is given occasionally in the course of the history of Chinese philosophy, but nothing original is offered so it is not worth mentioning.

Summing up the examination of the studies done in Europe on the *Book of Changes*, we unfortunately must notice first the striking diversity of opinions. Since the authors of these opinions have been mentioned above, here we limit ourselves, in the interest of conciseness and sharpness of the picture, to a list of opinions.

In European sinology it has been said that the *Book of Changes* is: (1) a divinatory text; (2) a philosophical text; (3) simultaneously a divinatory and a philosophical text; (4) the basis of Chinese Universalism; (5) a collection of proverbs; (6) the notebook of a politician; (7) a political encyclopedia; (8) an interpretative dictionary; (9) a Bactrian-Chinese dictionary; (10) a phallic cosmogony; (11) the most ancient historical document in China; (12) a textbook of logic; (13) a binary system; (14) the secret of the cubocubus; (15) the accidental interpretations and combinations of lines; (16) the tricks of street fortune-telling; (17) childishness; (18) delirium; and (19) a Han forgery. The most complicated and at the same time the simplest answer did not occur to anyone: that is, that the *Book of Changes* came into being as a text around the very ancient practice of divination and subsequently served as ground for philosophizing, which was especially possible since it (the *Book of Changes*), as a little understood and enigmatic archaic text, presents a wide scope for creative philosophical thinking.

CHAPTER 2

Noncommentatory Studies in the Far East

It is natural that the *Book of Changes* has been studied significantly more in the East than in Europe. In the East the historiography of the *Book of Changes* covers more than two thousand
years, and each author who wrote about it, even if he did not
know all the literature on the problem, was thoroughly familiar
with the document itself and usually followed one of his
predecessors. It is impossible to give here a complete account
of the entire literature devoted to the *Book of Changes*, but we
can make the task of a general survey of the Chinese and
Japanese literature of this kind considerably easier by dividing
it into four categories: (1) commentaries of various kinds which
were intended to immediately follow the text; (2) interpretative treatises on the content of the document; (3) treatises on
the technique of divination; and (4) treatises which developed
on the basis of a philosophical understanding of the *Book of
Changes*. In this chapter we are interested only in the treatises
of ideological content, including philological aspects.

It is appropriate to preface an examination of these works
(of course, only the major ones) by indicating the most ancient
references to this document, especially to divination according
to it.

First of all we should mention section nine of the chapter
"Hung-fan" in the *Shu-ching*. Here we read as follows:

The examination of what is doubtful. Choose and appoint people who
divine by the tortoise shell, and people who divine with milfoil stems,[1]

1. Divination with milfoil stalks lies at the basis of divination by the *Book
of Changes*. S.

and command them to divine. And they will tell you about rain, haze, mist, approaching storm, gale[2] and they will tell you about an internal sign and an external one.[3] There are altogether seven kinds of divination, five of which are with a tortoise shell, and two with the milfoil stems. This is to allow for doubts. And appoint these people and let them predict (with the tortoise) and divine (with the milfoil). If the three divine, follow the answer of at least the two who are in agreement. But if you have great doubt, then deliberate upon it, turning to your own heart; deliberate, turning to your retinue; deliberate, turning to the common people; deliberate, turning to the people who predict and divine.

If there is agreement among you, a tortoise, a milfoil, the retinue, and common people, it is called a great birth. And you personally shall be firmly and strongly established and good fortune shall meet your descendants. If there is agreement among you, a tortoise, and a milfoil, but the retinue and the common people oppose, then you shall have good fortune. If there is agreement among the people, a tortoise, and a milfoil, but you and the retinue oppose, then you shall have good fortune. If there is agreement between you and a tortoise, but the milfoil, the retinue and the common people oppose, then you shall have good fortune in the internal affairs of the kingdom, but misfortune in the external affairs of the kingdom. If a tortoise and a milfoil differ from the people, then good fortune shall meet those who are in inaction, but misfortune shall meet these who are in action.

As we see, great attention is paid here to divination with milfoil, but not a word is yet mentioned about divination by the text of the *Book of Changes*. However, this reference has some relation, for divination by the *Book of Changes* was in antiquity based on the selection of milfoil stems according to a definite order. Like the *Shu-ching*, the *Shih-ching* gives only an indication of the fact of divination itself: "And divine with a tortoise shell, and divine with milfoil stems" (see the *Shih-ching*, 1, Ode 5). This quotation is cited also in the *Li-chi*, chapter 30. On the basis of these quotations we can assume that if the *Book of*

2. All this refers to divination by the tortoise shell. S.
3. This is an internal trigram and an external trigram, that is, lower and upper parts of a hexagram. S.

Changes had not yet existed as a text then, there was neverthe-less the practice of divination in the course of which the text took shape in the oral tradition.

Furthermore, we have to discuss a number of references to the actual cases of divination which mentioned the text. One can encounter these references in the *Li-chi* and in the *Tso-chuan*. We shall talk further about these quotations from the *Tso-chuan* in more detail; here we limit ourselves only to the two places in the *Li-chi* where the *Book of Changes* is directly mentioned and quotations from it are cited.[4] First of all, we have a quotation: "An ox killed by eastern neighbors (as a sacrifice) cannot be compared to a small sacrifice of western neighbors (Hexagram 63, line 5). If you are upright, you shall indeed find good fortune!" It should be noted that this quota-tion concurs exactly with the present text of the *Book of Changes*. Secondly, in the same chapter of the *Li-chi* we find the following quotation: "To reap the harvest without having ploughed a field, and to use the field in the third year without having cultivated it in the first year brings misfortune." In the text of the *Book of Changes* this is stated somewhat differently: "[If] you reap the harvest without having ploughed the field, and use the field in the third year without having cultivated it in the first year, *then it will be favorable for you to have some place to go*" (Hexagram 25, line 2). The italicized words, apparently, are later additions originating from various com-mentatory schools. It can be assumed that these are schools of oral traditions, typical of the pre-Han period. Through these quotations we see the *Book of Changes* as a text studied by dogmatists. It is very difficult to determine when this dogmatic study began. However, it probably started in the pre-Han period, for the oral tradition, as is known, was especially pre-dominant before the Han period. However, even at that time the *Book of Changes* was not only mentioned as a divinitory text, or as a text about the ideal prototypes of behavior, but

4. See *Li-chi*, ch. 30. S.

also was the object of philosophical study. A passage from chapter 33 of the *Chuang-tzu* is apparently the first reference to the school of followers of the *Book of Changes* who regard it as a school of philosophy. It is known that this chapter does not belong to the great Taoist, but was written by one of the disciples of his disciples. Still, even with great skepticism, it cannot be considered later than the *Historical Records* of Ssu-ma Ch'ien, for this quotation is encountered in more advanced form in the *Historical Records* (*Shih-chi:* ch. 66, "Hua chi lieh-chuan"). Here is the context in which the *Book of Changes* is mentioned in this chapter, which is devoted to the analysis of the then existing philosophical schools in order to show the superiority of Taoism over the other schools.

Ah, what completeness the people of antiquity possessed! They were coordinated with the world of spirits, were pure between heaven and earth; they nourished everything existing, achieved harmony in the empire and were beneficent to all the clans of the people. They were enlightened concerning the number at the root and were not alien to the measure at the top. They acted everywhere; in the six infinite worlds, in the four quarters of the world, in the great and in the small, in the body and in the air. Out of those who were enlightened concerning the numbers and measures, many were writers on old laws and traditions descending from generation to generation. From out of those who were concerned with (literally, "abided in") the *Shih-ching* and *Shu-ching*, in the *Li-chi* and *Yüeh-ching*, the best people and the teachers of the realms of Chou and Lu, many could explain them [these books]. The *Shih-ching* talked about the intentions, the *Shu-ching* talked about events, the *Li-chi* talked about behavior, the *Yüeh-ching* talked about harmony, and the *Book of Changes* talked about darkness and light, and the *Chronicles* talked about differences of names (that is, definitions of terminology).[5]

If all we have here is a simple reference, there existed in China around the same period another text especially devoted to the *Book of Changes*. From this time on it began to be

5. Our italics. It is interesting to note that there is not yet a word mentioned here about divination by the *Book of Changes*. S.

included in the text of the book as Appendices. This is the oldest attempt to formulate theories which came to be included in the *Book of Changes* as the so-called *Hsi-tz'u chuan* or *Ta-chuan* (*Tradition on the* [appended] *Texts or great commentary* [decision]). The appraisal of these texts has varied over the centuries. Some, following the old version, ascribed them to Confucius, whereby they emphasized this enormous significance; others, on the contrary, completely denied their value. Among the first group we should mention K'ung Ying-ta (574–648), who says: "The teacher [Confucius] wrote the Ten Wings and in them developed the first and the second parts of the basic text. The text *Hsi-tz'u* is permeated paragraph by paragraph with fundamental ideas. It forms a special chapter generally called *Hsi-tz'u* [appended texts] and is divided into two parts" (*Chou I che-chung*, ch. 13, p. 16). Chu Hsi also supported the same opinion when he wrote:

The appended texts are, strictly speaking, the texts written by King Wen and the Duke of Chou. They are divided among the individual lines of the hexagrams and form the present basic text. This text (*Hsi-tz'u chuan*) is the interpretation of the appended texts given by Confucius. This interpretation sets forth the general thesis of the text as a whole; therefore, in it there are no specific passages to which one could relate it. It is divided into two parts.

Furthermore, Chu Hsi said: "When I attentively read over the text of the sixty-four hexagrams, then I understood that the words of the *Hsi-tz'u* represent the most hidden depth [of the text]. This is a summary of the *I* [*Ching*]" (*Chou I che-chung*, ch. 13, p. 16).

Side by side with such an interpretation, there existed other very impressive interpretations; for instance, the one held by a Japanese *I Ching* expert, Matsui Rashu (1751–1822), who in general ignored this text [the *Hsi-tz'u chuan* – Tr.].[6] The criti-

6. It was the same in China. See the commentaries by the scholars of the Sung period, Kung Yüan 龔原, *Chou I hsin chiang-i*, and by Li Kuo, *Hsi-ch'i-i-shuo*. However, although these authors do not include the *Hsi-tz'u chuan* in their editions, they took it into consideration. S.

cal approach to the *Hsi-tz'u chuan*, equally alien to both extremes, is represented by one of the most serious commentators among Japanese philosophers, Itō Tōgai (1670–1736). Concerning the text of the *Hsi-tz'u chuan* he made the following comment:

The appended texts are the line texts. Thus [in the *Hsi-tz'u chuan*] it is mentioned: "The sages established the hexagrams, contemplated their images, and appended the texts. And thus they explained fortune and misfortune." Furthermore, it is mentioned: "They appended the texts and thereby pronounced [fortune and misfortune]." This book [the *Hsi-tz'u chuan*] develops the significance of the hexagrams and the lines [which compose them], and generally interprets them. Therefore it is called *Hsi-tz'u* (appended texts). And here is the basis for this: "Judgments" and "images" are the Judgment and line texts. But the text, which entirely explains them, is also called "Judgments" and "images." [7] Some of the earlier Confucianists assumed that the appended texts are these explanatory texts. This is a mistake. Ssu-ma Ch'ien assumed that [the *Hsi-tz'u chuan*] was written by the Teacher [Confucius]. But his words are completely without foundation and we should neither believe nor follow him. I myself studied this book [and realize that] it combines within itself two principles—mantics and philosophy. And central in it is the feeling of duty and love. Does this not mean that in the period of *Ch'un-ch'iu* and *Chan-kuo* the trend of the experts of the *I Ching*, coupled with the learning of the Sage's [Confucius'] students, formed the foundation of these judgments (on the *Book of Changes*, that is, *Hsi-tz'u chuan*)?

Itō Tōgai, a remarkable scholar, rejects the authorship of Confucius with regard to the *Hsi-tz'u chuan*, and we can completely subscribe to his opinion. For this there exists a great deal of evidence: the fact that Confucius himself could not have called himself "Teacher" as is done in the *Hsi-tz'u chuan*; the fact that the terminology of this text is not identical with the terminology of the *Lun-yü*; the fact that the language of this text is considerably later than the language of the texts

7. Itō has in mind the abbreviated names *T'uan* [-*chuan*] and *Hsiang* [-*chuan*]. S.

connected with the name of Confucius; and finally the fact that Confucius himself emphasizes (*Lun-yü*, Ch. VII) that he does not "write" but only transmits. However, the *Hsi-tz'u chuan* is a text of great importance for the problem we are studying. It is, after all, the first attempt to evaluate and synthesize the material contained in the *Book of Changes*. Therefore, the basic subject of the present chapter—noncommentatory study of the book in the Far East—begins actually with the Judgments, which are scattered in the text of the *Hsi-tz'u chuan*. Everything previous was merely the "pre-history" to this question.

Thus the *Hsi-tz'u chuan* (Tradition on the appended texts) is an independent book which is now usually attached to the editions of the *Book of Changes*. It is divided into two parts: with regard to both its themes and its style, it is by no means a homogeneous text; it is, rather, a collection of short statements on the *Book of Changes* as a whole, and on various themes from the points of view of various experts of the *I Ching*. In general, the following themes are touched upon: (1) ontology; (2) reflections on the *Book of Changes* and the adequacy of these reflections; (3) origin of the book (two interpretations); (4) embryos of epistemology; (5) ethics; (6) history of culture and the *Book of Changes*; and (7) application of the book as a mantic text and the technique of divination by it. As is obvious, this is an extremely complex work; consequently, it is not surprising that it attracted the attention of scholars. Thus, for instance, Henri Maspero constructed his theory of the teachings of the *Book of Changes* not so much on the basis of the book itself as on the *Hsi-tz'u chuan*. This is obviously an incorrect substitution of the one book for the other, which is much later; but it is entirely understandable, for the *Hsi-tz'u-chuan* is the oldest text that synthesized the teachings. Of course, it would be futile to look for a critical approach to the text of the basic document in the *Hsi-tz'u chuan*. Nevertheless, it is correct to consider the *Hsi-tz'u chuan* the beginning of the study of the *Book of Changes* in China.

Therefore, it is not surprising that Wang Pi 王弼, the author of the first systematic treatise on the *Book of Changes*—the *Chou I lüeh-li* 周易略例 basically proceeded from the *Hsi-tz'u chuan*. The problem of Wang Pi, of his treatise, and of his philosophy, has already been studied at length by A. A. Petrov[8], therefore, we shall discuss the *Chou I lüeh-li* only to the extent that this treatise is related to the study of the *Book of Changes*. In this regard it is, as is the *Hsi-tz'u chuan*, an attempt to state the philosophy of the *Book of Changes*, completely ignoring problems of a philosophical order. It is true that Wang Pi introduced much clarity into the understanding of the technical terminology, but he treats it as a given, not subjecting it to historic-literary examinations. Wang Pi does not confirm the legendary origin of the book, but he does not deny it either. One can understand why all his attention was directed to one philosophical interpretation of the document, if one remembers that he above all protested the understanding of the *Book of Changes* by his predecessors, the Han commentators, who limited their energies exclusively to speculative-cabalistic arguments. In this chapter it is not our purpose to deal with the Han school, for it is merely commentatory; further on we shall have an opportunity to deal with its representatives in more detail. Protesting against them, Wang Pi outlines his views with special precision in the above-mentioned treatise; but he did not go far enough beyond them to establish a completely new interpretation of the document. Therefore, his work does not have any philological significance, though it has unquestionable philosophical value. As a commentator, Wang Pi is important only as far as he was the forerunner of the Sung commentators, who established a completely original school.

Similar to Wang Pi's treatise is the work of a T'ang scholar, K'ung Ying-ta, who supervised, as is known, the entire commission of the commentators of the classical books, one of

8. A. A. Petrov, *Van Bi* [Wang Pi]: *Iz istorii kitaiskoi filosofii*. S. [See Arthur Wright in *HJAS* 10. 1 (1947), 75–88. – Tr.]

which was the *Book of Changes*. His is not entirely a philological work. The commentary, approved by K'ung Ying-
ta[9], is so closely connected with the commentary of Wang
Pi that it can be better regarded as a sub-commentary to the
latter than as an independent work. In this regard, despite its
unquestionable merit, it is not of much value. K'ung Ying-ta
nevertheless understands the importance of the philological
aspect of study and attaches great significance to the criticism
of the record of the text. His observations on different editions
and his critical selection of interpretations are always sufficiently precise and well thought-out. In spite of this, K'ung
Ying-ta remains entirely under the spell of tradition in all
problems related to the *Book of Changes*. Together with necessary informative remarks about the *Book of Changes*, he states
his views in his rather extensive and interesting introduction.
We can point out the absence of criticism concerning the
problem of authorship and of the origin of the *Book of Changes*
as the weakness of this work, and as the strength—the fact
that this is the first work which was aware of the importance
of the philological approach to the text.[10]

9. *Chou I cheng-i* 周易正義 (683). S.

10. The formation of Confucianism as a specific philosophical current, took
place within Han philology—the science of ancient written documents, which
flowered in the period of the Han empire. The selection from the general
number of ancient documents (those which would comprise the "canon" of
this doctrine) was of the most important significance in this formation. Tung
Chung-shu (139–93) made this selection in the reign of Wu-ti (140–86). At
this time, the *Chou-i*, *Shang-shu*, *Mao-shih*, *Li-chi* and *Ch'un-ch'iu* went into
this canon. Thus the famous "Pentateuch" was generated. Wu-ti, who had
proclaimed this doctrine as the state ideology, in 136 B.C. established the
academic rank of *wu-ching po-shih* (Doctor of the Pentateuch).
Tung Chung-shu's activities were only the beginning: the process of formation of Confucianism was completed by the work of Cheng Hsüan (127–200).
Cheng Hsüan expanded the composition of the "canon" by the inclusion of
the *Chou-li* and *I-li* in the number of canonical books. Cheng Hsüan himself
succeeded in editing the texts and giving an interpretation to only six parts
of his "Septateuch": *Chou-i* (*I Ching*), *Shang-shu* (*Shu-ching*), *Mao-shih* (*Shih-
ching*), and the *Three Li* (*Li-chi*, *Chou-li* and *I-li*); the *Chronicles* of Confucius,

If in K'ung Ying-ta we see only the embryos of philological criticism, then we find this also in Ou-yang Hsiu's treatise *Questions of a Youth about the Book of Changes.*[11] Strictly speaking, this is the first critical treatise on the *Book of Changes*. Unfortunately, we do not have sufficient space in the present specialized study to give a complete translation of this treatise; therefore, we limit ourselves to point-by-point statements.

1) The theory of the Four Qualities 四德 developed in the commentary *Wen-yen chuan*, which tradition itself persistently connects with the name Confucius, in fact has nothing to do with him, for they are the words of Mu Chiang, the mother

11. *I t'ung tzu-wen* 易童子問 , quoted by *Sung-yüan hsüeh-an* 宋元學案, 卷四 (Shanghai 上海), p. 210. S.

the *Ch'un-ch'iu* (more accurately, the *Tso-chuan* version of the *Ch'un-ch'iu*) was treated, according to the records of Cheng Hsüan, by his pupil Fu Ch'ien. Thus was formed the system of ancient Confucianism.

Subsequently, a role similar to Cheng Hsüan's was played by K'ung Ying-ta at a new stage of the development of this doctrine. In 640, by edict of the emperor T'ai-tsung (of the T'ang) a special commission for a new edition of the "Pentateuch" was created. This commission was to establish a "correct" text for each book in the canon and also a "correct" interpretation. K'ung Ying-ta, who became the actual leader of this work, was placed at the head of the commission. Thus the *Wu-ching cheng-i* (The Pentateuch in correct interpretation) appeared. Knowledge of this "correct" Pentateuch became a compulsory requirement for the state examinations, which were then established for persons who aspired to enter government service.

The Pentateuch in K'ung Ying-ta's edition reflects the development of Confucianism within medieval scholasticism and is the end of the scholastic line in the history of Confucianism. At the same time, in this edition there is the clear stamp of the ideological picture of the early Middle Ages when, besides Confucianism and to a much greater extent than it, philosophical thought developed in the channel of Taoism and Buddhism. Wang Pi's treatise mentioned by Shchutskii, which is dated to the early period of the Middle Ages, testifies to the strength of Taoist philosophical thought: in his interpretation of the *I Ching* the influence of the ideas of Lao-tzu and Chuang-tzu is evident. Thus there is nothing surprising in the fact that the "correct interpretation" of the *I Ching* in the "Pentateuch" of K'ung Ying-ta was in general based on Wang Pi's commentary, supplemented by the pupil of the later Han K'ang-po.

For an understanding of the transition from K'ung Ying-ta (seventh century)

of Prince Ch'eng of the principality of Lu. They were in-corporated into the *Tso-chuan* in the year nine (fifth month) of Hsiang-Kung (563 B.C.).

2) In the text of the third line of the first hexagram there is an obvious lacuna which has not been noticed by anyone. In general, lacunae are not rare in the *Book of Changes*.

3) The symbolics of the numbers six, seven, eight, and nine must be understood as designations of changing lines (six-*yin* and nine-*yang*) and unchanging lines (seven-*yang* and eight-*yin*). From this, the vague phrases at the end of Hexagrams 1 and 2 can be explained.

---

to Ou-yang Hsiu (1017–1072) one must take into account that the latter belongs to a new stage in the history of Confucianism. The beginning of this stage is connected with the protest against the dogmatism of K'ung Ying-ta's school, against the dictating of an ideology approved by the government authorities. Signs of this protest began to appear even in the second half of the eighth century and in the beginning were expressed in the form of a very critical attitude toward the texts of the Pentateuch established by K'ung Ying-ta and the text of the interpretation which accompanied it. Li Ting-tsu subjected the *I Ching* to a new analysis; Ch'eng Po-yü, the *Shih-ching*; and Tan Chu, Chao K'uang, and Lu Ch'un, the *Ch'un-ch'iu*.

These thinkers, however, only cleared the road for a real reconsideration of the entire ideology of Confucianism, which the Sung school conducted. The first serious blow against the scholastic dogmatism of K'ung Ying-ta was dealt by Han Yü (768–824), who passed from "interpretation" of the canonical books to criticism of the general trend of medieval Confucianism, and who liberated philosophical thought from the fetters of dogmatism. Simultaneously, Han Yü carried on a struggle with the elements of Taoist quietism, and Buddhist aloofness which had penetrated Confucianism. The chief aim of Han Yü was the "return to antiquity," i.e., the reestablishment of Confucianism in its original, as he thought, purity. Ou-yang Hsiu followed the same road, but worked primarily as an historian. However, a genuinely new system of Con-fucian philosophy, and at the same time the basic line of Chinese philosophy of a new era, was created by the illustrious representatives of the Sung school, especially Chou-tzu (Chou Tun-i, 1017–1073), the Ch'eng brothers, Ming-tao (1032–1085) and I-ch'uan (1033–1107) and Chu-tzu (Chu Hsi, 1130–1200), who brought to conclusion all this enormous work. They created a profound and comprehensive philosophy which absorbed into a transformed and de-veloped form a greater whole, which included Confucianism and some elements of the philosophy of Taoism and even Buddhism. K.

4) There exists a contradiction between the predictions of Hexagram 3 according to the text itself and to its interpretations in the *T'uan-chuan* and the *Hsiang-chuan*. The contradiction is explained by the fact that these texts are directed to different people; "do not act" is directed to commoners and "act" to a noble person (*chün-tzu*).

5, 6) A commentary is given to Hexagrams 4 and 5.

7) A commentary to Hexagram 6 is given, and the necessity is explained for the words "there will be no errors" which are found in the text.

8–36) Explanations of a commentatory nature are given of contradictory and vague passages in a series of hexagrams. These points do not contain substantial material and are of a casual nature; therefore we ignore them and pay greater attention to the following point (37).

37a) Contrary to tradition, it is asserted that not only the *Hsi-tz'u chuan* but also the rest of the Appendices have nothing to do with Confucius. Furthermore, they are generally scattered and confused judgments not belonging to any single person.[12]

---

12. Since this passage plays an important part in Ou-yang Hsiu's treatise, we shall cite it in its entirety:

童子問曰：繫辭非聖人之作乎？曰：何獨繫辭焉？文言說卦而下皆非聖人之作，而象說淆亂亦非一人之言也。昔之學易者雜取以資其講說，而說非一家。是以或同，或異，或是，或非。其擇而不精，至使害經而惑世也，然有附託聖經。其傳已久。莫得究其所從來，而遂其眞偽。故雖有明智之士或貪其雜博之辯，溺其富麗之辭，或以爲辨疑。是正君子所愼。是以未始措意于其閒。

A youth asked: "Was the *Hsi-tzu* [-*chuan*] not composed by the Sage (i.e., Confucius)?" I answered: 'Why only the *Hsi-tz'u* [-*chuan*]! The *Wen-yen* [-*chuan*] and the *Shuo-kua* [-*chuan*] and all the works which followed them were not composed by the Sage, but [are] a mixture of various interpretations which do not even belong to one person. The scholars of the *I Ching* in antiquity unsystematically introduced the [material] for the basis of their discussions and interpretations, and their interpretations [do not belong] to one school. Therefore, they either concur, or differ; either are correct or incorrect. And if we are to select them without cautious attention, we [shall] go as far as to do harm to the classical book and to mislead the

37*b*) Ou-yang Hsiu reached these ideas completely independently, having no corresponding teaching tradition.

37*c*) In the Appendices there are so many repetitions and
pleonasms, etc. that it is impossible to recognize in them
Confucius' style. It is also clear that they could not have been
written by one person. They are rather a collection of quotations from various authors, whose names were not preserved.
Besides, this selection is arbitrary and hasty.[13]

37*d*) Confucius' style, as is known from the *Ch'un-ch'iu*, is
simple and profound. In it, pleonasms and contradictory
interpretations on one and the same [subject] are completely
intolerable.[14] The so-called Four Qualities are simultaneously

---

future generations. However, [there is something in them which] is in line
with the books of the Sage and is based on them. This tradition has existed
since olden days, but it is not possible to trace its sources and distinguish in
it the truth from the untruth. Therefore, even men possessing brilliant
wisdom, who avidly attempt complicated and far-reaching discussions, are
lost in its precious and brilliant phrases, or they assume that [tradition] has
solved the doubts. In this a noble person [should be] cautious. Therefore, I
have never included my ideas in its midst." S.

13. In order to clarify what Ou-yang Hsiu means by repetitions, we translate, albeit partially, his words (p. 8b): "A youth said: 'I venture to ask about
this in general lines.' I answered: 'Under the first strong line of the Hexagram
Ch'ien [1] it is said 'submerged dragon. Do not act.' A sage [not necessarily
Confucius. Ou-yang Hsiu talks about an anonymous person – S.] in a commentary on the image says: 'The force of light is found below' [the hexagram].
Why not say that this text is clear and its meaning is sufficient? But the author
of *Wen-yen* [*chuan*] still says: 'This is a person who possesses the quality of a
dragon and is hidden.' Furthermore, he says: 'The force of light is found
below [the hexagram].' And further, 'The tendency of the light is submerged
and hidden.' And further, 'To be submerged means to hide and not to appear
. . .' [Further, a long passage introducing the same tautology from the *Hsi-
tz'u chuan*]. . . . To say that this originated from one person is to say something
confusing, vague, unsystematic, and petty. If following this we ascribe it to
the sage [Confucius] then it would be an especially great mistake.' " The
material introduced by Ou-yang Hsiu is sufficiently convincing. I shall return
seriously to the problem of authorship of Confucius again later on. S.

14. On this point Ou-yang Hsiu is not quite correct. Remember only the
different understandings of *Ch'un-ch'iu* in the *Tso-chuan* and *Kun-yang chuan*.
In spite of this, his thesis remains valid, for it is not a matter of commentaries,
but of text. S.

explained either as four independent words isolated in a syntactical relationship, or as a united and inseparable phrase. It does not make sense that this assumption originated with one and the same person.

37e) In the *Hsi-tz'u chuan* there are two interpretations of the origin of the trigrams. One is that Fu Hsi allegedly received them as a gift from heaven.[15] The other asserts that they were inventions of Fu Hsi himself, based on his own perception of the world (observations, made under contemplation of footprints of animals and birds, and hence—reflection about the external world and about himself). In addition, in the *Shuo-kua chuan* still another interpretation is given: that the trigrams developed in the practice of divination. The assumption of a single author for all these interpretations likewise does not make sense. It is more correct to assume that they are the fragments of disputes among various commentatory schools which subsequently fell into oblivion.[16]

37f) If it is generally impossible to ascribe the Appendices to a single author, then in particular, the tradition about the authorship of Confucius is inadmissible.

37g) From these theories it can be regarded as rational

15. 河圖 (*ho-t'u*), a drawing borne by a mythical monster from the Yellow river. S.

16. Three versions of the origin of the *I Ching* cited by Ou-yang Hsiu are important for understanding that since antiquity various attitudes toward this document were observed. Some saw in the *I Ching* something based on the wonderful revelation given to people through the "writing of Lo" and the "sketching of Ho," i.e., through mystical signs on the back of magical tortoises, which came from the Lo-shui river and the dragon-horse, which came from the Huang-Ho. Others attempted to understand the *I Ching* rationalistically as the result of observations on reality—on the world of Heaven and Earth. A third group connected the *I Ching* with cultural history, with life practices, thinking that in it was reflected a definite system of divination. Actually, it is this which has significance for the history of the understanding of the *I Ching* and not the controversy over Fu Hsi, King Wen, the Duke of Chou, and Confucius as "authors" of various parts of this ancient document. These arguments are important only in the sense that they deal with the discussion of the time of combination of the various parts of the document and on its composition. K.

truth that the doctrine of the Four Qualities stated in the
Wen-yen chuan is a fiction, that the myth of the gift of trigrams
from heaven is a fiction, and that the tradition of mantics,
though it is known to us, was not attested to by Confucius.

37*h*) Nevertheless, not all these Appendices are devoid of
use: we should remember only that they are commentaries,
not the basic text.[17] Before the Han period it was called *Ta
chuan* (the Great Commentary), and only during the second
Han dynasty (not from Ssu-ma Ch'ien) did it receive the
name *Hsi-tz'u* [*chuan*]. It is incorrect to say that they are
monolithic and come from Confucius, but it is correct to say
that there are valuable ideas in them for the study of thought,
for they were not far removed in terms of time from the
period of the formation of the basic text. It is necessary only
to take a critical approach to them.

37*i*) Since Mu Chiang from Lu divined by the *Book of
Changes* and obtained an answer in the form of teachings on
the Four Qualities fifteen years before Confucius' birth, it is
clear that the corresponding quotation in the *Wen-yen chuan*
is not the words of Confucius.

37*j*) The concept that the author of the *Tso-chuan* supposedly introduced into its text Confucius' words on the Four
Qualities from *Wen-yen chuan* is inadmissible. By this he
would have made his own text less authoritative, for it is
impossible to include in the text ascribed to the already elderly
Confucius words which sound like those even before he was
born. At the time of the compilation of the *Tso-chuan* Confucius was not regarded as the author of *Wen-yen chuan*.
Therefore, the quotation from the *Wen-yen chuan* included
in the text of the *Tso-chuan* did not confuse anyone. The
theory that Confucius is the author of the *Wen-yen chuan* is a
later invention.

37*k*) The attempts to reconcile the contradictory interpre-

17. This thesis lies at the basis of our judgment of the document as a whole
as it is edited now. It is necessary to single out the basic text in it. But we go
further, differentiating its three diachronic layers. S.

tations on the origin of trigrams are so strained that one would chastise those who deign to confirm them. Incidentally, the interpretation of the "human" origin of the trigrams was developed in the *Hsi-tz'u chuan* in more detail than the "miracle" theory of their origin.

37*l*) The interpretation of the mantic origin of trigrams is strained and embellished by elements of miracle. But the trigrams can be understood rationally without regard to mantic.[18]

37*m*) It would be a mistake to deny the influence of the Confucian school on the authors of the Ten Wings, but this influence was never comprehensive; such texts as the *Shuo-kua chuan* and *Tsa-kua chuan* reflected the influence of the school of diviners, not the Confucian school.

Such is the general outline of the contents of Ou-yang Hsiu's treatise. In it we see a serious critical approach to the problem. However, his treatise presented to the later experts of the *I Ching* a merely insignificant influence which was limited, essentially, to the fact that some of them no longer regarded it possible to emphasize the authorship of Confucius. Among the rest, the *Book of Changes* was, as before, interpreted only from the philosophical aspect without regard to Ou-yang Hsiu's views. Thus, soon after Ou-yang Hsiu's death there emerged a commentary which was judged as playing a leading role for centuries not only in China but also in Japan. This is the commentary of Ch'eng I-ch'uan (1033–1107).[19] It is sufficient to read the introduction to it in order to clarify the point of view of the famous *I Ching* expert:

18. However, we are inclined to think that the "mantic" theory of the origin of the trigrams is closer to reality than any other theory. For the practice of divination, as we have already seen, was attested to sufficiently well. In any case this is better than to turn to the figure Fu Hsi, who, according to the "human" theory of Ou-yang Hsiu, should be regarded as the inventor of the trigrams. S.

19. 易傳 (*I-chuan*)—written apparently at the end of the nineties of the eleventh century. S.

The "changes" are the transformations in which we change according to time, in order to follow the Way of world development (Tao). This book is so wide and all-embracing that through it we hope to stand in right relationship to laws of nature and fate, to penetrate all the causes of what is evident and what is concealed, to exhaust all the actuality of objects and events, and through it to reveal the way of discovery and perfection. And it can be said that its sage authors reached a peak in their concern for the following generations. Although we are already far from those ancient times, the basic texts bequeathed by them have been preserved for us. However, commentators of former periods lost the meaning and preserved only the words. Their followers only recite these words and forget about their essence. Beginning with the time of the Han [the text has: Ch'in – Tr.] dynasty the tradition of this teaching, perhaps, no longer exists.

Living a thousand years later, I am afraid that this writing will fade away and disappear, and I wish that people of future times would trace the source through this development. This is the reason why I set out to write the present commentary.

In the *Book of Changes* there are four ways to perfect wisdom: (1) to approach the understanding of the text through words; (2) to approach the understanding of transformation through action; (3) to approach the understanding of images through the construction of instruments; (4) to approach the understanding of the oracle through divination.[20]

20. Since this difficult text can be transmitted by different words, we shall clarify what he means by the four ways of understanding the content of the *Book of Changes*. The first is the genuinely philological way proceeding from an exact understanding of terminology of the document and leading to a correct account of the text. The second is the way of practical action in which the "law of transformation" (which we would call movement) is directly understood. This is possible since the book was regarded by the experts of the *I Ching* as the teachings adequately reflecting the world. Thus, those who study in practice the transformation of the world are studying above all the basic law of the teaching of the *Book of Changes*. Thirdly, according the Ch'eng I-ch'uan's opinion, the construction of instruments in agreement with images of the hexagrams leads to an understanding of the figurative content of the document. In other words, what is meant is the creative activity of man in the world, in which he must conform to the regularities expressed in the image of the hexagrams. Fourthly and finally, the understanding of the *Book of Changes* is possible through the study of its oracles, which are understood in the practice of divination. It is important to note that in this sentence Ch'eng

The law regarding increase and decrease of good fortune and misfortune, and the way of advancing and retreating movement of safety
and death—all these are in their entirety included in the texts of the
Book of Changes. Understanding the text and studying the hexagrams,
we can understand the transformations. The images and oracles are
already included in them. "A noble person (*chün-tzu*) in time of repose
contemplates the images and understands the texts, and in time of
action he observes the transformations and understands the (essence
of) the oracles."[21] It is possible that while understanding a text one
does not understand its ideas, but it is impossible to understand the
ideas without fathoming the text. Most concealed is its law, and most
obvious is its image. But its essence and effect are united in their
source, for there is no space between the secret and the evident. If we
contemplate them in their mutual penetration, and above all put into
practice the regular procedure of discipline, then everything will be
decisively inferred from these texts. Therefore, those who well (understand) the teaching, grasping (the meaning of these) words, will
without fail, proceed from the closest (that is, directly from the given).
Those who proceed more differently than from the closest, do not
understand anything of the words.

That which I transmit are texts. And to find ideas based on these
texts depends more on the person himself.

In the reign of Sung, the second year Yüan-fu (1099), the first
month. Ch'eng I from Ho-nan.

In order to understand this introduction one should keep
in mind the fact that for its author the clarification of the
ideological contents of the document comes first. This is
possible only on the basis of analysis of the text, but Ch'eng
I-ch'uan understands this analysis not in a philological but in
a philosophical sense. As the author of a number of philosophical works, Ch'eng I-ch'uan is naturally more interested
in the philosophical interpretation of the document. In spite
of this, he reveals a greater keenness of historical reality than

I-ch'uan repeats the words of chapter 10 of the *Hsi-tz'u chuan* with which he
apparently completely agrees. But these words, as quoted, are taken by us in
this translation in quotations. S.

21. See *Hsi-tz'u chuan*, ch. 2. S.

the acknowledged philologist Chu Hsi. To note this, it is enough to read just the first sentences from the commentaries of Ch'eng I-ch'uan and Chu Hsi. Ch'eng I-ch'uan writes: "When in extreme antiquity the sages drew the eight trigrams for the first time, the three world forces (Heaven, Earth, Man) were already expressed in them. Beginning with them, they doubled these trigrams in order to express completely that which is transformation in the entire world. . . ."

Chu Hsi starts his commentary in a completely different tone.[22] His is the tone of a teacher trying to make a pupil conform to tradition. Explaining the title *Chou I*, he says: "*Chou* is the name of the dynasty; *I* is the name of the book. Its hexagrams[23] are based on those drawn by Fu Hsi. They

22. Chu Hsi has two works specially devoted to the *I Ching*: the *Chou I pen-i* 周易本義 or *Basic Thought of the Chou* (*I Ching*) and the *I-hsüeh ch'i-meng* 易學啓蒙 or *The doctrine of the I Ching for beginners*. The first work is a large (twelve chüan) treatise, in which the author attempts to reveal the basic conception of the *I Ching*. In his interpretation of this conception, Chu Hsi once again strongly emphasizes the mantic side of this ancient document which some *I Ching* scholars—among them to a significant degree Ch'eng I-ch'uan —lose sight of, being attracted by the philosophical side of the *I Ching*. At the same time, Chu Hsi fully understands this side of the *I Ching* too and attempts to reveal it, without destroying artificially what is very firmly united within the book itself. Thus this work of Chu Hsi is one of the more profound and comprehensive investigations of the *I Ching*.

The second work is a sort of "introduction to I Ching studies." This is a textbook, composed by Chu Hsi, as a professor for an audience starting to study the *I Ching*. If we speak of the popularizing line of Chu Hsi-ism, as Shchutskii does, then we must understand just this second work of Chu Hsi, but not the first. In connection with this, statements about the "deterioration" of criticism among the learned Confucians are hardly just. The very objection of Chu Hsi to the mantic side of the *I Ching* testifies to the healthy respect for this document and at the same time the critical regard for the former tradition. Shchutskii's statements, strictly speaking, are provoked by the fact that Chu Hsi mentions Fu Hsi, but this reference should not be taken as evidence of any belief that the trigrams were created by just this Fu Hsi. For Chu Hsi, as for many others, the reference to Fu Hsi is a simple fact of tradition; the main thing for such *I Ching* scholars is the content of the document. K.

23. That he means hexagrams, not trigrams, is clear from the following statements introduced by us. S.

have the meaning of mutual interchange and transformation. Therefore (this book) is called *I* (Changes). Its texts were added by King Wen and the Duke of Chou. . . ." Further, dealing with the first hexagram, Chu Hsi begins his explanation as follows: "The six lines are the hexagrams which were drawn by Fu Hsi. . . ." From a comparison between Ch'eng I-ch'uan and Chu Hsi it becomes clear how far the criticism among the Sung Confucianists had degenerated by the time of the latter. It is possible to assume that this has something to do with the general decline in the nature of social life toward Chu Hsi's time.

A more comprehensive comparison of Chu Hsi, a late Sung Confucianist, with the Confucianists who founded the Sung school, only confirms this observation made by us on the basis of the quotations introduced above. However, precisely this uncritical and popularized line of the Chu Hsi school later received a wider circulation. This can be explained above all by the fact that the commentary of Chu Hsi is much easier to understand for a man who is not especially familiar with the problems of the *I Ching*. The main contingent of readers of commentatory literature were the people preparing for the state examinations for service in the bureaucracy, and who studied the text of the *Book of Changes* only as a compulsory process, not by their own interests. However, despite all the differences between Ch'eng I-ch'uan and Chu Hsi, their relationship to the *Book of Changes* proved possible to reconcile. This synthesis was done by the commentator Tiao Pao (1603–1699).[24]

24. Going from Tiao Pao (1603–1669) to the next investigators of the *I Ching*, Shchutskii enters a new period of Confucianism, which extended into the Ch'ing dynasty (1644–1911), i.e., into the last declining phase of feudal absolutism. As Shchutskii says, many diversified works, devoted to the classics of Confucianism, appeared in this period. In order to understand their appearance and their content, it is necessary to take into account the following circumstances.

Philosophical rationalism, on the basis of which there occurred in China the liberation of philosophical thought from the fetters of medieval dogmatic

In this chapter we shall not touch upon the commentatory literature and shall later discuss Tiao Pao as a commentator. Here we take into consideration merely the introduction to his work on the *I Ching*, dated 1660.[25] The author begins his discussion with a quotation from a famous Taoist of the tenth

---

Confucian scholasticism, leading to the flowering of philosophy in the Sung dynasty, had exhausted itself and could not provide for further movement of philosophical thought. It could only turn into dogma, accessible only to an essentially scholastic treatment. This occurred in China in the eighteenth–nineteenth centuries. This is an age of classicism, which is characteristic in general for periods of feudal absolutism.

However, this classicism was marked by two tendencies: the conservative and the critical. The conservative tendency, represented by the ideologues of the governing regime, treated the classical legacy of Confucianism in the spirit of the Sung school, mainly the spirit of Chu Hsi. The critical tendency, represented by the ideologues of the Enlightenment, which at that time was the most important form of social opposition to the reactionary regime of the Manchu government, studying the same classical heritage, aspired to undermine the very bases of the official version of classicism. This was done by studying the same classics, in order to show the bankruptcy of the Sung interpretation of them. On these grounds the critical line of Ch'ing classical philology developed. As a rule, it did not go beyond the bounds of the circle of problems common to Confucianism, but did a great deal on parts of the critical investigations of old documents—their origins, their texts, their contents.

This critical line of classical philology clearly appeared in the preface to the *I Ching* in the work of Hu Wei 胡渭 (1633–1714), *I-t'u ming-pien* (Elucidation of the sketches of the *I Ching*). This work considered the question of the "Sketches from the Ho river" and the "writing from the Lo river" and it is shown that neither have any relationship to the *I Ching*. In this way, Hu Wei attempted to undermine the very basis of the interpretation of the *I Ching* which was given by Chu Hsi. It must be noted that the Sung thinkers, the object of whose researches was the philosophical content of ancient documents, did not give serious significance to this side of the tradition which grew up around the *I Ching*.

It is very characteristic that among the representatives of the critical line of classical philology of Ch'ing times there were also historians. Chang Hsüeh-ch'eng, who is mentioned by Shchutskii, was such an historian. The activities of Chang Hsüeh-ch'eng extended into the period of the great flowering of critical philology (the 1730s to the 1820s). K.

25. We used the 1843 edition. S.

century, Ch'en Hsi-i 陳希夷 , with whose name tradition persistently connects the origins of Sung Confucianists.[26] Ch'en Hsi-i assumed that the hexagrams were created by Fu Hsi, but that for him they were images rather than historical evidence. He emphasized that the hexagrams are symbols of representation which had existed before the establishment of writing. Tiao Pao subscribes to this opinion on the basis of his study, according to which "under Fu Hsi" all the names of hexagrams had already existed. Tiao says that the establishment of Judgment texts and line texts are ascribed to King Wen. But it was known to him that only a few dogmatists (for example, Pan Ku and Yang Hsiung) regarded King Wen as the author of the line texts. The others (for example, Chiao Hung) regarded the Duke of Chou as the author.

Having set forth this theory, which was widespread in his time, Tiao Pao rejects it, since in the line texts there is mentioned, for instance, Chi-tzu 箕子 , whom King Wen, living earlier, could not, of course, have known.[27] Therefore, Tiao,

---

26. Ch'en Hsi-i, otherwise Ch'en T'u-nan 陳圖南 (d. 989) is a representative of the philosophical thinking of China in the transitional period encompassing the last decades of the T'ang dynasty, the years of the interregnum (Wu-tai), and the beginning of the Sung dynasty. The tendency toward philosophical syncretism, consisting of the desire to consider the basic positions of Confucianism, Taoism, and Buddhism as mutually supplementing each other, is characteristic of him, as it is of that time in general. This syncretism served as the grounds on which subsequently grew up the philosophy of the Sung school in which the combination of Confucianism with some elements of Taoist and Buddhist philosophy had already lost the syncretic character, but served only as a means to create a fully independent philosophical system. Ch'en Hsi-i is considered a forerunner of the Sung school primarily because he was the first to advance the concept of "the unity of Heaven-Earth and all things," i.e., the unity of all beings, which is based on the unity of "material nature" [ch'i] and the "natural law" [li] that permeates this nature. The followers of Taoism thought that this concept came from the doctrine of Lao-tzu and Chuang-tzu and on this basis claimed that the success of the philosophy of the Sung school was indebted to these two founders of philosophical Taoism and that the concepts of "matter" [ch'i] and "law" [li] which comprise the most essential part of Sung philosophy, come directly from Ch'en Hsi-i. K.

following Ch'eng I-ch'uan and Chu Hsi, is inclined to ascribe this part of the text to the Duke of Chou. Tiao also follows tradition when he does not dispute the legend of Confucius as the author of the Ten Wings. Further, Tiao speaks about the construction of the document and proceeds to an assessment of the two commentaries of Ch'eng I-ch'uan and Chu Hsi, finding them comparatively good. He does not give a clear preference to either one of them, but attempts to synthesize them, thinking that they supplement each other, while clearly understanding their difference. This he discovers by the fact that "those who study the *I* [*Ching*] achieve breadth thanks to the tradition of Ch'eng [I-ch'uan] and concreteness thanks to the commentary of Chu [Hsi]. . . ."[28] However, after extensive reading of his commentary there is no doubt that Ch'eng I-ch'uan is rather closer in spirit to our author than Chu Hsi. And it is understandable why this is so. Indeed, Ch'eng I-ch'uan inherited and developed the style of an understanding of the *Book of Changes* established by Wang Pi, who proceeded mainly from the *Hsi-tz'u chuan*; and this later text, according to Tiao, originates from Confucius. Therefore, wishing to restore the understanding of the *Book*

---

27. Chi-tzu, one of the tribal leaders at the end of the Yin kingdom after the fall of the latter (in 1122 B.C., according to traditional chronology), together with his tribal group (historical legend mentions about 5,000 people), moved to the Korean peninsula where the tribe settled in the northern part of the peninsula in the area of the later Pyong-yang. Having based their kingdom here, old Chinese historiography gave it the name Ch'ao-hsien 朝鮮 . King Wen, the head of the Chou tribe and ruler of the Chou kingdom before its conquest of the Yin domain died in 1120 B.C. Thus, if we follow the traditional chronology, King Wen was about one generation older than Chi-tzu. K.

28. We cannot but notice that Tiao Pao is inclined to somewhat unprincipled eclecticism, which is generally characteristic of him. Introducing very frequently different points of view of other authors into his commentary, he notes their indiscriminate acceptability. This excessive tolerance makes Tiao Pao's work, which is very useful in many respects, somewhat dull. Therefore, Tiao probably did not raise himself to the level of independence, and the *Ssu-k'u ch'üan-shu tsung-mu* soundly regards his work merely as a subsidiary text to the analysis of Ch'eng I-ch'uan and Chu Hsi's work. S.

of Changes by Confucius, Tiao is in the most intimate way connected with the tradition of Ch'eng I-ch'uan. He gives barely appropriate attention to Chu Hsi and his cosmogonistic concepts based on the *Book of Changes* and inherited from Chou Tun-i, the teacher of Ch'eng I-ch'uan.

However, the psychological understanding of the *I Ching*, so to speak, is most characteristic for Tiao Pao. In this he proceeds from Kao Chung-hsien 高忠憲 .[29] Thus, in complete accordance with him, Tiao Pao states his basic thesis on the *Book of Changes* as follows: "This crystallization of consciousness is the Great End. That this crystallized consciousness does not have either an object or an image on which it would be based is the Infinite." Thus, "the Infinite which is also the Great End," rests precisely on internal contemplation. As in the *Book of Changes* there is the Great End, so in the consciousness there is the Great End. Therefore, in Kao-tzu [Kao P'an-lung] it is said that in the world there is "the consciousness which is not transformation, but there is no transformation which would not be consciousness." Furthermore, "In transformation[30] (that is, in the *Book of Changes*) there is the Great

29. Also known as Kao P'an-lung 高攀龍 (1561–1626), one of the Confucian scholars of the late Ming dynasty. We consider it necessary to characterize, though briefly, his philosophical outlook in order to make Tiao Pao's view on the *I Ching* more understandable. Kao P'an-lung, like many of his contemporaries, experienced the strong influence of Wang Yang-ming (1472–1528). Perhaps the following statement most clearly characterizes him: "The science of common people is to work on the external [world] and to neglect the internal world, to admire things and to ruin their own will, for [people] do not turn to themselves in order to seek ideas. But [if] you seek ideas, is it possible to talk about something internal and external? The ideas contained in the consciousness and the ideas contained in the external things are one. In the entire world there are no things which lie outside of nature and likewise there are no things which lie outside the consciousness. The fact is like objects being illuminated by sunshine; it is here and there but the sun is only one! It is impossible to divide it, and why should one expect the sun to become one, only having been reunited?" S.

30. Untranslatable play on words: 易 ("transformation" and abbreviated name of the *Book of Changes*). S.

End. In the consciousness there is [also] the Great End. If we do not see the Great End in our consciousness, then we lack that with which we [can] see transformation."

Then Tiao takes another quotation from Kao P'an-lung in which it is said: ". . . internally we contemplate the secret of an undivided transformation of our consciousness, and externally we contemplate the flow of an undivided transformation of our body. But the consciousness, the body, and the transformation are merely one." In this connection Tiao remarks: "What we have here[31] can be called a true study of the *Book of Changes* [of transformation], and what we have here can be called a sagacious study of Kao-tzu [Kao P'an-lung]." Starting from such theoretical premises Tiao compares the *I Ching* with the *Shu-ching* and with the *Ch'un-ch'iu*: "The teaching is begun in the *Shu-ching*, is established in the *Ch'un-ch'iu* and finds its completion in the *I Ching*." Tiao Pao ends his treatise by recognizing the perfection of the "four authors" of the *Book of Changes*—Fu Hsi, King Wen, the Duke of Chou, and Confucius, and thinks that only Ch'eng I-ch'uan and Chu Hsi, who supposedly revealed the meaning of Ch'eng I-ch'uan's commentary, are the peerless commentators.

However, among the numerous and various commentators on the *Book of Changes* there were thinkers of a quality different from Tiao Pao, whom we have just examined. In this regard, the historian Chang Hsüeh-ch'eng 章學誠 (*tzu*, Shih-chai 實齋) is interesting. He wrote a collection *Wen-shih t'ung-i* 文史通義 (General interpretation of the literary and historical [documents])," which was published for the first time in 1832 and republished with European punctuation in 1924. The first three treatises of the collection are devoted to the *Book of Changes*.[32]

31. In our edition, there is an obvious misprint: 比 instead of 此. It is correct in the second half of the phrase. S.

32. The fact that Chang Hsüeh-ch'eng's work, examined by Shchutskii, was reprinted in 1956 in the People's Republic of China testifies to its significance. It must be emphasized that Shchutskii was the first of the Western sinologues to evaluate this work properly. K.

2. *Studies in the Far East*

First of all, he considers the *Book of Changes* a text which states not only theory but also facts and on this basis he does not regard it in principle as different from the rest of the classical books. However, this factual character of the *Book of Changes* is different from that which is inherent in other classical books. This is factual character not of historical events, but of innate achievement. In this respect it is wider than the other classical books. It "clothes the sky in images and the earth in laws." It is difficult, perhaps, to employ this factual character merely because, as Chang Hsüeh-ch'eng says below, the expressive style of the ideas in the *Book of Changes* is special: it is figurative, but not conceptual.

The *Book of Changes* as known to us is not the sole document of this kind, for we have historical evidence concerning other analogous books such as the so-called *Kuei-tsang* and the *Lien-shan*.[33] Like the *I Ching* they also served as mantic texts, but the idea of transformation is inherent only in the *I Ching* and the other two books (which are not preserved, but mentioned in the *Li-chi*) were never called *I*—"Changes." This idea— central to the *Book of Changes*—finds its expression in the symbols of the changing lines of the hexagrams, which, without this transformation, are devoid of any meaning that, in Chang Hsüeh-ch'eng's opinion, is confirmed by the traditional practice of divination where everything is based on the changes of lines.[34] Therefore, the Judgment texts could not have

33. The *Chou-li* contains the information that in antiquity there were three divination books: *Lien-shan*, *Kuei-tsang*, and *Chou-i*. The first, according to the *Chou-li* dates to the time of the Hsia kingdom (2205 B.C., according to traditional chronology), the second to the Yin kingdom (1766 B.C.), and the third to the Chou (1122 B.C.). Traces of the first two books have never been found, but references to them even in some details (e.g., which hexagram in each of them is in the first place) are encountered (e.g., in the *Shan-hai-ching*). Even such authorities as Cheng Hsüan speak of the *Lien-shan* and the *Kuei-tsang*. However, K'ung Ying-ta, transmitting the opinion of Cheng Hsüan who believed in the existence of these ancient books, declared that there were no documentary grounds for such a belief. K.

34. Such an argument is hardly acceptable, for it is obviously based on the premise of immutability of the techniques of divination. However, even at

existed without line texts. Both texts took shape simultaneously,[35] but were formed only after the establishment of the Chou dynasty. It is hardly correct to say that King Wen was the author of these texts, but it is correct to say that Confucius transmitted the traditional understanding of this text to future generations. Chang Hsüeh-ch'eng asserts Confucius' familiarity with the *Book of Changes* on the basis of the quotation of the *Li-chi*.[36]

I [Confucius – S.] [wished] to see the teaching of Hsia, [therefore I went] to Chi. [There], however, there was not enough evidence, but I found there the Hsia Calendar. I [wished] to see the teaching of Yin, [therefore I went] to Sung. [There, however,] there was not enough evidence, but I found there "Earth and Heaven"...

Chang Hsüeh-ch'eng himself clearly understands that it is

present there exist different methods of divination (no fewer than three) and it is obvious that the technique of divination on which Chang Hsüeh-ch'eng bases his theory cannot be the first. Therefore, we distinguish between the first, the second, and the third layers of the text of the *Book of Changes*. S.

35. Here Chang Hsüeh-ch'eng, a captive of his own idea, sins by means of insufficient criticism. S.

36. Chang Hsüeh-ch'eng quotes the *Li-chi*, apparently by heart, and consequently incorrectly. The words omitted by Chang Hsüeh-ch'eng are inserted by us in square brackets. It should be noted also (Chang Hsüeh-ch'eng does not consider this) that this chapter (9) of the *Li-chi* could be written only by one of the disciples of Tzu Yu, a disciple of Confucius, and cannot be regarded as a fully valuable document for judgment about Confucius himself; beside, Chang Hsüeh-ch'eng does not make the extremely important comparison of this quotation with Confucius' own words (*Lun-yü*, ch. 3, 9): "The Master said, how can we talk about the ritual of the Hsia. The state of Ch'i supplies no adequate evidence. For there is a lack both of documents and of learned men. But for this lack we should be able to obtain evidence from these two states." [Waley's own translation here – Tr.] And nothing more! In whatever way we should read it, this text does not say a word about the availability of the *Book of Changes*. Instead of seeing in the *Kuei-tsang*, the book about "Earth and Heaven," a forerunner of the *Book of Changes*, it seems to us closer to the truth, following Chang Hsüeh-ch'eng, if we assume that the *Book of Changes* was not known to Confucius (and generally in his time); and only after it received great circulation a spurious text of it was included in the saying attributed to Confucius by the author of this chapter of the *Li-chi*. S.

difficult to surmise Confucius' enthusiasm for the *Book of Changes* as a divinatory book, for such a text must have been completely foreign to a rationalist like Confucius. Chang Hsüeh-ch'eng tries to overcome this contradiction by the theory of the twofold *I Ching* or more correctly, of its double understanding: (1) rational understanding which sees in the text of the *Book of Changes* only the records of ancient customs and ceremonies, in other words, of ritual, *li*, which supposedly comes from Confucius; and (2) mantic understanding, or more correctly, a distortion of the document which has nothing in common with Confucius himself.[37]

Analyzing the term *I* ("Changes") itself, while rejecting the two interpretations based on the analysis of the Character *I*, Chang Hsüeh-ch'eng is generally inclined to understand the term as did Chu Hsi, who ignored the pictographical analysis.[38] This is in complete harmony with his style of interpretation, assiduously avoiding everything that cannot be externally documented, in which there is even the smallest hint of a hypothetical character. However, Chang Hsüeh-ch'eng does not finally notice the whole hypothetical character of his own judgments, to which he is brought by the assertion that Confucius allegedly studied the *Book of Changes*, the assertion constructed on an unauthentic quotation from the *Li-chi* and on the uncritical relationship to the aphorism from the *Lun-yü*, in which the name of the *Book of Changes* appeared only as a result of the scribe's carelessness.[39] In any case Chang Hsüeh-ch'eng is consistent when he devotes the entire end of

37. This theory clearly does not stand up to criticism, for the mantic role of the *Book of Changes* was attested to by the oldest references to it. Rational interpretation is the later attempt to preserve a canonical text under trial of thought. S.

38. As is known, the term 易 was understood either as a pictogram depicting a chameleon, hence the meaning "changeability" (as it is explained in the *Shuo-wen*) or as a synthetic character consisting of characters of "sun" and "moon" in their rotations. S.

39. On the detail of this quotation, see translation of Itō Zenshō, 1771, below (pp. 114–118) S.

his second treatise to the proof of the rationalalistic understanding of the *Book of Changes* by Confucius.

Chang Hsüeh-ch'eng's third treatise is the most interesting
one. It is true that he does not raise philological problems in
it, but is concerned merely with the philosophical understanding of the basic conceptions of this document; and since
it is so original, we should dwell on it in detail. In order to
understand correctly the author's argument, it is necessary to
bear in mind that he proceeds (without sufficient philological
criticism!) from an undifferentiated text, basing his interpretation mainly on the materials of the *Hsi-tz'u chuan*. Consequently, despite his series of acceptable judgments on this
text, one cannot entirely agree with him when he transfers
these Judgments to the *Book of Changes* proper.

In order to understand Chang Hsüeh-ch'eng's point of
view, it is necessary to understand what place among other
classical books his system gives to our document,[40] in which
he perceives the basic method of thinking reflected in the
Book of Changes. Thus he assumes that, if the thought in the
Ch'un-ch'iu is expressed in examples, in the *Li-chi* in its hierarchical nature, then in the *Shih-ching* it is expressed in its
influence on emotion through the medium of metaphor, and
in the *Book of Changes* in the images. From this comparison
it becomes clear what Chang Hsüeh-ch'eng means by images:
the metaphor in poetry is also an image but an image which
chiefly influences emotion. The images of the *Book of Changes*
are understood correctly when they lead, not to an emotional
expression, but to the knowledge of ideas invested in them
and to the realization of the basic ideas of transformation
(movement, we would call it now).

There is no possibility of reducing these images to simple
representations, for they are saturated with a much greater
and many-sided content than a representation abstracted from
observation. They are, as it were, loaded with a wide content

40. Here Shchutskii refers to the *Hsi-tz'u chuan*. Tr.

which is taken up in many forms. Therefore, Chang Hsüeh-ch'eng says: "That which the images embrace is wide. Not merely the *I Ching*, but each of the Six Arts grasps it in common. In general (it) is the Tao's structure (frame) when it is about to take form and has not yet been manifested." Of course, that kind of image is encountered also in other classical books, but there they transmit only the representation abstracted from some kind of concrete event, object, situation, etc. The images in the *Book of Changes* are different.

The *I Ching* is on a level with heaven and earth. Therefore it is able to fill up and entwine the Way of heaven and earth. When the myriad things and affairs are in the midst of coming from stillness and begin to move, the forms and traces are not evident, but the image is indeed visible. Therefore, the Tao cannot be seen; when men in seeking the Tao seem to have occasion to glimpse it—in such a case it is always its image.[41]

Thus, if representation is inseparably connected with a concrete and always past factor, then the images of the *Book of Changes*, in Chang Hsüeh-ch'eng's understanding, are the images anticipating something which is not yet known. However, for the account of our author's philosophy it is necessary to raise a question: from where do such images appear in man? If images can appear, in Chang Hsüeh-ch'eng's opinion, in a man independently from the world, he is of course an idealist. If they are the reflections of the world, then he is a materialist (though only in a gnosiological sense).

Chang Hsüeh-ch'eng did not avoid this cardinal problem. He differentiates the "natural images of the world" and "the constructed images of human consciousness." And, speaking of the latter, he declares unequivocally that

. . . a man, differentiating himself from everything that exists between Heaven and Earth, cannot but be subjected to [the influence of]

41. These two passages have been checked with the original and retranslated directly from Chinese to English for more clarity. Cf. Chang Hsüeh-ch'eng, *Wen-shih t'ung-i*, p. 5. Tr.

increase and decrease of the forces of Light and Darkness. The structure of the consciousness, the changeability of the senses (of an emotional order), create them. This changeability is provoked by contacts with the world of people [society], and is created on the basis of the forces of Light and Darkness (i.e., the forces of nature).

Thus the constructed images of human consciousness in turn proceed from the natural images of the world.

If this is not materialistic reasoning, in any case it is something close to it. Chang Hsüeh-ch'eng, of course, could not yet on the basis of natural science, substantiate his theory. However, having apparently worked a great deal on the problem of the images of the *Book of Changes*, he reached the thought that they are related to the poetical images of the *Shih-ching*, as the internal aspect of the external. Even though recognizing the perfection of the images of the *Shih-ching*, he nevertheless thinks that only the images of the *Book of Changes* (proceeding ultimately from the natural images of the world) carry system and harmony in themselves. Therefore, the teaching of the *Book of Changes* is more complete than that of the later philosophers. It is true that they (the philosophers) proceed from the same ancient source, but they deviate so far from it that they no longer express the most important and basic ideas. And only Buddhism, genetically not connected to Chinese tradition, possessing a completely independent terminology, still basically "proceeds from the teaching of the *Book of Changes*" and "does not differ from the words of the sages." [42] Of course, the escape from the world, characteristic of Buddhism, is entirely foreign to the practical concepts of the *Book of Changes*. However, the imagery of Buddhism, with its complicated pantheon, shocks the Confucianists for no good reason, since it is only imagery. Besides, the *Book of Changes* is not devoid of fantastic and symbolic images.

42. This thesis is too strong, but not without meaning. In any case it supports our opinion of Wan I's Buddhist commentary to the *Book of Changes* as the most interesting philosophical interpretation of the *I Ching*. S.

We must note that Chang Hsüeh-ch'eng is basically a confirmed Confucianist. But, because of those ideas which strongly distinguish him from other authors who wrote about the *Book of Changes*, we cannot but recognize him as one of the most original and interesting thinkers in the development of Chinese philosophy.[43] Turning to the modern period, we must first get acquainted with the treatise of P'i Hsi-jui 皮錫瑞 (1850–1908).[44] In the introduction to this work P'i Hsi-jui speaks as a confirmed Confucianist.[45] In his opinion, it is necessary to restore the teaching of Confucius to its authentic form. Only after this, applying it to practical life, will one be able to perfect this practical life. Let us examine what P'i Hsi-jui does for the explanation of the, as he thinks, "authentic" teaching of Confucius. For this we shall give an account of the treatise chapter by chapter.

Chapter i. Concerning the general meaning of the *Book of Changes* as transformation and nontransformation.

In this chapter the author states his basic purpose in his approach to the study of the classical texts of Confucianism. In order to interpret correctly a particular text, first of all it is necessary to clarify its leading idea. For the *Book of Changes* such a leading idea is the concept *I*, in which the mutually exclusive ideas of transformation and nontransformation and the idea of their unity are formally combined. In essence such an idea is inherent not only in the *Book of Changes*, but also in a whole series of other ancient Chinese texts with philosophical content. Some commentators fit them to the under-

43. See David S. Nivison, *The Life and Thought of Chang Hsüeh-ch'eng* (Stanford Univ. Press, 1966). Tr.

44. Shan-hua P'i Hsi-jui, *Ching-hsüeh t'ung-lun* 善化皮錫瑞 , 經學通論 (General treatise on the study of classical books, n.p., 1907). The book was printed in wood block during the lifetime of the author and the author's introduction was dated in 1907. We used the first volume devoted to the *Book of Changes*. S.

45. P'i Hsi-jui is one of the last great representatives of the critical line of classical philology in old China who worked in the last decades of the Ch'ing empire, in the Kuang-hsü period (1875–1908). K.

standing of the idea of the unity of contradictions and correspondingly constructed their explanations. For this they
were often subjected to attack by those who could not go
beyond simple formalism to ideas of a higher order.[46] Let us
take examples from chapter 1 of P'i Hsi-jui's treatise, which
apparently indicates the ability to think, if not yet dialectically,
then no longer in terms of formal logic. Thus he writes:

Not only the *I Ching* talks about it [that is, about simultaneous transformation and nontransformation and their direct connections – S.]
but all the classical books talk about it. This is most clearly said in
chapter 16 of the *Li-chi, Ta-chuan*:[47] "[They] correct a system, change
the color of clothes, introduce a difference in distinctive signs, distinguish difference of weapons, differentiate [the form] of clothing. All
of this is that which is subject to change in connection with [the life]
of people. But there is also that which is not subject to change. This is
respect for the esteemed, the kindred relationship, exaltation of elders,
differentiation between men and women. This is what does not change
in connection with [the changes in life] of people." This subjection
to change [in the language of the *Book of Changes* – S.] means "transformation" and nonsubjection to change is "nontransformation."

From this quotation it is obvious that for P'i Hsi-jui the object
is the changing process of the development of social institutions on the one hand, and the preservation of social differentiation on the other.[48] It is recommended to the ruler to

46. It is possible, however, to err by ascribing to P'i Hsi-jui dialectical views
of a scientific understanding of this problem. At first it appears that in him we
encounter a real understanding of the unity of contradictions, but after a
closer examination, he does not, of course, have such a view. S.

47. P'i Hsi-jui, as the Chinese dogmatists often did, quotes the text apparently
from memory; therefore his first phrase is somewhat changed. In the *Li-chi*
we read: 立權度量 考文章 改正朔云云, that is, "[The wise rulers] established
measures of weight, length, and capacity, they grasped the meaning of the
written documents, they reformed the calendar . . . , etc." [for a different
translation see Legge, II, 61 – Tr.] P'i Hsi-jui starts with the words: 改制度
("reform the system"). It is easy to see that he instinctively submitted himself
to a threefold rhythm. The meaning as we see, is also slightly altered. S.

48. It is clear that P'i Hsi-jui could not venture upon a sermon on elimination
of classes! S.

adhere in the first field to the teaching of transformation, and in the second the teaching of nontransformation.

It is not difficult to notice that there are two objects here which are distinguished from each other, despite the fact that both can be incorporated into the composition of some general whole. But here there is not yet an assertion of the dialectical unity of contradictions in one whole, but only the contradictory characteristics of different parts of it. Such characteristics are permissible also within the limits of formal logic, but it is not without interest that P'i Hsi-jui's thought is turned to these polarized elements of the object, reflection on which could subsequently facilitate the elaboration of dialectical thinking. The thought of the typical *I Ching* expert, as was P'i Hsi-jui, is found in the approaches to dialectical thinking. Thus we see that the first chapter of this treatise is basically devoted to the problem expressed in its title, but the author limits this level of theorization and philosophical development to this chapter. The following chapters are philology rather than philosophy. All of the ideological tone which occupies the first chapter is also preserved further. This is seen, for example, in the very beginning of the second chapter of P'i Hsi-jui's work.

Chapter II. Concerning the fact that Fu Hsi created the *I Ching* and handed down teachings, the meaning of which is to regulate the relationship of ruler and subject, father and son, husband and wife.

The entire political significance of the creation of the *Book of Changes* amounts to the fact that the differentiations of society should be confirmed with its assistance. In it is taken into consideration the status of the primitive tribe which, not having been differentiated in the main (for Confucius at least) was not distinguished from a herd of animals. Therefore, it is assumed that with the transition to a differentiated society there appeared such institutions as (correctly organized?) food, clothing, tools, hunting and fishing equipment, and a division into ruling and ruled. Up until that time there could be only matriarchy and collective marriage for, according to the evidence of the old encyclopedia *Po-hu t'ung* 白虎通 ,[49] there was no fundamental basis of families[50] in ancient times and people knew only their mothers and did not know their fathers. . . . Fu Hsi changed matriarchy on the theoretical basis of the *Book of Changes*. For this, first of all, it was necessary to establish individual marriage as the basis of the family in order to develop a differentiated society from it.[51]

Thus Fu Hsi himself is the first emperor, and if Chuang-tzu's school disputes this it is simply because it does not know the teaching of the *Book of Changes* and does not know what Fu Hsi achieved. As soon as a differentiated society can be governed as a unit, it becomes a human society. In other words, in P'i Hsi-jui's opinion, the entire meaning of the *Book of Changes* is reduced to the fact that "the success of the venture of the hexagrams (or rather trigrams – S.) consists mainly in a serious recognition of the differences between emperor

49. P'i Hsi-jui's appeal to this ancient source is very characteristic of representatives of the critical line of classical philology in Ch'ing China: they endeavored to draw on all sorts of sources as supporting material, including those which somehow had been neglected. Among such sources is the *Po-hu t'ung* 白虎通 . Chinese bibliography traces this document to a discussion held in A.D. 79 by experts on the ancient written texts about the questions of the origins and material of the *Ching* (*I Ching, Shih-ching, Shu-ching, Li-chi*, and *Ch'un-ch'iu*), who gathered for this purpose in a place called the Po-hu-kuan 白虎觀 . The historian Pan Ku (32–92) who recorded this discussion, introduced this name into the title of his book *Po-hu t'ung-i* 白虎通義 or, more briefly, *Po-hu t'ung*. This book, which is actually of an encyclopedic character, contains a mass of the most detailed information on antiquity and this is why it attracted Ch'ing philology. Its position outside of the main line of sources of Confucianism, as it were, is perhaps explained by the fact that it contains material related not only to the *ching* 經 but also to the *wei* 緯 or *ch'an-wei*, i.e., not only to the "manifest" line of Confucianism, but also its "secret" line, which, incidentally, has not been studied at all by European sinology, which follows the orthodox version of Confucianism. [On this book see Tjan Tjoe Som, *Po Hu T'ung*, 2 vols. (Brill, Leiden, 1949 and 1952) – Tr.] K.

50. San-kang Liu-chi 三綱六紀 . S.

51. 有夫婦然後有父子。有父子然後有君臣。伏羲設卦觀象定嫁娶以別男女。始有夫婦有父子有臣君。然則君臣。自伏羲始定 . S.

and subject." [52] This is also expressed in the text of the Hexagram *Lü* [53] (Hexagram 10, Offensive). [54]

The upper part [of the hexagram is the symbol] of heaven and the lower part is swamp. [This is the image] of offensive. A noble man distinguishes higher men and lower men by this [image] and determines the aspirations of the people. The fact that in the *Book of Changes* there exist hexagrams which, on the contrary, indicate a combined action of higher and lower (for example, Hexagrams 10, 11, and 12) does not contradict this assertion. Since such hexagrams deal with the actual events in which the higher and lower interact then in this hexagram they are understood as unchangeable fundamental positions, the representatives of which, of course, act together, for they are in the indivisible world and indivisible society. But the Hexagram *Lü* (10) speaks of [fundamental] positions and the hexagrams *T'ai* and *P'i* (11 and 12) of reality. [55]

Though subsequently this leading idea was forgotten, nevertheless, the entire essence of the precept traced to Fu Hsi is to bring into order the human relations and elucidate the rulers' way. In what P'i Hsi-jui says, a fact of extremely great significance clearly shows through: The ideology at the basis of the *Book of Changes* (but, of course, not in the later layers) could not appear in a still undifferentiated, pre-class society. Thanks to this, Fu Hsi, though legendary, remains symbolic; this is a landmark on the border between the two types of social systems.

Chapter III. Concerning the fact that it is necessary to agree with Ssu-ma Ch'ien, Yang Hsiung, Pan Ku, and Wang Ch'ung, and regard King Wen as the author of the redoubled trigrams. [56]

52. 畫卦之功。 首在厚君臣之別. S.

53. 履。 上天下澤。 履。 君子以辨上下。 定民志. S.

54. In his list of hexagram names in ch. 1, part II, S. translates this term as "stepping." Tr.

55. P'i Hsi-jui overlooks the fact that this is not the basic text but merely the commentary *Ta-hsiang chuan* (which P'i Hsi-jui quoted in the first two sentences. – Tr.) S.

Before raising the questions of the textual authorship of the
Book of Changes it is necessary to decide who doubled the
trigrams and by doing so turned them into hexagrams. This
question was raised more than once, and the answers to it
given by different authors are different. K'ung Ying-ta introduces the four solutions to the problem. We know from him
that the doubling of trigrams was done by (1) Fu Hsi himself,
as Wang Pi thinks; (2) Shen-nung, as Cheng Hsüan assumes;
(3) the founder of the Hsia dynasty Yü, as Sun Sheng thinks;
and (4) King Wen, as Ssu-ma Ch'ien maintains.

K'ung Ying-ta assumed that the last two interpretations fall
apart by themselves, for according to the *Hsi-tz'u chuan* there
were already in existence at the time of Shen-nung, the forty-
second hexagram "Increase" and the twenty-first "Clenched
Teeth." However, he assumes also that the interpretation
about Shen-nung's authorship was not yet proved. It can and
needs to be verified by the texts. The doubling of trigrams is
ascribed to Shen-nung falsely, since in the *Shuo-kua chuan*
what is mentioned is the creation 作 of the *Book of Changes*,
not its transmission 述 , as would have followed had Shen-
nung only developed something that had been created before
him (under Fu Hsi). From the text of *Shuo-kua chuan* it follows
that the doubling of the trigrams should inevitably be traced
to Fu Hsi. P'i Hsi-jui, however, looks at this problem differently. He says that the tradition of the *Book of Changes* from
Confucius to Ssu-ma Ch'ien is well known. Based on this

56. The list of authorities which P'i Hsi-jui drew up attracts attention. There
are the two historians: Ssu-ma Ch'ien (145–86 B.C.) author of the famous
History (*Shih-chi*) and Pan Ku (32–92) the main author of the no less famous
History of the Early Han Dynasty 前漢書 , the compilation of which was begun
by Pan Piao. Yang Hsiung—who was never included among the typically
Confucianist thinkers and who was recognized by the latter as a master of
certain of the doctrines of the "Sage." Wang Ch'ung (27–97)—also a representative far from the basic line of Confucianism. This list, as was noted above
in the treatment of the *Po-hu t'ung*, testifies to the fact that the representatives
of the critical line of classical philology were to a significant degree free from
dogmatism, even in the utilization of sources. K.

tradition, Ssu-ma Ch'ien also says that King Wen doubled the trigrams at the time of his confinement in Yu-li. This theory, incidentally, was known to K'ung Ying-ta. Yang Hsiung in his *Fa-yen*, the "I-wen chih" section in *History of the First Han Dynasty*, and Wang Ch'ung's treatise, *Lun-heng*, also support this theory. In other words, this opinion was maintained until the beginning of the second Han dynasty inclusively.[57]

However, it is hardly possible, says P'i Hsi-jui, to consider K'ung Ying-ta and Cheng Hsüan's evidence convincing, for they both are based on identical texts, but the one (Cheng) thinks that the trigrams were doubled by Shen-nung, and the other (K'ung) thinks that this could only be before Shen-nung, under Fu Hsi. Such a confusion of opinions proves only the flimsiness of both authors' argumentation. But the theory of Cheng Hsüan and K'ung Ying-ta is rejected not only on this ground. This theory is, indeed, entirely dependent on the conviction that the cultural institutions were founded according to the images of hexagrams.[58]

However, this point of view is not shared by all in China. Thus Chu Hsi assumed that while the *Hsi-tz'u chuan* speaks of the thirteen hexagrams, according to the images of which some implements existing under Shen-nung were allegedly established, this still does not mean that there were hexagrams and their names in the beginning, and that the objects were made only in imitation of them.[59]

It is rather, the contrary: the objects were made earlier and independently from the hexagrams, and only afterwards was

57. Is it not because until just that time the oral tradition was strong? Later with the appearance of the written tradition great independence of opinion appeared. For the detail of this change from oral tradition to written tradition, see Honda, pp. 211–218. S.

58. We have already indicated the falseness of such views criticizing Wilhelm. The further text of P'i Hsi-jui's work only confirms our judgment. S.

59. Incidentally, this is self-evident, and we speak of it here only because we are stating the content of P'i Hsi-jui's work, and also because apparently it is not clear to everyone (for example Wilhelm, who is convinced of the opposite). S.

resemblance to the images of the *Book of Changes* found. Shen Yü 沈寓 [60] and Ch'en Li 陳澧 [61] support such views with, however, the difference that in their opinion these images could have come into being under Shen-nung, and King Wen, having doubled the trigrams, reflected them only afterwards in the *Book of Changes*. On the other hand, Lo Pi-lu doubts this role of King Wen, but his argumentation is based on a text which is now recognized as spurious. Similarly, Ku Yen-wu 顧炎武 assumed[62] that the sixty-four hexagrams already existed under the Shang-Yin dynasty. His assumption was based on quotations (earlier mentioned in our discussion of Ou-yang Hsiu's treatise) from the *Tso-chuan*, which, as he maintains, came into the *Tso-chuan* from the old mantic literature. However, Ku Yen-wu is incorrect, for it is impossible for Tso, a truthful disciple of Confucius, to have permitted an unauthoritative quotation from mantic literature to get into his text. Probably it was that Confucius employed this quotation and Tso adopted it, for he could garnish his text with quotations from the *Book of Changes* only as long as Confucius employed them.

In other words, P'i Hsi-jui says in this chapter that King Wen doubled the trigrams, since, first of all, the oldest uninterrupted tradition ascribed the doubling of the trigrams to King Wen, and secondly, the scholars who disproved this tradition and related the doubling of the trigrams to the time of Shen-nung and earlier did so incorrectly, either not understanding the quoted text, or quoting a spurious text. Thus, for P'i Hsi-jui, the opinion that the doubling of the trigrams belongs to King Wen is proved, and the argument against it

60. Little-known Confucianist of the Ch'ing dynasty. S.

61. Famous philologist in the middle of the nineteenth century. S.

62. The name of Ku Yen-wu mentioned by the author deserves comment. Ku Yen-wu (1613–1682) is one of the pioneers of criticism in classical philology of the Ch'ing. Being in general a follower of the Sung school, he wanted to continue, and to develop further as much as possible, its investigatory line. Therefore, he drew into the study of the classics the most diverse sources, critically weighed and evaluated. K.

seems groundless.[63] With this he ends the chapter, but even he remarks that the problem of the other mantic texts of the pre-Chou period, analogous to the *Book of Changes*, had not been solved by him. He considers this problem in the following chapter.

Chapter IV. On the *Lien-shan* 連山 and the *Kuei-tsang* 歸藏.

According to K'ung Ying-ta, the *Lien-shan* and *Kuei-tsang* were first mentioned in the *Chou-li* (in our opinion this source is quite doubtful – S.). Even in older times the question of authorship of these lost texts was raised. The answers to this question vary. Tzu-ch'un assumed that the *Lien-shan* belonged to Fu Hsi and the *Kuei-tsang* to Huang-ti. One of the most original commentators of the *I Ching*, Cheng Hsüan,[64] distributes these texts by dynasties. He relates the *Lien-shan* to the Hsia dynasty, the *Kuei-tsang* to Yin, and the *Chou-i* to the Chou dynasty. However, he does the last not because the name *Chou-i* is ordinarily understood as the "Chou I [Ching]". He tries to interpret all these names: "*Lien-shan* ("mountains [standing] behind each other") means: '[this] depicts mountains appearing from behind clouds, standing out one after another without interruption' 象山之出雲連不絕."

The basis of such an interpretation is apparently the legend that in the *Lien-shan* there stood at the first place the Hexagram *Ken* 艮 ("mountain"), in which the trigrams == are arranged one above the other and depict mountains appearing one after another.[65] According to the same tradition, in the *Kuei-tsang* there stood at the first place the Hexagram *K'un* 坤 ("Earth") which was considered the storehouse to which everything originating from it sooner or later returns. (This idea is also reflected in the *Tao-te ching*: "All beings reach

---

63. P'i Hsi-jui's point of view is hardly convincing; for us, Confucius' familiarity with the *Book of Changes* itself is a great question. S.

64. See Cheng Hsüan's work, 易贊 and 易論 . S.

65. That is, since even now in Chinese landscape paintings, mountains extended in the distance are depicted arranged one over the other and are divided by strata of clouds. S.

bloom, but each will return to its root.") Therefore, Cheng Hsüan says that the expression *Kuei-tsang* means "to return to and are kept in it (in the Earth—*K'un*)."[66] The term *Chou-i*, as Cheng Hsüan assumes, says that the system of transformation [*I Ching*] is, like a circle,[67] universal and devoid of any incompleteness. However, Cheng Hsüan does not (according to K'ung Ying-ta) confirm this (very interesting) conjecture by any of the texts and in our time, says P'i Hsi-jui, no one shares Cheng Hsüan's point of view. On the contrary, it is known that Shen-nung was called Lien-shan-shih 連山氏 and Huang-ti was called Kuei-tsang-shih 歸藏氏.

Since these terms were names of periods, then *Chou* in the name of *Chou-i*, by analogy to the *Chou-shu* (*Book of records* [*of the period*] *Chou*) and *Chou-li* (*Book of rituals* [*of the period*] *Chou*), must also be understood as the *Book of Changes* [*of the period*] *Chou*. The epithet "Chou" could have been added to the *Book of Changes* before the official beginning of the Chou dynasty, at the time when King Wen was in confinement at Yu-li. Precisely as a method of protest against the Yin dynasty, the overthrow of which he prepared, King Wen gave his text the name of his clan, considering it independent from the culture of the preceding dynasty. Incidentally, apocryphal literature (易緯) also indicates that the name *Chou-i* was given according to the dynasty.[68]

There were, it is true, attempts to combine both understandings of the term. But this is a hardly admissible eclecticism. Thus Huang-fu Mi figured that the word means, in the name of our document, both the Chou dynasty and *chou* in the sense of "complete" by force of the universal completeness of the teaching in this text. This completeness is the result of the "doubling of the trigrams" which was done

66. 万物莫不歸藏于其中. S.

67. A play on words: 周 ("Chou") is a component in the term "*Chou I* [*Ching*]" and together with it has the meaning "circle" "complete," "perfect," and "entire." S.

68. 因代以題周。是也. S.

by King Wen. It is true that the text *Hsi-tz'u chuan*, speaking of the *Lien-shan* and the *Kuei-tsang*, is not reliable. However, in the subsequent period the majority is inclined to the opinion that the *Lien-shan* relates to the Hsia dynasty, the *Kuei-tsang* to the Yin, and the *Chou-i* to the Chou. But is this true? If one were to think that the *Kuei-tsang* is not a special text, but the same text as the *Chou-i* arranged in a different order, then it is impossible to ascribe it to Huang-ti, for in the text[69] one encounters the references to the Yao and Yin kings who were after Huang-ti. Therefore, Huang-fu Mi thought that the name *Lien-shan*, like the story about it, could have appeared only under the Hsia dynasty, when the *Book of Changes* was removed from Yen-ti [i.e., Shen-nung – Tr.], and the *Kuei-tsang* under the Yin dynasty, when it was removed from Huang-ti.

Though it is a different solution to the problem than from that of Tu Tzu-ch'un, it still relies on him. We have seen that *Chou* in the combination *Chou-i* was understood by Cheng Hsüan, not as the name of the dynasty, but as a meaningful word. P'i Hsi-jui prefers Cheng Hsüan's interpretation and finds in it the following assertion: if the *Lien-shan* and the *Kuei-tsang* are the names of the period, then their differences from the usual names Fu Hsi and Huang-ti are strange. Furthermore, had it been the name of the dynasty, then after them the character *I* must have been added by analogy to *Chou-i*, i.e., it should have been *Lien-shan i* and *Kuei-tsang i*. But this is not the case. It means that Cheng Hsüan is right when he understands the word "chou" in its literal meaning, but he bases his understanding of this word as well as the understanding of the *Book of Changes* on the *Hsi-tz'u-chuan* which says: "*I* [*Ching*] is a book which washes in circular succession [like the sea] the six empty places"[70] (i.e., the entire cosmos is found within it). Therefore, K'ung Ying-ta is wrong when he says that Cheng Hsüan does not document his ex-

69. But in the text of the Appendices, not in the basic text! S.

70. 易之爲書也：周流六虛. S.

planation. P'i Hsi-jui further points out that the *Hsin-lun* 新論 , a treatise written by Huan T'an 桓譚 of Han times, states that in the text of the *Lien-shan* there were eighty thousand words and in the *Kuei-tsang* forty-three thousand words. This calls forth a doubt, for it is not probable that a text at the time of the Hsia dynasty was more developed than a text of the Shang-Yin dynasty. P'i Hsi-jui says that in the *Pei-shih* (History of the Northern Kingdoms) it is mentioned that the *Lien-shan* is the forgery of the famous Liu Hsiang.[71] Obviously the *Kuei-tsang* is also a myth.

It is known that the selection of the classical books was begun with the editorial work of Confucius. Before him the *Chou-i* was mentioned together with the *Lien-shan* and the *Kuei-tsang*, just as the *Chin Chariot* 晉之乘 and *Ch'u Memoirs* 楚之檮杌[72] were mentioned together with the *Ch'un-ch'iu*. But Confucius gave preference merely to the last text. Likewise the *Chou-i* is the only text selected by Confucius. Only the teaching approved by Confucius received wide circulation, and the apocrypha *Lien-shan* and *Kuei-tsang* could not stand in the same rank with the classic *Chou-i*.

It is entirely probable that the *Lien-shan* and the *Kuei-tsang* were not even texts, but only systems of divination. It is possible to assume that before Confucius the *Chou-i* was also merely a system of divination and that a written text did not exist.[73] In other words, the attempts to prove that there were three different versions of the *Book of Changes* dating to various periods are weak, for at the outset the *Chou-i* was the name of one system of divination alongside the *Lien-shan* and *Kuei-tsang* systems. But Confucius provided only the *Chou-i* system, which then still lacked a written text. Therefore, it is useless to search for the texts of the *Lien-shan* and the *Kuei-tsang*, since there were no such things, and the text of the *Chou-i* is not older than Confucius.

71. Shchutskii has "Liu Hsüan," which is probably a slip. Tr.

72. Names of old chronicles – Tr.

73. 故周易 , 當孔子未贊之前 , 疑亦止有占法而無文辭也。 S.

Chapter v. There is no evidence to show that the Judgment texts were written by King Wen and the line texts by the Duke of Chou. One should consider in P'i's opinion both the creations of Confucius. According to K'ung Ying-ta it is known that there existed two answers to the problem of authorship of the *Kua-tz'u* (Judgment texts) and the *Hsiao-tz'u* (line texts). The first answer is that both texts were created by King Wen. The argument comes down to the fact that in the *Hsi-tz'u chuan* there are the words: "The origin of the *Book of Changes* probably dates to middle antiquity 中古 [74]. Its author probably was concerned about something." "The origin of the *Book of Changes* probably dates to the end of the Yin dynasty and the beginning of the Chou dynasty, probably to the time when King Wen had the confrontation with Chou-hsin." According to these texts Fu Hsi created the hexagrams, and King Wen the entire Judgment and line texts, and Confucius—the Ten Wings. Ssu-ma Ch'ien and subsequently Cheng Hsüan adopted this interpretation. The second answer is that one must first of all pay attention to the fact that in the text of the *Hsiao-tz'u* there are many places speaking of events which happened after King Wen; for instance, in Hexagram 46, line 4, "The King had to penetrate the mountain Ch'i." This refers to events which took place after King Wu overthrew the Yin dynasty, i.e., after King Wen. Only then was the title "Wang" (King) posthumously given to King Wen. In other words, even this text was written after the victory of King Wu over Yin. Furthermore, in Hexagram 36, line 5, the Chi-tzu is mentioned. This, also, could not have been written before King Wu. Furthermore, in Hexagram 63, line 5, Yin and Chou (it is true, only in the understanding preserved by the commentatory tradition, and

74. "Middle antiquity", according to the notions reflected in the *Hsi-tz'u chuan*, is the time generally encompassing the period of the Hsia and Yin kingdom, i.e., according to the traditional chronology, 2205–1122 B.C. Apparently, the *Hsi-tz'u chuan* has in mind the last part of this period—the time of the fall of the Yin and the rise of the Chou. K.

not literally) are mentioned as equals, i.e., this likewise cannot be dated to the period of King Wen. Consequently, one has to think that the *Kua-tz'u* belong to King Wen, and the *Hsiao-tz'u* to the Duke of Chou. Ma Yung and Lu Chi support this opinion.

It is this solution, says Pi Hsi-jui, that is widely accepted in our time. If there is sometimes mention of three sage authors, the Duke of Chou is automatically implied among them on the basis of the fact that King Wen was already added to the three. However, as we have seen, Cheng Hsüan asserted on the basis of the text of the *Hsi-tz'u chuan* that the *I Ching* was created by King Wen.[75] The apocryphal literature indicates, as we have seen, that the participation of King Wen in the creation of the *Book of Changes* must be understood in in the sense that he expanded 演 it, i.e., he did not double the trigrams, but added the texts to them. But since in the *Hsiao-tz'u* there is unquestionably proof of their origin later than the time of King Wen, they are ascribed to the Duke of Chou. There are many other interpretations, but they are all no more convincing.

On this matter of the two answers to the question, P'i Hsi-jui says that neither of them can clearly and definitely be confirmed by the text. But the criticism of these theories is not indisputable. It is sometimes based on the fact that in the text written by King Wen there would not have been the name Chi-tzu 箕子, but on the other hand Chao Pin assumed that there is a slip of pen here: i.e., this is not a proper name but the combination of words "his son" 其子. It was also said that the "mountain Ch'i" was already known in the dynasty of Hsia, i.e., earlier than King Wen by many hundreds of years. On these foundations the experts on the *I Ching* of the second Han dynasty accepted the authorship of King Wen.

75. It is true that in this text the period at the end of Yin and the beginning of Chou is mentioned, but all who refer to this text forget that even for its author problem was doubtful, to say the least, for in the text there is a construction with the character 耶. Even at that time this problem was unclear. S.

However, the former Han *I Ching* experts (Ssu-ma Ch'ien, Yang Hsiung, Pan Ku, and Wang Ch'ung) say merely that King Wen doubled the trigrams but do not ascribe the texts to him, considering Confucius their author. Against this conclusion the following objections could have been raised: if in the *Tso-chuan* there are references to an older application of the *Book of Changes*, it is impossible to accept, on the basis of these references, that these texts took shape only under Confucius and not earlier. However, this objection is incorrect. These references could have been incorporated into the *Tso-chuan* not from the oldest mantic materials—which might not have been convincing to the author of this text, a Confucianist —but only as a later insertion, from the text accepted by Confucius.

In other words, P'i Hsi-jui maintains that the attempts to ascribe the *Kua-tz'u* and the *Hsiao-tz'u* to King Wen or the *Kua-tz'u* to King Wen and *Hsiao-tz'u* to the Duke of Chou appeared only under the second Han dynasty. Much earlier authors definitely thought that the texts belonged to neither King Wen nor the Duke of Chou. The only author from the "three sages" (i.e., the compilers of the *Book of Changes*) to whom they can yet be ascribed is Confucius. The appearance of the reference to the *Book of Changes* in the *Tso-chuan* is not the quotation of ancient (for Tso Ch'iu-ming) material, but an insertion of a text which was contemporary with him, as an explanation of ancient events.

Chapter VI. Concerning the fact that the *Book of Changes* became known only under Confucius, and at this time the scholars and local officials began to esteem and recognize it.

It is known that in antiquity the *Li-chi* (the Book of rules) and the *Yüeh-ching* (the Book of music) were part of the compulsory program of education in spring and autumn courses, and the *Shih-ching* (the Book of poetry) and the *Shu-ching* (the Book of history) in summer and winter courses. If the *Book of Changes* was not included in the realm of compulsory education, it was only because at that time there existed only the hexagrams, and not the text to them. This was merely the art of divination, i.e., a specialty outside of general education. It is still another piece of evidence of the fact that neither King Wen nor the Duke of Chou were the authors of the *Kua-tz'u* and the *Hsiao-tz'u*. Had the *Book of Changes* been a text at the time, then why would it not have been included in the general education together with the other texts?

Ssu-ma Ch'ien speaks of the ardent study by Confucius of the *Book of Changes*. But it is also known that he taught his rank-and-file disciples only ritual (*li*), music (*yüeh*), songs (*shih*), and history (*shu*). Apparently he entrusted the text of the *Chronicles* (*Ch'un-ch'iu*) and the *Book of Changes* only to the most capable disciples.[76] Moreover, he treated the *Book*

___

76. The question of "rank-and-file" disciples and the "most able" demands some clarification. In the *Lun-yü* there is a place which might be taken as an indication that Confucius valued his disciples unequally.

"Ai Kung asked: 'Whom among your disciples do you consider a lover of learning?' The Teacher replied: 'There was Yen Yuan [sic]. He loved learning. He did not give in to anger. He did not commit a mistake twice. Unfortunately his life was short and he died. Now he is no longer. And now I no longer hear that anyone loves learning'" (*Lun-yü*, VI, 2).

Did this mean that Confucius had some special "program" of studies for Yen Yuan? Hardly. The *Lun-yü* points out: "The Teacher constantly spoke of the *Shih*, *Shu*, and the observance of the *Li*" (*Lun-yü*, VII, 17), i.e., of what is contained in the *Shih-ching*, *Shu-ching*, and *Li-chi*. There is one more place which is so curious that it deserves to be cited as a whole.

It occurred to one of Confucius' disciples that the Teacher did not reveal everything to his disciples, and there was something that he transmitted only to the select. So the disciple decided that above all Confucius should have taught his own son as the person closest to himself. In view of this, meeting his son he asked him:

"Is there something special which you have heard [from your father]?" The other replied, "No! Once the Teacher was standing alone. At this time I ran through the court. He asked me, 'Have you already learned the *Book of Songs*?' I replied, 'Not yet.' Then he said, 'If you do not learn the *Book of Songs*, you will have nothing to talk about.' Then I went and began to study the *Book of Songs*."

"Another time the Teacher was again standing alone. At this time I ran

of Changes merely as a philosophical theory, giving a key to the understanding of things and events. Therefore, Hsün-tzu says that those who divine by the *Book of Changes* do not understand its true significance. And in the prominent Confucianists at the end of the Chou dynasty one can constantly encounter references to the *Book of Changes* as a text explaining this or that event, and the *Book of Changes* was turned into the starting point of philosophizing. Therefore, Confucius advanced and, perhaps created, the text of the *Book of Changes* as a kind of compendium of everyday wisdom. But tradition considers Confucius the author of merely the Appendices. Chapter VII of P'i Hsi-jui is devoted to a refutation of the tradition.

Chapter VII. Concerning the Fact that the Judgment texts and line texts are the *Hsi-tz'u*. Their interpretation, as included in the compositions of the Ten Wings, is not confirmed by the ancient texts.

The thesis that Confucius is the author of the *Kua-tz'u* and the *Hsiao-tz'u* cannot be established by the ancient texts; however, there are no texts disproving this thesis either. We must remember that under the Han dynasty the *Kua-tz'u* and the *Hsiao-tz'u* were called *Hsi-tz'u* and were distinguished from the commentary *Hsi-tz'u chuan*. It is in the *Hsi-tz'u chuan* that we find a number of places where it is mentioned that "the sage added the Judgment and line texts"[77] (繫辭). Therefore, the *Kua-tz'u* and the *Hsiao-tz'u* are the "appended texts"[78] (繫辭). If in the text which is now called the *Hsi-tz'u shang-hsia*[79] the *Hsi-tz'u* is mentioned four times, then it is impossible

---

through the court: He asked me, 'Have you learned the *Book of Rules*?' I replied, 'Not yet.' Then he said, 'If you do not learn the *Book of Rules*, you will have nothing on which to stand.' Then I went and began to study the *Book of Rules*. That is what I have heard about these two things." (*Lun-yü*, XVI, 13)

This place seems written especially to show that there was no special program for selected disciples of Confucius. K.

77. 繫辭 *hsi* (predicate), *tz'u* (object) S.
78. 繫辭 *hsi* (attribute), *tz'u* (determinatum) S.
79. With the absence of a word 傳. S.

for Confucius to refer to himself repeatedly in the *Hsi-tz'u chuan*. Furthermore, it is impossible that he, as the author of the *Kua-tz'u* and the *Hsiao-tz'u*, called himself in the *Hsi-tz'u chuan* a sage.[80] Thus, the *Kua-tz'u* and the *Hsiao-tz'u* are the *Hsi-tz'u* which is the text created by Confucius, and the *Hsi-tz'u-chuan* is the text created by the disciples of Confucius. This is especially clear because in the *Hsi-tz'u chuan* the expression "the Teacher said," which is so common to the *Lun-yü*, is often used. It is obvious that the text written by Confucius is a canon 經 and the commentary of his disciples is a commentary 傳 to it.[81] And if it is mentioned in the *Hsi-tz'u chuan* that "the sage added the text to solve [questions] of good fortune and misfortune," then this was written by one of Confucius' disciples, who calls him a sage, and not by Confucius, calling King Wen and the Duke of Chou sages.[82] Cheng Ch'iao[83] supports this theory in *Discussion on the Secret Meaning of the Six Canonical Books*.[84]

K'ung Ying-ta subscribes to a different point of view, considering the basic text as belonging to King Wen, and the *Hsi-tz'u chuan* and other Appendices to Confucius; he erred and did not understand that before Confucius the notion of

80. In the *Lun-yü* the denial of the fact that he was a perfect sage is ascribed to Confucius. S.

81. Let us remark here that P'i Hsi-jui overlooks that Confucius, talking about himself, always emphasized: "I transmit, but do not write." Besides, as we shall see below, the language of the *Book of Changes* and the language of the *Lun-yü* are completely different. S.

82. Contrary to P'i Hsi-jui's opinion it is not difficult to quote from the same *Hsi-tz'u-chuan* where it is mentioned that the *Book of Changes* was created in antiquity (古). For Confucius' disciples his time was not yet antiquity, but simply the past (昔). It is true that the text of the *Shuo-kua-chuan* starts also with the exact words: "In the past the perfect sage created the *I* [-*chuan*]," but the *Shuo-kua·chuan* is a text which is not entirely reliable, being written in different times by different and obscure people. One cannot rely on it. S.

83. Cheng Ch'iao (1104–1162) is one of the Confucianists of the Sung school who was distinguished from its other representatives by his special attention to philological work on the ancient documents. K.

84. *Liu-ching ao-lun* 六經奧論. S.

canonical texts was generally absent. In the meantime, Ou-yang Hsiu understood that Confucius did not believe in the supernatural or magical. Therefore, he put under question the reliability of these places in the *Hsi-tz'u chuan*, where the legendary and miraculous origin of the *Book of Changes* are spoken of (河圖·洛書), which the sober skeptic Confucius would not allow in his text. But Ou-yang Hsiu did not know that the *Hsi-tz'u chuan* did not belong to Confucius, but to his disciples.

Thus the only outline of the creation of the text of the *Book of Changes* acceptable to P'i Hsi-jui is as follows:[85] (1) Fu Hsi invented the eight trigrams; (2) King Wen doubled them and created the sixty-four hexagrams from 384 lines; and (3) Confucius added to them the Judgment and the line texts (but not the Appendices).

While the *Shih-chi* mentions that Confucius wrote the *Shuo-kua chuan*, these words are merely a later addition to the text of the *Shih-chi*, for even in Wang Ch'ung (see *Lun-heng*, ch. 4), there is a reference to the fact that the *Shuo-kuo chuan* was found by some woman from Heng. Like the *Shuo-kua chuan*, two other Appendices of the Ten Wings, namely, the *Hsü-kua chuan* and the *Tsa-kua-chuan*, have nothing to do with Confucius. These are the least reliable of all the Appendices of a later period. It should be noted that the term "Ten Wings" itself was used widely only under the Eastern Han dynasty. There is no basis to verify it. However, the question of the rest of the *chuan* is not solved by these examples. P'i Hsi-jui devotes chapter VIII to this problem.

Chapter VIII. If Confucius wrote the *Kua-tz'u* and the *Hsiao-tz'u* and also wrote the *T'uan-chuan*, *Hsiang-chuan*, and the *Wen-yen chuan*, it means that he authored these texts and also wrote the commentaries himself.

In the preceding arguments P'i Hsi-jui states his thesis that Confucius should be regarded as the author of the basic text.

85. We are already sufficiently armed by the preceding discussions to reject this mythical scheme. S.

However, still according to the translation acceptable to P'i Hsi-jui, Confucius is incidentally the author also of the *T'uan-chuan*, the *Hsiang-chuan*, and the *Wen-yen chuan*. Thus, it is accepted that Confucius himself wrote the text and commented on it at the same time. Such a theory at first glance appears as strange, to say the least. Foreseeing the objection to this point, P'i Hsi-jui says that if the fact that Confucius himself wrote the text and commented on it confuses anyone, this confusion is unfounded. The auto-commentary is possible in principle—as the desire to make a complicated and laconic text understandable for future generations; and in practice—for example, no one is confused by the fact that in the *T'ai-hsüan ching* (the Book of the Great Mystery) Yang Hsiung, as is known, added an auto-commentary to his work which was written in imitation of the *Book of Changes*. Therefore, we can affirm that Confucius himself wrote the text of the *Book of Changes* and himself commented on it. This is, strictly speaking, the most important and most original thesis in the entire treatise of P'i Hsi-jui. In a radical way he solves the problem of authorship, but it is impossible to agree with him entirely for a number of reasons.

In view of the importance of this thesis in the context of the entire treatise we are compelled to dwell on it in a little more detail. P'i Hsi-jui is mistaken here because (1) the language of the *Hsi-tz'u* and the language of the *T'uan-chuan* (especially the *Hsiao-hsiang chuan*) and the *Wen-yen chuan* are completely different; (2) the language of the *Hsi-tz'u* at first glance (but not under detailed analysis, which will be mentioned in the second part of the present work) seems similar to the language of the *Ch'un-ch'iu* and *Lun-yü*, but it is impossible to notice even such a similarity in the language of the *T'uan-chuan*, the *Hsiang-chuan* and the *Wen-yen chuan*; the language of these texts is significantly later—clear and precise; (3) Yang Hsiung and his *T'ai-hsüan ching* cannot serve as evidence, for he imitated the already existing *Book of Changes*, and since he could not expect that his text would be commented upon, he himself commented on his lapidary text. The author of the text of the *Book of Changes* (P'i Hsi-jui assumes that this author is Confucius, but we cannot agree with him) lived in the period when the technique of writing was considerably less developed than under Yang Hsiung and he (the author) could hardly have allowed himself such a luxury as an auto-commentary.

It is known that Confucius refused all authorship: "I only transmit, but do not write," he said. Hence it is impossible to regard him as the author of the *Hsi-tz'u*. We must discard the assumption that he did not write, but merely transmitted, the text of the *Hsi-tz'u* which had existed before him, and that he himself nevertheless wrote a commentary to it as well as the *T'uan-chuan*, *Hsiang-chuan* and *Wen-yen chuan*. The language of these texts is much younger than the language of the *Lun-yü*, which is the text written not by Confucius, but later by his disciples and by the disciples of his disciples. On the same basis the authorship of Confucius must be rejected with regard to the rest of the Appendices as well. Thus P'i Hsi-jui, contrary to tradition, denies Confucius a particularly honorable role among the authors of the *Book of Changes*, but breaks tradition not just in that direction: Confucius is not only *not* the author of the basic text, as P'i Hsi-jui wishes, but further and contrary to naive tradition, not a single passage in the entire book known to us as the *I Ching* belongs to him. Neither can he be recognized as its commentator. For if Confucius had played a role as a commentator, he would first of all have tried to comment upon the *Shu-ching* and the *Shih-ching*, which he constantly referred to, and not the *I Ching*, the reference to which in the mouth of Confucius was, to say the least, problematical. With this chapter ends P'i Hsi-jui's discussion concerning the period of the creation of the basic text of the *Book of Changes* and its author. The rest of his work is directed to a study of the tradition of commentatory schools which took shape around the *Book of Changes*.[86]

86. Shchutskii in a more complex form explained the content also of the following chapters of the treatise. Since Shchutskii notes that they do not have a direct relationship to the main theme of his work, the corresponding text in the present edition is omitted. K.

This is the content of P'i Hsi-jui's treatise.[87] In the course of discussion, we have repeatedly pointed out the unacceptability of the basic conceptions of P'i Hsi-jui, i.e., his conviction that the text of the *Book of Changes* was written by Confucius. Before P'i Hsi-jui, the authorship of only the Ten Wings was attributed to Confucius, which has more than once been repudiated. P'i Hsi-jui also discards tradition, but in a diametrically opposed direction. We do not know of a more radical solution to the problem. However, though one cannot deny P'i Hsi-jui's originality, there is no possibility of agreeing with him on this thesis either. His entire treatise is proof. Nevertheless, while disagreeing with the basic concepts of our author, we

87. In the enormous literature which has grown up around the *I Ching* over more than a thousand years, two main trends clearly took shape. The first trend came from the conception of the *I Ching* as a system of "symbols" (象) and "numbers" (數); the second found "meaning" (義) and "law" (理) in the *I Ching*. Within each of these main trends several different currents were revealed. In the first trend, one current regarded the "symbols" and "numbers" of the *I Ching* as a reflection of the structure of the real world—nature and human life; the second considered the "symbols" and "numbers" as the laws of cosmic forces in their operation, the comprehension of which made it possible to understand the present and predict the future; the third current saw in the "symbols" and "numbers" a picture of the development of the world. The first current developed mainly among the Han *I Ching* specialists; the second also in the Han among the representatives of the doctrine of the "Two Forces" (*Yin-yang*) and the "Five Elements" (*Wu-hsing*), especially in Ching Fang 京房, who even found the scale of musical harmony in the *I Ching*; and the third, among certain parts of the thinkers of the Sung, especially Ch'en T'u-nan 陳圖南 (d. 989) and Shao K'ang-chieh 邵康節 (1011–1077)—created an entire mathematically meaningful picture of the development of the world.

The second trend is also represented by several currents. The first thought that the *I Ching* was a unique statement of those ideas which comprised the basic doctrine of the founders of philosophical Taoism—Lao-tzu and Chuang-tzu; the second discovered in the *I Ching* a kind of physics of nature and a nature-philosophy based on it; and a third perceived in the *I Ching* a reflection of the process of development of human culture. Among the representatives of the first current we must mention primarily Wang Pi 王弼 ; the second current is represented by such philosophers as Ch'eng I-ch'uan 程伊川 and Chu Hsi; Yang Wan-li 楊萬里 (1124–1206) might be mentioned as a representative of the third. K.

cannot but recognize that his was a colossal study of the *Book of Changes* and that his treatise is full of the most valuable information not yet taken into account in the European study of China. Our point of view on the "authorship" of the *Book of Changes* will be precisely stated in the second part of our work. Here it remains for us to examine again the verdicts on the *Book of Changes* from contemporary Chinese sinology and also the opinions of Japanese scholars about it. Naturally, even in a specialized monograph there is no possibility of covering in detail the content of this entire grandiose literature, and we are compelled to limit ourselves to references to the works which are most typical or which introduced new views.

The work of a contemporary Chinese scholar, Yü Yung-liang 余永梁, deserves attention.[88] It consists of five chapters: (1) the relationship of the cultures of Shang and Chou; (2) under the Shang dynasty (Yin) there was neither the eight trigrams nor divination with a milfoil; (3) comparison of the Judgment texts and the line texts with the texts of divination by means of the bones of animals and tortoise shells; (4) historical evidence of the fact that the Judgment texts and the line texts were created at the beginning of the Chou dynasty; and (5) confusion concerning the authorship of the *Book of Changes*.

The first chapter, based on sufficiently abundant materials, shows the difference between the cultures of the Shang and Chou tribes. At the moment of their historical encounter the Shang had a more developed stage of culture than the Chou. But the culture of Chou itself was higher. The Shang were still mainly hunters whereas the Chou were chiefly an agricultural people. The Shang were already experiencing the period of decline when they met the Chou, who were emerging. In this regard, their cultures were different. Thus, for example, under the Shang dynasty there still existed the inheritance from the older brother to the younger, a law which is typical for nomads, but under the Chou dynasty the inheritance was from

88. 易卦文辭的時代及其作者。歷史言語研究所，集刊第一本，第一分 (*Kuo-li chung-yang yen-chiu-yüan*). S.

father to son, as it happens among sedentary agricultural people. Among the Shang, wine was in great demand, whereas the Chou literature warns against the abuse of wine. The writing of the Shang documents is poorer than that of the Chou and more confused. Nevertheless, the Chou unquestionably inherited their writing from the Shang and perfected and developed it. Among the Shang, divination with animal bones and tortoise shells was widely practiced, whereas among the Chou, divination with stalks of milfoil appeared.

The last theory is elaborated in the second chapter. According to the nature of the graphical method of writing, the system of trigram-drawing can be traced far back to the early period. This cannot be said about the maps with which the *Ho-t'u* (Diagram from the Huang-ho) and the *Lo-shu* (Diagram from the river Lo) are written. They are, apparently, only a device of the Han period. The lines of the hexagrams were first used as signs of calculation. But under the Shang dynasty there were not the eight trigrams. There is much evidence for this.

1) From the standpoint of writing. In the bone inscriptions *kua* 卦 ("trigrams or hexagrams"), *shih* 筮 ("divination with stalks of milfoil"), *shih* 蓍 ("milfoil") are not encountered. It is true that the sign *pu* 卜 ("divination with bones and tortoise") is encountered, but in Shang documents written on bones and tortoise shell it is not written as the binomial *pu-shih* 卜筮 or *shih-pu* 筮卜 as it is under the Chou. In the *History of Shang* only the word *pu* 卜 and not *shih* 筮 is encountered.

2) The range of divinatory objectives by bones is extraordinarily broad. There is divination on campaigns, travels, servants, guests, performances, sacrifice-offerings, uprisings, doubts, generals, kings, arrivals, drawings of a bow, quivers, gems, the power of the sun, etc., etc. Had divination with milfoil stalks been adopted then the divination on bones would have been limited.

3) It is perfectly clear that the Shang worked out the animal oracles since they were predominantly hunters and constantly

had bones of animals at hand. It is also clear that the Chou, being basically an agricultural people, elaborated on a vegetable oracle for they could always obtain the stalks of a milfoil.

4) From all the quotations and materials of which we avail ourselves, it is clear that divination with bones is much earlier than divination with milfoil.

Divination with bones undoubtedly existed in antiquity, for we find even now among some nationalities of southwestern China (among the Yi) divination with rooster bones. This divination in China was mentioned in the text of the *Han-shu*. There exists also evidence that along with bone divination the pronouncements were newly improvised or, in case of analogy, older and already famous ones were changed. And if one is to compare the texts which have come down to us engraved on bones and tortoise shells with materials of the *Book of Changes*, then the demarcation between these two methods of divination becomes immediately clear. While on the bones there rarely exists an inscription which deals with, for example, a marriage, in the *Book of Changes* marriage occupies an important place. And, on the contrary, while in the *Book of Changes* little attention is paid to the problem of hunting and sacrifice-offerings, on bones many inscriptions about them are preserved. It is obvious that the problems which were more connected with the personal life of man were within the competence of the *Book of Changes*, whereas the problems dealing with the life of tribes are related to the mantics on the bones. In addition, divination by the *Book of Changes* is technically easier than the complicated bone divination. Therefore, divination by the *Book* was more widespread and gradually replaced the preceding system.

The third chapter is devoted to illustrated materials: similar (but only rarely identical) quotations are cited in parallel columns.[89] On the basis of this material the author thinks that

89. We think, however, it necessary to make a reservation: this similarity is less significant than the striking first-glance differences, particularly in the language. The most similar prove to be only those quotations which are com-

the Judgment texts and the Line texts originated from these inscriptions on bones and tortoises.

The fourth chapter is devoted to the collation of materials in the *Book of Changes* with historical evidence of an ethnological order; there the author studies the names mentioned in the *Book of Changes*. Cases of captured brides and conversion into slavery of captives and criminals which, in Yü Yung-liang's opinion, are witnessed in the text of the document, indicate that it could have appeared only before the Eastern Chou dynasty (i.e., the eighth century B.C. according to the traditional chronology). The analysis of the names and the events points to an earlier date for the origin of the document. It could not have been earlier than King Ch'eng of Chou (1115–1078 B.C.). At this time the *Book of Changes* was, in general, already formed and was subsequently supplemented merely by additions.[90]

The fifth and concluding chapter of Yü Yung-liang's work is directed against the attempts to ascribe the *Book of Changes* to King Wen, the Duke of Chou, or Confucius. The author introduces a series of quotations from the works of K'ang Yu-wei, who always attempted to prove that the *Book of Changes*

monplace and which are completely unexpressive and are encountered in almost any text. Therefore, this material which is in the author's article on the basic argument, does not seem to us convincing. S.

90. It seems to us that the author approaches his materials with insufficient caution and attention. Thus, for example, because in the text, slaves, shells in the role of money, and other terms characteristic of the beginning of Chou are mentioned (now and then), he traces the entire document to this period. He does not consider the fact that these terms are encountered in the text only sporadically, and are not characteristic of it. It is easy to explain them as archaisms, if one is to think that this text took shape no earlier than the eighth century B.C. Yü Yung-liang obviously constructs this hypothesis under the influence of the quotation from the *Hsi-tz'u chuan*, which speaks of the origin of the *Book of Changes* at the period between the Yin and Chou dynasties. But, first of all, there is no foundation to believe blindly the *Hsi-tz'u chuan*, and secondly, it, indeed, speaks of the origin of the book, but not the creation of its basic and main parts. In this regard, as in some others, our point of view is not the same as Yü Yung-liang's. S.

was the fruit of Confucius' creative activities (the author here forgets that K'ang Yu-wei is not original). This theory, however, is based on a misunderstanding; if it were true that the first commentatory treatment proceeded from the pre-Han Confucianists, then the advocates of Confucian authorship are not entirely Confucianist. Among them there are the Geomantists and the Taoists. Here (Yü Yung-liang says perfectly correctly) no one has paid attention to the most important fact: that the mantic tone so peculiar to our document is absolutely alien to Confucius. Having thoroughly investigated the problems connected with these questions, Yü Yung-liang comes to the conclusion that the *Book of Changes* actually has nothing in common with Confucius and his school, and it was created at the beginning of the Chou dynasty, namely, in the twelfth century B.C. One cannot but agree with him here, but we assume that the date indicated by Yü Yung-liang is too early (on this, see below).

Japanese scholars have done a great deal in the study of the *Book of Changes*. Even in a specialized monograph it is not possible to examine all the works of Japanese sinologists. We limit ourselves to three works by Japanese authors, more original than the others, *Shūekikyōyoku tsukai* 周易經翼通解, written by one of the greatest philosophers of old Japan, Itō Tōgai, and the articles of T. Naitō and N. Honda.

Itō Tōgai's work was published in 1771 by his son Itō Zenshō who provided this edition with an introduction. Since this introduction reflects very well the author's attitude toward the *Book of Changes*, we shall cite here a complete translation of this introduction.[91]

---

91. Itō Jinsai 伊藤仁齋 (1627–1705) and both of his famous sons, Tōgai 東涯 and Rangu 蘭嵎 (1693–1778) are the greatest representatives of the so-called School of Ancient Studies (古學派) which arose in Japan during the Tokugawa period (1600–1868), in the last period of feudalism in that country. In this respect the Tokugawa period is analogous to the Ch'ing dynasty in China (1644–1911): The regime which had been established in Japan, like the regime of the Ch'ing empire, was in general close in form to what is called feudal

During his reign, the Emperor Pao-hsi examined what is above, what is below, what is in front, and what is at the back, and traced eight trigrams with the help of which he contemplated the qualities of the world and arranged reality by kind. He doubled these eight trigrams and created the sixty-four hexagrams which, having given the basis for the system of his world view, came into their complete existence.

Concerning the origin of the divinatory hexagrams from the *Draft from the Yellow River*, I do not know whether or not this interpretation is correct. Is the origin of the *Book of Changes* to be traced to the end

---

absolutism. Thus, just as in China, this period is, in the realm of cultural history, one of Classicism and Enlightenment.

Just as in Ch'ing China, the governmental circles of Tokugawa Japan declared the Chu Hsi version of Sung Confucianism the official ideology; and just as in China, a social struggle was conducted in every possible way against this implanted ideology. In China this struggle was conducted mainly through philological criticism, which attempted to undermine the authenticity of those ancient sources on which Chu Hsi and his school based themselves; in Japan the struggle was conducted along two paths: the opposition to Chu Hsi-ism by the doctrine of the Ming philosopher Wang Yang-ming (1472–1528), which was hostile to it, and the demonstrative refusal to base oneself on anything but the very oldest sources. The School of Ancient Studies was active in this latter trend, hence its name. It goes without saying that under such a name there actually developed an independent philosophical trend of thought, which was inimical to the official ideology of the reactionary Tokugawa regime.

In the general orbit of the School of Ancient Studies, the works of Itō Jinsai and his sons and followers occupied an independent place. The special attention paid to the *I Ching* is very indicative of it. As is said in Itō Jinsai's preface, translated by Shchutskii, the founder of this trend, Itō Jinsai himself began to study the *I Ching*, but he succeeded only in writing a small work devoted to the investigation of the "ancient meaning" of the first two hexagrams (周易乾坤古義). The monumental work devoted to the entire *I Ching*, i.e., to the basic text and its "Wings" was done by Jinsai's son, Tōgai 周易經翼通解 . It was published by the latter's son Zenshō. Furthermore, the same Tōgai wrote a very interesting work devoted to an analysis of the discrepancies in the various commentaries to the *I Ching* which had appeared in China (周易傳義考異). Finally, Jinsai's other son, Rangu, wrote two works: one devoted to "Questions of *I Ching* studies" (易疑) and the other claimed to reveal "the basic content" of the *I Ching* (周易本旨). All the works enumerated deserve the greatest attention. Shchutskii dwelt on the first and most important work of Tōgai, as more fully reflecting the views of Itō Jinsai and his school. K.

of the Yin dynasty, or to the zenith of the Chou dynasty, or to the period of struggle between [Chou] King Wen and [Yin] Chou Hsin? In the Great Commentary[92] there are clear statements [on this problem], but it is still impossible to establish with precision the name and the period of the author of the *Book of Changes*. It is said that the Judgment texts were written by King Wen and the Line texts by the Duke of Chou, but in my view this is the opinion elaborated by the Confucianists of the Han period, and does not have any clear evidence in the text of the *Book of Changes* itself.[93]

In its contents this book is broad and all-dimensional, sophisticated and does not miss anything; with the help of the changes of decrease and increase of the cosmic forces—light and darkness—it explains the mechanism of progress and retrogress, existence and downfall in the path of mankind and interprets the success and failure [of action] and the occasions of remorse and regret [in it]. [According to this theory] avoiding overdevelopment, living in self-restraint and vigilantly observing the correctness of one's relationships with people and one's position among them by a strenuous disciplining of oneself in these respects, it is possible to reach perfection. Working for the good, one should act as far as possible, but should not distinguish the possibilities and impossibilities of a given temporary situation; and wish to accomplish [the good] despite the prevailing conditions, not only should one never surrender to them, but one should even overcome these conditions.[94] This is what the *Book of Changes* teaches. If one says [that it teaches] to endeavor for the good and avoid the harm, then this is a superficial opinion.

In the *Book of Changes*, from olden times there were two aspects—philosophical and mantic. Noble people in times of inaction treated it philosophically in order to evaluate critically their personal conduct, but in periods of action they divined by it in order to solve questionable

92. That is, in the *Hsi-tz'u chuan*. S.

93. This place reflects the basic position of the School of Ancient Studies: not to consider anything but the document itself. In view of this, not only did they not recognize the Sung literature on the *I Ching*, but they did not even recognize the Han literature, i.e., actually the oldest literature. K.

94. A very significant place! The oppositional relation toward the regime existing at that time clearly shows through in this place. Incidentally, these words should be considered in connection with Tōgai's interpretation of the Hexagram Ko 革 . K.

problems. In the *Lun-yü* Confucius says: "If I were to be given more
years to live, I would devote fifty years more to study the *Book of
Changes* and I would not make major mistakes" (*Lun-yü*, ch. 7).[95]

The Teacher (Confucius) chose only what should be followed, and
followed it. It is possible to understand why he chose just this [book]
and not any other one.

The Ten Wings were written at different times, and, based on
different schools, convey opinions of different authors. Here the case
is exactly the same as in the later commentatory literature with its
different opinions. Therefore, both philosophical and mantic interpretations are given in it. This multiplicity of interpretations is in
general alien to the *Book of Changes* [itself], but each author bases
himself on what is known to him. In these texts there is such praiseworthy assurance that even raising doubts is a deviation from the
teaching of the perfect sages. And it is completely mistaken to regard
the entire text as entirely belonging to the Teacher (i.e., Confucius),
without considering these circumstances.

When books of the early three dynasties were burned under Ch'in,
only the *Book of Changes*, being a mantic text, was not destroyed. And
when books began to be collected under the Han dynasty many books
of various kinds turned out to have been lost, and the *Book of Changes*
in these circumstances turned out to be preserved in the best shape.

95. This phrase from the *Lun-yü* inspired extremely different interpretations
in the entire commentatory literature. The debate is mainly concerned with a
problem of words— 五十 ("fifty"): whether they should be understood as
"toward fifty years of age" or "fifty years more." In parallel there is another
problem: at what age was it said by Confucius? Some maintain it was 70;
and others, 45–46. Finally, the most radically inclined Sung commentator, Liu
An-shih 劉安世 suggested that there is a mistake here: 五十 ("fifty") should
have been 卒 ("in the end.") It is possible to agree with Kanno Michiaki 簡野
道明 , *Rongo kaigi* 論語解義 , pp. 220–221) in his critique of Chinese scholastic
commentatory literature and accept the most probable interpretation that
Confucius was 45–46 years old, and understand it in a way as is done here.
But we find more fundamental criticism in an extremely serious and philologically precise work of Honda Nariyuki, *History of Chinese Classicism*, which
proves that as a result of damage to the text they mistakenly think of the *Book
of Changes*, in fact the word 易 (the *Book of Changes*) is merely a mistake for
亦 ("also"). This does not exclude by any means the fact that the *Book of Changes*
was known to Confucius in some way. S.

But in antiquity the basic texts and the commentaries existed separately, and together consisted of twelve chapters. For the first time a commentator of the Han period, Fei, placed the Judgment texts and Image texts after the corresponding hexagrams. Beginning with this period, the order of the text was already different in the editions of different commentators.

At the time of the Wei dynasty, however, Wang Ts'u-hsi (Wang Pi) developed a free interpretation of the text, and Han Po-hsiu (Han K'ang-po) commented on the Ten Wings without considering the mantic interpretation, explaining it only from the philosophical viewpoint. His views are correct and deserve to be accepted. But in the period of the Wei and Chin dynasties mysticism[96] was highly esteemed, and as a result the traditions of the teachings of Lao-tzu and Chuang-tzu became popular for the interpretation of the books of the perfect sages [i.e., The Classics – Tr.]. Such views could be correct but in their interpretation there were errors. These traditions explained the system of the perfect sages, but did so in such a way that it can be said they misrepresented the system.

Under the Sung dynasty Ch'eng-tzu (Ch'eng I-ch'uan) composed a commentary which is exclusively a philosophical interpretation and considers as its task the explanation of the system of the sages. His views are correct, sublime, and clear, and it can be said that it is the most excellent book since the time of the "Three Periods."[97] But its author reconciled the interpretation of Judgment texts to the hexagrams, and the interpretations of the Judgments of the Image texts and of the commentary *Wen-yen*. Therefore, in his commentary there are some awkwardness and artificial generalizations, mistakes which he could not avoid. Chu-tzu (Chu Hsi), when he wrote [his commentary] *Basic Content of the Book of Changes*, explained the text and the commentary in accordance with their specific content. Among his philosophical and philological explanations there are many things which can be accepted. According to our Teacher,[98] the *Book of Changes* is a philosophical work but Chu-tzu again treats it as a mantic work, therefore we must look at [his interpretation] with suspicion.

96. Shchutskii translates Lao-tzu's term 虛玄 as "mysticism." K.
97. Periods of Hsia, Yin (Shang), and Chou are taken into consideration. S.
98. Confucius. S.

My late grandfather[99] in his declining years began to comment on the *Book of Changes*, explained the first two hexagrams up to the sections of Images, and named his work *The Ancient Meaning [of the Book of Changes]*. My late father[100] had been for a long time deeply interested in the *Book of Changes*, analyzed the differences and similarities of the commentatory schools, and remarked about them. [All this he did] with great care and with all his power and with extremely careful analysis. My late grandfather used to say of his work: "[It] is nearly unyielding to [any work] of the ancient experts on the *I Ching*." Since my grandfather died without completing *The Ancient Meaning*, my father, on the basis of the guiding ideas of the tradition of our house and critically comparing the commentatory schools, established his interpretation and named it *The Complete Explanation of the Book of Changes and Its Oldest Interpretations*. In this work he directly follows the basic meaning of the *Book of Changes* in order to teach future generations how to apply it to human affairs. As far as the Ten Wings are concerned, and particularly those places in them which do harm to the teaching of the perfect sages, he also explained them directly according to their meaning without straining his interpretations, so that what is correct and what is not correct becomes clear. In this way, both the basic texts and the Wings are restored to their actual meaning, avoiding general chaos.

About the methods of divination there are different interpretations among the Sung Confucianists. My father paid special attention to the exposition of the ancient meaning of these methods, and interpreted them in detail in his book. With regard to the arrangement of the materials he followed Ch'eng-tzu. From my point of view, in this interpretation the *Book of Changes* was distinguished from the later layers. This year, starting to put this book into print and make it generally known, I, as before, consulted like-minded people and only then submitted it to print in order to promote knowledge in society of this book's content, and in order for it not to perish in the future.

> 8th year of Meiwa (1771), new lunar
> 11 month. Itō Zenshō,
> With deference, wrote this.

99. Itō Jinsai. S.
100. Itō Tōgai. S.

While some criticism (following, apparently, Ou-yang Hsiu) is contained in Itō's words, the work of a present-day scholar, Naitō, is entirely critical in its approach to the document. This is not surprising, for Naitō Torajirō 內藤虎次郎 combined in himself the ancient Chinese dogmatist, brilliantly familiar with the materials, with the scholar in command of European philological methods. His article, as its title indicates, is a critical one.[101]

It is not our purpose to speak of the versatility of the author in the problem we are studying. He himself makes clear what line of study he will follow. This is the line beginning with the criticism of Ou-yang Hsiu, and finding its complete development in the works of Itō Tōgai and the contemporary Japanese sinologist, Honda Nariyuki (see below). But continuing this line of studies, Naitō is especially concerned with the problem of the original materials of the *Book of Changes*. The fact that such texts as the *T'uan-chuan* and the *Hsiang-chuan* are of later origin, and that in them the ancient understanding is not represented, but only a later interpretation has been known since the time of Chu Hsi. But no one had yet raised the problem of the more or less ancient parts of the *Book of Changes* on which its basic text is arranged.

A difference in the understanding of the basic text has been mentioned up until that time in the different commentatory schools, but the fact that the basic text is not uniform and monolithic has never been mentioned. But by careful study of the basic text one cannot fail to notice that in the various hexagrams it is constructed not according to one plan. Naitō finds the main evidence for this in the fact that only in some hexagrams is there one image which goes through the entire text of the hexagrams like a red thread and is repeated in each Line text. In other hexagrams this common image is mentioned not with every line, but only with some. Thus, for instance, in the

101. "Ekigi" 易疑 . S.

first hexagram the dragon image is mentioned five times: "a submerged dragon," "emerging dragon" "a flying dragon" "a proud dragon," and "all dragons." We find such a fivefold reference in Hexagrams 1, 4, 5, 19, 24, 27, 31, 53,[102] 58, and 59, and sixfold appearances of such common images in hexagrams 47, 48, and 52. There are cases when a common image is repeated only four times (in Hexagrams 13, 15, 16, 33, and 60), and three times (in Hexagrams 10, 18, 20, 22, 23, 39, 54, and 55). Hence, there are three hexagrams with sixfold references; ten hexagrams with fivefold references; five hexagrams with fourfold references; eight hexagrams with threefold references. Altogether there are twenty-eight hexagrams in which there is an image repeated in the text.[103] In all of them (except Hexagram 1) this image corresponds with the name of the hexagrams. Besides, in the Line texts in almost half the hexagrams, one can find rhymes (five to a hexagram). For example, the Line texts to Hexagram 2: *lü-shuang* [*chih-fang*], *han-chang*, *kuo-nang*, and [*huang-shang*].[104]

Introducing some less significant observations, Naitō draws the conclusion that the symbols originally consisted not of six lines each, but of fewer (and not necessarily identical) numbers of lines, and that only subsequently were they supplemented in order to achieve some uniformity of the text. This is the textual revision known now, which was done not long before the Ch'in dynasty, that is, before 221 B.C.

102. Hexagram 53 actually belongs in the sixfold group. Tr.

103. Shchutskii represents here Naitō's reasoning only in part. Actually Naitō does discount some of the appearances of the hexagram name in some of the Line texts for good reasons. Shchutskii's reduction of Naitō's argument to a word count is actually misleading. Naitō's thesis that the hexagrams were originally pentagrams to which one line was later added cannot be sustained by a word count alone, even if correct. The number five as an emphasized number arose in China only comparatively late. Six is a much older "sacred" number. Tr.

104. The rhyme in the sixth line, *hsüan-huang*, has been disregarded by Naitō and Shchutskii. Tr.

Naitō's assumption is based on phenomena which are noticed in half of the materials. This is a sufficiently firm basis. From our point of view, we could reinforce his theory by the fact that the mantic terms "beginning," "penetration," "determination," and "steadiness" exist only in half (almost) of the hexagrams. And in the materials introduced by Naitō there can be noticed a tendency on the part of the text not to the sixfold form of line texts but rather to the fivefold ones.

With regard to this problem the hypothesis may be made that the hexagrams were developed from older pentagrams by adding to each alternatively a line: light or darkness. Such pentagrams could have been only thirty-two in number, and the creation of fivefold divinatory texts, in light of the general tendency to fivefoldness in China, is completely natural (compare five poems, five flowers, five tones in the Chinese scale, etc.)

Thus we see that Naitō's work casts some light on the history of composition of the hexagrams. Naitō does not dwell on a series of other problems, important for the study of our document, because they were already studied in Honda's work. He later combined this work with a series of his other articles and published them as a chapter of the book *History of Chinese Classical Studies* mentioned above. Honda begins his chapter on the origin of the *Book of Changes* by referring to two lists of traditions concerning the document. One list is found in a section of "Biography of Disciples of Confucius," in the *Historical Notes* (by Ssu-ma Ch'ien), and the other in the section "Biography of Confucius," in the *History of Han*. They are identical neither in sequence of names nor in their selection, but both start from Confucius. This merely indicates that under the Han dynasty the *Book of Changes* was already closely connected with the name of Confucius; but this is, of course, not undebatable evidence of Confucius' familiarity with it. We can show why there is no basis for connecting the *Book of Changes* with Confucius by setting forth Honda's views here.

List of Disciple-Experts of the *Yi-ching*

According to the *Historical Notes*	According to the *Han History*
Confucius	Confucius
Shang Ch'iu	Shang Ch'iu, *tzu* Mu
Han Pi, *tzu* Hung	Ch'iao Pi, *tzu* Yung,
Ch'iao, *tzu* Yung, Tz'u	Han Pi, *tzu* Kung,
Chou, *tzu* Chia, Shu	Chou Ch'ou, *tzu* Chia,
Kuang, *tzu* Cheng, Yü	Sun Yü, *tzu* Ch'eng,
T'ien, *tzu* Chuang, Ho	T'ien Ho, *tzu* Chuang
Wang, *tzu* Chuang, T'ung	Wang T'ung, *tzu* Chung
Yang Ho	Yang Ho

With this the list ends.

The list is continued by successors of T'ien Ho, *tzu* Chuang, who were, in addition to Wang Tung, *tzu* Chuang: (1) Chou Wang-sun, (2) Ting K'uan; and (3) Fu Sheng. In addition, Ting K'uan had a successor, T'ien Wang-sun, and the latter had successors: (1) Shih Ch'ou; (2) Meng Hsi; and (3) Liang-ch'iu Ho. [S. has Liang-ch'iu Chia – Tr.]

With this ends this later (more nearly perfect, if not more correct) list.

Even a cursory comparison of these lists indicates significant discrepancies. Sometimes it is a transcription by different characters of the same word *yung*,[105] sometimes it is a change of characters. The fact that the second list is longer than the

---

105. As in the case of Ch'iao, *tzu* Yung. Tr.

first is perfectly natural: it was written later.[106] Honda thinks that both lists "essentially concur and differ only in detail." In passing, Honda notes that the path of the *Book of Changes* from Confucius to his successors indicated by this tradition strongly differs from the path of the other classical books, which went through the hand of Tzu-hsia and was widespread in the central regions of China, differing from the *Book of Changes*, which was originally widespread on the periphery. Further, Honda goes on a consideration of the historical evidence of the time of the document's creation, and having declared categorically that mention of it in the *Tso-chuan* does not deserve credibility, goes on to an analysis of the material of the *Hsi-tz'u chuan*.[107] Then, Honda examines some commentatory judgments on the time of the origin of the document, and on whether the sixty-four hexagrams were created simultaneously with the eight trigrams or later, etc. After this, on the basis of the abundant material of quotations, archaeological documents, and pictographical analyses of some terms, Honda shows that the system of divination with tortoises is earlier than divination with milfoil stalks which is the basis of the *Book of Changes*.

The first system of divination, as the oracle bones of Ho-nan[108] prove, existed, in any case, before the Chou dynasty. Under Chou the system of divination by milfoil not only already existed, but also was incomparably wider spread than the divination by tortoise or bones, though theoretically the latter was recognized as more complete. Honda sees the cause of victory of the vegetative oracle over the animal oracle in its great simplicity and the easy accessibility of the system of divination by milfoil. But these causes given by the Japanese scholar are touched upon only casually; he is more concerned

106. We assume that both lists are greatly distorted by the tradition of centuries. The discrepancies in the names (for example, Kuang, *tzu* Cheng, Yü and Sun, Yu, tzu Cheng) and in the sequences of the names are explained by this fact. S.

107. Are these more reliable than the text of the *Tso-chuan*? S.

108. For detail see Iu. V. Bunakov, *Gadatel'nye kosti iz Khe-nani*. S.

with a statement of facts than the causes of their appearance. In any case, the evidence of the victory of one system of divination over the other Honda sees in the fact that the divination by milfoil is recorded in the *Tso-chuan* sixteen times and the divination by tortoise shells, only once.[109] From this Honda goes on to the problem of the date of creation of the *Book of Changes*. He points out that the quotation from chapter 7 of the *Lun-yü*, the only reference to the *Book of Changes* in early Confucian literature is insufficiently documented, since in a more authoritative version of the *Lun-yü* 魯論語 the word "Changes" is absent in this phrase, and a word with a similar sound meaning "also" (in this context meaning "even") stands in its place; that is, instead of "if I had been given several years, fifty [years] for the study of the *Book of Changes*, it would be possible not to commit great mistakes, thanks to this,"[110] it must be read: " . . . and fifty (years) for study, then even I could be able to avoid great mistakes thanks to this."[111] This quotation shows that despite the testimony of Ssu-ma Ch'ien, based on the incorrect quotation from the *Lun-yü*, Confucius did not have anything to do with the *Book of Changes*. Honda reaffirms this conclusion by Confucius' words on his negative attitude toward divination. Thus, disengaging our document from whatever connection with Confucius there might be, Honda points out that an approximate date for the creation of the book can be determined from the fact that it was not mentioned by Mencius and was by Hsün-tzu. Honda draws the conclusion that the revision known to us appeared soon after Mencius.[112]

109. In such argumentation, one cannot but notice contradictions, for several pages before Honda doubts these phrases of the *Tso-chuan*, which speak of divination by the *Book of Changes*. S.

110. 加我數年 , 五十以學易 , 可以無大過矣 . S.

111. 五十以學, 亦可以無大過矣。

112. Honda's hypothesis is not quite convincing, for under the conditions of this period, with weak contacts among the population of individual states, it is completely possible that the *Book of Changes* existed at the time of Mencius, and perhaps even before him, but it was not known to him. Honda, examining the problem exclusively from the philological point of view, does not take into consideration the content of the document. S.

Furthermore, somewhat contradicting himself, Honda finds a significant similarity between the language of the *Book of Changes* and the language of the oldest commentary to the *Ch'un-ch'iu*—the language of the *Tso-chuan*—and on this basis he states his assumption that the supposed author of the *Tso-chuan*, Tso Ch'iu-ming, is the author of the text of the *Book of Changes* as known to us. He states this very cautiously, but from the context of his work it is clear that it was written for the sake of this hypothesis of which the author himself is entirely convinced.[113]

Thus what we have mentioned here are the works devoted to the problems of the *I Ching*, the most difficult to interpret among the documents of ancient Chinese literature. In these works (we must do justice) they have done much; but the basic thing that characterizes all the works of these scholars and dogmatists, bourgeois authors and feudal authors, be they in Asia or Europe, is a suspicious mixture and a discord of opinions. It has to be noted that the representatives of bourgeois European scholarship broke all records in this respect. The representatives of bourgeois university scholarship in the East have more unity, but having adopted a specific technique, they suffer from excessive formalism and are limited by the blinders of narrow problems, not taking into account contiguous problems in all their dialectical entirety.[114]

This stimulates us to an independent and a new study of the *I Ching*, the first book in the catalogue of Chinese libraries.

113. Further, we shall see that the "closeness" of the *Book of Changes* to the language of the *Tso-chuan* is merely apparent. Honda cannot imagine the famous document without a famous author. As a person who was educated in the spirit of philological criticism, he cannot, of course, agree with the story of the authorship of Confucius, but neither can he think of the possibility of an anonymous author (more correctly, authors) of the *Book of Changes*. S.

114. We should remember that these passages were written thirty years ago. K.

PART II

Introduction

While the first part of this work is only a brief summary of what has been done in the study of the *Book of Changes*, this second part has as its aim the sharing of those insights which came to the writer of these lines in the study of the document and the texts connected with it. First of all I had to pose the question: To what extent is the text of the document reliable? In working on the history of Chinese philosophy, at every step I encountered the need to turn to the *Book of Changes* in order to explain some philosophical text. In spite of such important works in the history of Chinese philosophy as Wang Pi's treatise *Chou-i lüeh-li* and those of the Sung school, which as a whole grew out of the ideas of the *Book of Changes*, the need to trace references to it haunted me at every step, even in such texts as Tu Kuang-t'ing's. It was most natural to turn to already existing translations and researches of the *Book of Changes*, but their inadequacy forced me to undertake an independent study of the document. This was in the summer of 1928 when I was studying the philosophy of Chou Tun-i, the founder of the Sung school. The very first lines of both his treatises demanded a complete understanding of the terminology of the *Book of Changes*, but most important for the gnosiology of Chou Tun-i, the text (ch. 4 of his *T'ung-shu*) turned out to be the Rubicon which I could not cross without long and complex philosophical and linguistic study of the term *chi* ("the moment of enlightenment") which Chou Tun-i takes from the *Book of Changes*.

Gradually it became clear that not one of the existing translations could be called fully scholarly, since none of them was based on a text which had been subjected to preliminary philological criticism. Its beginnings (and then just in the view of the translator, not supported by rational argumentation) could be found only in Richard Wilhelm's introduction to his translation. Taking, in essence, the traditional view, which, as is known, made no distinction between historical facts and myths, Wilhelm could only bring himself to express doubt that the *Wen-yen chuan* text belonged neither wholly to Confucius nor to his closest students. It is unnecessary to mention the completely uncritical approach of the rest of the translators.

While the translations of the *Book of Changes* are completely bound to Chinese tradition, as we have seen, the points of view expressed by European sinologists on this document, on the contrary, err in their complete disengagement from Chinese materials. Thus European scholarship has been banal or uninformative or has expressed completely fantastic opinions on the subject. In European scholarship, Maspero (greatly indebted to contemporary Japanese works) stands out especially since he understood that the *Book of Changes* was a work of Chinese culture which had been created in the circle of court shamans and clerks. In spite of this, up to the present not a work has been produced which one might regard as indispensable for a conclusive opinion on the document itself and its place in Chinese literature. It was necessary to have a philological critique of the text which resolved the following problems: (*a*) the monolithic nature of the present text of the *Book of Changes*; (*b*) the differentiation of the text according to the content; (*c*) problems of thought; (*d*) language; (*e*) the dialect of the basic text and its relationship to other dialects of archaic Chinese which have already been studied; (*f*) the chronological coordination of part of the *Book of Changes*; (*g*) the reflection of the social system in the basic text and, connected with this, the determination of the approximate date of the formation of the basic text; (*h*) the history of the study of the document by various commentatory schools and their differentiation; (*i*) the different commentatory schools' interpretation of the work; (*j*) the influence of the *Book of Changes* on Chinese philosophy; (*k*) the problem of a philological and interpretative translation.

CHAPTER I

Monolithic Nature of the Text

There is no doubt that for the street diviner the *Book of Changes* is an indivisible unity. He does not even ask himself if what he has before him is a monolithic text or a collection of aphorisms which belong to various authors and which were created at various times. His relationship to it is singularly practical; for him it is merely a handbook for divination, and whence it came and when it arose are not essential. The only thing that one can expect of such a diviner is his confidence in the fact that the trigrams were drawn by Fu Hsi and that the Ten Wings were written by Confucius. This point of view also penetrated the "studios" of Japanese "*I Ching* scholars." In a secondhand book shop in Osaka, I managed to find a book, by one of the magicians of contemporary Japan, entitled *Lectures on the Science of Divination by the Book of Changes with Practical Examples and Real Life Judgments.*[1] In this three-volume "work" the writer is not at all interested in the authorship of the document, since he does not comment on the whole text which could be found in the editions of the *Book of Changes.* Thus he leaves out the *Hsi-tz'u chuan* and the rest of the Wings. At first glance one might see this as criticism, but it is explained more simply: It is known that the *Hsi-tz'u chuan* and the other Appendices are not taken into account in divination. Thus these texts do not interest Ohata; he "explains" only those which "occur to" the diviner. In the form in which Ohata printed the *Book of Changes*, the texts were used as a completely monolithic unity.[2]

1. 大烟重齋, 實例活斷易學講, 東京, 1926 S.

At whatever level of development of critical thought the Chinese writers concerned with the text of the document stood, its heterogeneity is so obvious that even tradition points to the "four-sage" authors; to Fu Hsi belong the eight original trigrams, on the basis of which he formed the sixty-four hexagrams; King Wen added the Judgment texts to them; the Duke of Chou created the Line texts; and Confucius himself wrote the Appendices, the Ten Wings. Subsequently, many different opinions were expressed. What was Fu Hsi, an individual or an epoch? Even if we admit that he was a man, even if we admit that the eight trigrams were created by him, then what about the sixty-four hexagrams? Were they created by him or did they appear later? The first point of view is customary in historical tradition, but in antiquity, other opinions were expressed. Thus Cheng Hsüan suggested that Shen Nung created the hexagrams; Sun Sheng suggests that Yü did; Ssu-ma Ch'ien, Pan Ku, and Yang Hsiung ascribed them to King Wen.

"We do not have available the historical facts on the basis

---

2. Besides the ordinary—commentatory and noncommentatory—literature devoted to the *I Ching*, a literature elucidated by the author in the preceding parts of his work, in the East—in China, Korea, and Japan—there was an extensive literature of a radically different type devoted *not* to *I-hsüeh* 易學 , *I Ching* studies in the true sense of the word, but to *I-tuan* 易斷 , divination according to the *I Ching*. This is a very special branch of the literature which grew up around the *I Ching*, having its own traditions, its own schools, its own history. Among the masses of compositions of this type there are all kinds, from very serious, elaborate mantic systems of the *I Ching* to marketplace diviners' books. There are also books of the "manifest traditions," i.e., published for general information and books of the "secret tradition," transmitted only, so to speak, to the initiated. Similar works are published even in recent times, many of them intended for wide distribution and they are sold in ordinary bookstores. The book which Shchutskii acquired in Japan is related to this type of publication. It is necessary to remember in this connection that as the mantic aspect of the *I Ching* is not subject to the slightest doubt, it is hardly admissible to ignore such literature in the study of the *I Ching*. Of course, elements of philological criticism are absent in such literature. But this literature is important for the understanding of the role of the *I Ching* in the everyday sphere. K.

of which we could select one of the opinions and stay with it," writes Endō Ryūkichi.[3] I think that in general we do not have available reliable historical evidence for any serious discussion of the traditional "four-sage" authors. The account about them took shape at a time when the distinction was not made between historical document and legend; when it was not known that while a legend can refer to reality, it is totally different from an historical document. The researcher's problem is not to take the legend naively as realistic, but also not to dismiss it high-handedly. One must see through the appearances of the legend (a work of art) to the facts standing behind them.

The legend of the four-sage authors explains primarily the heterogeneous nature of the text of the document. For if this text were really homogeneous in all respects it would never have occurred to anyone to talk about a plurality of authors. It is completely immaterial to which of the legendary heroes one or another of the scholastic commentators ascribes this or that part of the *Book of Changes*. It is important that even such commentators felt that the *Book of Changes* was a collection of different texts. I think that even the basic text of the *Book of Changes* is not uniform. I have in mind here not the simple interpolations (attention has already been paid to this; see, for example, the article by Naitō mentioned earlier); I am thinking of the *multilayered nature of the basic text itself*, if we strike out all the later insertions mentioned in the critical literature. As far as I know attention has not yet been paid to this in the literature.[4]

---

3. 哲學大辭典, 東京, 同文館卷, p. 183. S.

4. The work of Conrady, indicated in the first part of the work, is not taken into account, for Conrady thinks that such terms as *chi* ("fortune"), *hsiung* ("misfortune"), etc. are only later interpolations, not being concerned with the multilayered nature of the text. The embryo of thoughts concerning the multilayered nature of the text can perhaps be found only in Wilhelm, but in application not to the basic text, but to the text of the commentary *Wen-yen chuan*. S.

In the basic text, the Judgment texts and the Line texts are very clearly separated. In the former, one does not find even an allusion to the lines of the hexagram, while the latter can be understood only in relation to individual lines. Furthermore, the Line texts are understandable only on account of the specific qualities of the six positions within the hexagram and the two types of lines. I shall cite a part of my interpretative translation of Hexagram 2 which is based on the commentaries of Wang Pi, Wan I, and Itō Tōgai.[5] Both the second and fifth lines of this hexagram, being the middle lines of the upper and lower trigrams, express one of the most important qualities: even-temperedness 中,[6] understood as the ability to be always in the proper place without extremes. This central position is expressed in an image which demands interpretation. The fact is that according to ancient Chinese ideas, the color spectrum consists of five colors and that yellow occupied the central position among them. Thus, in the texts of the second and fifth lines, one often encounters the image with the epithet "yellow." Furthermore, yellow is the "earth color."[7] The fifth line in this hexagram is the main one and occupies the most advantageous position in the upper trigram signifying the external and symbolizing the possibility of external display. The external is represented by a type of clothing. But since here the hexagram deals with the Earth, its position, lower in relation to the Heaven, finds its reflection in the fact that the lower part of a Chinese garment, the "skirt," is indicated in the image. The favorable nature of this position makes it possible to speak here not only of "fortune," but even of "eternal fortune."[8]

After these explanations perhaps the text no longer seems strange and incomprehensible: "A weak line in the fifth position: a yellow skirt, eternal fortune." That is why the

---

5. On the selection of commentators see ch. 9. S.
6. The Chinese term means "centrality" or "the mean" – Tr.
7. The second hexagram has as its image "earth." S.
8. "Supreme good fortune" in the Wilhelm/Baynes version. Tr.

Line text has to be thought of as a special (and also, in view of its sophistication, a later) text. If we differentiate the Judgment texts as the older layers of the basic text then, with more attentive consideration, the book turns out not to be monolithic. One can notice that in a number of hexagrams one encounters (wholly or in part) the divinatory terms: *yüan* 元, *heng* 亨 [亨], *li* 利, and *chen* 貞. We shall study their role in the texts in more detail in order to analyze the texts which I tentatively call the older layer of the basic text.

In the commentatory literature there are two systems for explaining these terms. Some commentators (e.g., Chu Hsi) paired these four characters in a formula and, combining them with the name of a hexagram into one phrase, suggest that these are two predicates to the common subject—the name of the hexagram. In this case we get the phrase *ch'ien yüan heng li chen* 乾元亨利貞, which (taking Chu Hsi's glosses into account) should be translated: "The creative heaven is the great all-penetrating and the proper steadfastness." However, it is difficult to agree with such an interpretation since a construction so highly developed in grammatical relations would hardly be possible in such an archaic text.[9] Other commentators (e.g., Ch'eng I-ch'uan, continuing the tradition of Wang Pi and the *Wen-yen-chuan* commentaries on the Manchu translation of the *I Ching*—*Han-i araha ubaliyambuha Jijungge nomun*) consider these four words as independent, not connected in the context of a sentence. This, they suggest, is only the enumeration of the "Four Qualities" (四德) of creation. Proceeding from this tradition, the Japanese philosopher Kumazawa Banzan (1619–1692) even created an entire theory of the cosmic manifestations of these Four Qualities of creation. He produces the following scheme of his cosmology[10] (see fig., p. 137). This is how Kumazawa interprets it:

9. Thus Wilhelm's translation: "... Erhabenes Gelingen, fördernd ist die Beharrlichkeit" (... sublime success/Furthering through perserverance) does not translate the archaic meaning of this phrase either. S.

10. 熊澤蕃山, 集義和書, 東京, 1927, pp. 155ff. S.

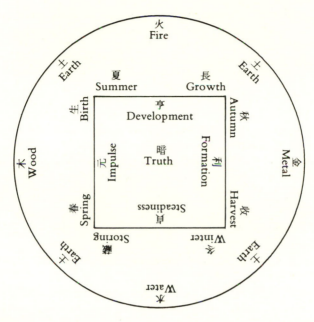

The square is the image of the silent and immovable [spirit]; the circle is the image of the overflowing and vital [matter]. The square is the depiction of form; the circle is the depiction of matter. The cosmos is but form and matter. The Heavenly Way is absolutely true and intangible. Thus in the middle I write the word "truth": i.e., truth is the Heavenly Way. It comprises spontaneously the stages: impulse, development, formation, and steadiness. These are called the four attributes of Heaven. The four attributes are strictly speaking, indivisible form and non-dimensional spirit. However, from the moment a cosmogony began and images and bodies began to exist, everything found its place. Wood occupied the place in the East; the spirit of wood is impulse and we place it to the left. Fire occupied the place in the South; the spirit of fire is development and we place it in front. Metal occupied the place in the West; the spirit of metal is formation and we place it to the right. Water occupied the place in the North; the spirit of water is steadiness and we place it behind. The form of impulse excites the matter of wood, it overflows and everything is born; this is Spring. The form of development excites the matter of fire, it overflows and everything grows; this is Summer. The form of determination[11] excites the matter of metal; it overflows and gathers everything like a harvest; this is Autumn. The form of steadiness excites the matter of water, it overflows and all is stored; this is Winter. Earth occupies the center. The spirit of earth is truth. But by accident earth is in correspondence with all seasons of the year so we place it [earth] in [all] four corners. The sequence resulting from the inter-acting [of these elements] is wood, fire, earth, metal, water. Since fire is the mother of earth, earth achieves the highest point of its develop-ment in the Southwest corner.

Here we have the absolute form which is the creating of heaven and earth, demons and spirits, and which is an inexhaustible treasure house.[12]

It is necessary to note that Kumazawa is not the originator of these ideas; basically, they are taken from the *Wen-yen chuan* commentary, so it is impossible to consider them later specu-lations which have nothing in common with the ancient conception of the *Book of Changes*.[13] Kumazawa only sys-tematized the material known from time immemorial.

This commentatory school's point of view on the Four Qualities is more valid than the Chu Hsi-ist conception of them. However, I cannot wholly agree with such an interpre-tation, for these Four Qualities, if understood in Kumazawa's sense, are such a systematic development of the creative act that creation is impossible in the absence of one of these links. Of course, in Sung philosophy (e.g., in Chou Tun-i) these terms were understood thus: (1) the impulse [*yüan*] necessary for the creative act of being, to be directed toward its appear-ance in the *meon*; (2) the penetration (-development) [*heng*] of being into the *meon*; (3) the formation (-determination) [*li*] of

11. I change Banzan's terms to avoid a tautology: "form of formation." S.

12. For an example of poeticization of the image "inexhaustible treasure" see my translation of Su Tung-p'o's "Red Wall" in *Vostok*, first collection (1935). S.

13. It is this passage from the *Wen-yen chuan* which is quoted in the *Tso-chuan* under the year 563 B.C., so such an interpretation is actually earlier [than Confucius – Tr.]. S.

being by the *meon*; and (4) the steadiness [*chen*] of what has already been created. But this systematization just does not allow the absence of any of the steps of creation. If this understanding of the Four Qualities was correct in the Appendices to the *Book of Changes*, then the all Four Qualities would only appear together in the texts. But is this so?

The chart below gives a graphic example of how unsystematic the appearance of the terms *yüan*, *heng*, *li*, and *chen* is in the oldest layers of the basic text. (In this chart the hexagrams are designated by numbers where "1" is a solid line and "2" is a broken line; the first number to the left is the corresponding lowest line of the hexagram and the number on the extreme right is the topmost line. Thus converted into numbers, the hexagrams can be distributed in a systematic order in which it is easy to find any of them.) The minus sign means the absence of the Four Qualities and the plus sign, their presence.

111111 +	121111 −	211111 −	221111 +
111112 −	121112 −	211112 −	221112 +
111121 +	121121 +	211121 −	221121 −
111122 +	121122 +	211122 +	221122 +
111211 +	121211 −	211211 −	221212 −
111212 −	121212 +	211212 −	221221 −
111221 +	121221 +	211221 +	221222 +
111222 −	121222 −	211222 +	222111 −
112111 −	122111 +	212111 −	222112 −
112112 +	122112 +	212112 +	222121 −
112121 −	122121 +	212121 +	222122 +
112122 −	122122 +	212122 −	222211 −
112211 −	122211 −	212211 +	222212 −
112212 +	122212 +	212212 −	222221 −
112221 −	122221 −	212221 +	222222 +
112222 +	122222 +	212222 +	

Thus we see that the Four Qualities are absent in thirty-two hexagrams (that is, in exactly half of all the cases!). In those hexagrams where the Four Qualities are mentioned they occur either wholly or in part; namely: one quality is mentioned in fourteen hexagrams, two in nine, three in three, and four in six hexagrams. From this it is obvious that the presence of all the Four Qualities in a hexagram is not the rule, but rather the exception.

Thus, while the theory of the first of the schools mentioned above is not correct in finding syntactical relations between the words *yüan*, *heng*, *li*, and *chen* where these relations do not exist, the second school is mistaken in regarding them as links in the ideological content of philosophical statements, links inserted by this school into the meaning and succession of these words.

What indeed do they mean? The term *yüan* 元 in the commentatory tradition was understood as "beginning," "primordial," or "great." But paleographic analysis of the sign which designates this character, an analysis supported by philological criticism,[14] leads to the reconstruction of the basic meaning of the word: "head," "chief," "initial." Pictographic analysis also supports this, for the two upper lines in the character *yüan* (as in many other characters) is equivalent to the present-day *shang* 上 ("above") and the lower complex to *jen* 人 ("man"). Thus the entire character means the "upper part of the body," "head," etc. Since this word appears in the context of the first hexagram as a quality, an attribute of creation and its first moment, it is most natural to assume in it the meaning "impulse," "initiative," etc. In those contexts in which this word clearly appears adjectivally, it can be translated as "primordial."

All commentators explain the term *heng* 亨 with the gloss *t'ung* 通 ("to penetrate"). The pictographic analysis of this character given by Hsü Shen establishes in it a graphic element

---

14. See the commentary 長井金風 , 周易時義 . Nagai first made a systematic study of the *Book of Changes* by research in the field of terminology, and with proper criticism and verification, this work can be useful. S.

of the synthetic category, composed of an abbreviation of the character *kao* 高 ("high," "height"), and *jih* 日, in place of the present-day element 了, which in the archaic Chinese writing system meant the filled sacrificial cup. Its basic meaning is to sacrifice to and serve the spirits. The offerings are raised upward, thus it was written with the character *kao*. Unfortunately, we have not yet found materials which indisputably prove the correctness of such an etymology of the character; however, it can be admitted as a hypothesis. It is supported in Takada's serious and well-documented paleographic dictionary.[15] According to Takada, the term *heng* means "to sacrifice" and "to partake of an offering" in dealing with gods, parallel to the term *hsiang* 饗 ("to entertain a guest," "to partake") in dealing with people.

Among the many (120) variants of the character *heng*, Takada cites forms which, apparently, reflect the notion of mirror likeness and of the identification of the priest conducting the sacrifice and the divinity accepting the sacrifice, a notion, which, as is known, is present in every cult. This is based on the conviction that the sacrifice[16] penetrates to the divinity. Hence, the meaning "to penetrate → to reach → completion" and as a further semantical development in the philosophical reasoning of the commentators → "development." All this, of course, proceeds from the archaic meaning of the word "the raising of the sacrifice to be taken by the divinity," an act by which the priest is identified with the divinity.

The contexts of the *Book of Changes* persuade one to settle on the meaning "completion," and now and then "development," i.e., development and completion of what was conceived in the initiative of the first moment *yüan* ("impulse").

Paleographic analysis (in the *Shuo Wen* and by Takada) reveals the term *li* 利 as an abbreviation of the character *ho*

15. See Takada Tadasuke, *Dictionary*, vol. 73, pp. 34ff. S.

16. The Russian text reads "sacrifice;" this might, however, be a misprint for "sacrificer." Tr.

141

和 ("harmonious combination," "close contiguity") and *tao* ("knife" → "to divide"); cf. the function of this element in *fen* 分 ("to divide" → "lot," "part," etc.). If we take into consideration that each side delimiting an object, to one extent separating it from some objects, and to the other uniting it with others, makes an object contiguous, then it is understandable why in a philosophical context this word means "formation," "determination"; see Kumazawa Banzan's chart cited above, p.139. Hence, it means "corresponding," "suitable" (common to commentators of glosses of both *li* and *i*),[17] "favorable." These meanings are also reflected in the Manchu translation *acabun* ("... correspondence, ... use, ... meeting").[18] Another meaning of the word *li* ("to sharpen a knife," "keen") probably comes from the transference to this character of the meaning of another word *li* 礦 ("whetstone," "to sharpen").

The context persuades us in this case to select the meaning "favorable."

The term *chen* (also *cheng*)   the commentators understand as *cheng-ku* 正固 ("correct and firm"). Paleographic analysis[19] shows that in the present form of *chen* (*cheng*) we have the combination of the characters *cheng* (*chen*) and *ting* ("tripod," "stability"). Strictly speaking, the term *chen* (*cheng*) is composed of the characters *pu* 卜 ("to divine," "to request a decision of an oracle") and *pei* 貝 ("cowrie") as an abbreviation of the character *chih* 贄 ("offering," "gift"). At the time when this character was created, it was believed that the highest wisdom in deciding the questions of life was given in the answers of the oracle which was consummated by an offering.

The people who believed this created the character *chen* with the meanings given above, and since they were related to the decisions of the oracle as to something stable, (1) the

17. 利 is equal to 宜. S.

18. See I. Zakharov. *Polnyi man'chzhursko-russkii slovar'* (1875), p. 48. Compare also the verb *achambi*. S.

19. See Takada Tadasuke, *Dictionary*, vol. 29, pp. 21, 22. S.

appearance of the meaning "stability," "steadiness," "correctness" in this character is natural and (2) the reason for its
combination with *ting* ("tripod," "stability") is understandable.

The contexts of the *Book of Changes* persuades me to select
the meaning "steadiness" for the translation of the word *chen*.

One more observation is essential for the understanding of
these four terms: in the context of the *Book of Changes* they
are not in close connection with the entire phrase, if it is not
composed of only these four characters; they are inserted in
the text like *chi* 吉 ("fortune"), *hsiung* 凶 ("misfortune"), *hui*
悔 ("repentance"), and other similar words which, according
to a theory originated by Conrady, are later additions. I do
not contend here that they are really later additions, but only
refer to the true linguistic flair of the German scholar, who
senses the heterogeneous nature of *Book of Changes* the text
and these terms standing, as it were, outside the structure of
the phrase. Only *yüan* 元 and *li* 利 sometimes are organically
part of the context of a sentence. Furthermore, the words
heng and *chen* are met in isolation in the text, but *yüan* and
li only in connection with other (succeeding) words; hence,
they are attribute and predicate.

Thus we can draw the conclusion that these terms represent
some special layer of the text. I can suggest only the following
hypotheses to explain their presence: the sentences made out
of the characters *yüan*, *heng*, *li*, and *chen* are mantic formulae,
the meaning of which has been lost. However, their completely amorphous synthesis testifies to the fact that these
formulae are much older than the rest of the text. Probably
they are the remnants of a much earlier system of divination.[20]

---

20. We can see the structure of an allusion to this in the character 卜 (*pu*),
which is part of the character 貞 (*chen*), and mainly in that 卜 (*pu*) means "to
divine on tortoise shell," i.e., this term comes from the lexicon of an earlier
(hunting and not agricultural) system of divination. This seems especially
persuasive to me for the following reasons: (1) hunting is older than agriculture; (2) divination with tortoise shells has no relationship to the life of the
agriculturalist, since the worldview, reflected in the *Book of Changes*, as a whole

In this hypothesis there is no need for me to regard them as later additions to the text, as Conrady does. What inclined him to this notion was the assumption that the basic text was a dictionary which suddenly began to be used in divination and in which were made explanatory additions. It is much more natural, in my opinion, to imagine the following: The system of divination by milfoil took shape under the influence of another older system from which the terminology was also partially borrowed. Originally this system had only the names of the divination categories (the names of the hexagrams) and formulae constructed of the terms *yüan*, *heng*, *li*, and *chen*.

In view of their laconic and polysemantic nature, it was these formulae that demanded explanations composed of generally accepted poetic images, cultic apothegms, proverbs,[21] etc. These comprise, as a later layer, the text of the *Book of Changes*.

In order to study in more detail the genuinely oldest layer of the document—the names of the hexagrams and the mantic formulae constructed of the words *yüan*, *heng*, *li*, and *chen*— I shall mention that only half the hexagrams contain these mantic formulae. The mantic terms are encountered in mantic formulae: *yüan*—nine times, *heng*—twenty-eight times, *li*— twelve times, and *chen*—fourteen times. In the entire text of the hexagrams (both in formulae and text) correspondingly we meet *yüan*—four times, *heng*—twelve times, *li*—twenty-nine times, and *chen*—nineteen times.[22]

comes from representations of agriculturalists; 3) Yü Yung-liang proves, convincingly enough, that divination with tortoise shells is older than divination with milfoil according to the *Book of Changes*; and (4) cults as a rule preserve archaisms. Thus the term is older than the system of divination—*chen* was preserved in a newer system of divination as a linguistic archaism. S.

21. Only in this limited sense is Waley correct. His article is mentioned in the first part of this work (pt. 1, ch. 1, n. 67). S.

22. Shchutskii apparently differentiates between two different usages of the terms *yüan*, *heng*, *li*, *chen*: (1) uses in "oldest layer texts" which in his translation of the Judgment texts in the third (presently untranslated) part he puts into brackets, and (2) applied use of these terms in "second layer texts." The

The mantic formulae are absent in thirty-two hexagrams, i.e., in 50 percent of the cases. Formulae of one term are in fourteen hexagrams, of two terms in nine, of three in three, and of four in six, i.e., in 50 percent of the cases.

In the work *I-hsüeh ch'i-meng* 易學啓蒙 (Science of the *I Ching* for beginners) Chu Hsi develops an entire theory (based on the material of the *Hsi-tz'u chuan*) of the gradual increase of lines in the symbols of the *Book of Changes*: (*a*) two symbols of one line, —, --; (*b*) four symbols of two lines, ⚌, ⚍, ⚎, ⚏; (*c*) eight symbols of three lines, ☰, ☱, ☲, ☳, ☴, ☵, ☶, ☷; (*d*) sixteen symbols of four lines, ▤, ▥, ▦, ▧, etc.; (*e*) thirty-two symbols of five lines, ▤, ▥, ▦, ▧, etc.; (*f*) finally the sixty-four hexagrams.[23] Thus the sixty-four hexagrams could be produced from thirty-two symbols composed of five lines each to which was added one line, — or --.

Naitō is inclined to think that the oldest text of the *Book of Changes* was composed of symbols made up of five or fewer lines but not of six.

From these considerations it might follow that at some time before the appearance of the sixty-four hexagrams and their texts, there were only thirty-two symbols of five lines; to these symbols then was added the corresponding text which in a significantly expanded form became the *Book of Changes* we know. However, no matter how attractive this hypothesis, is it true?

If the hexagrams developed from thirty-two pentagrams which did not have mantic formulae (or, on the contrary, to which they were added) then *a priori* it should turn out that among the complex of hexagrams with mantic formulae or among the complex of hexagrams without them, there should not be within one or the other complex corresponding pentagrams obtained by removing one line of the hexagrams.[24]

---

first counting apparently applies to "the oldest layer" in Judgment texts only. If this assumption is correct his figures do *not* bear recounting. What the second counting refers to is unclear. Tr.

23. This is originally Shao Yung's theory which Chu Hsi accepted. Tr.

Thus, for example, if it is true that the hexagrams having the mantic formulae were produced from a pentagram to which were added above the lines — or --, then are increase in the number of grams to sixty-four was thus produced. That is, if it is true that, for example, ☶ and ☴ were produced from ☳, then these two hexagrams should be in different complexes, and in hexagrams of one and the same complex there should appear an indifference to one of the types of lines [solid or broken – Tr.] even if the sixth line could be added in any position. The following list shows that this is not so.

The hexagrams having mantic formulae are: 1, 2, 3, 4, 7, 9, 14, 15, 17, 18, 19, 21, 22, 24, 25, 26, 30, 31, 32, 33, 34, 45, 46, 47, 51, 55, 58, 59, 60, 62, 63, 64.

Indifference cannot be in the top line for with its removal, Hexagrams 4 and 7 are indistinguishable (212221 and 212222). The same is true for the fifth position: 1 and 14 (111111 and 111121). Also the

> fourth position: 1 and 9 (111111 and 111211);
> third position: 21 and 30 (122121 and 121121);
> second position: 19 and 24 (112222 and 122222);
> first position: 2 and 24 (222222 and 122222).

Hexagrams lacking the mantic formulae are: 5, 6, 8, 10, 11, 12, 13, 16, 20, 23, 27, 28, 29, 35, 36, 37, 38, 39, 40, 41, 42, 43, 44, 48, 49, 50, 52, 53, 54, 56, 57, 61.

Indifference cannot be in the top line for with its removal, Hexagrams 38 and 54 (112121 and 112122) are indistinguishable. The same is true for

> fifth position: 61 and 42 (112211 and 112221); also the
> fourth position: 10 and 61 (112111 and 112211);
> third position: 37 and 42 (121211 and 122211);

---

24. Shchutskii's assumption seems to be that by adding a sixth line, either solid or broken, to a pentagram two categories of hexagrams are created which should be characterized at the same time by the presence or absence of the formula. Tr.

second position: 43 and 49 (111112 and 121112);
first position: 20 and 42 (222211 and 122211).

Consequently, neither the hexagrams with the mantic formulae nor the hexagrams without them could be considered pentagrams to which solid or broken lines were added in any place. For if it were so, at any position in them there would be indifference to the line being solid or broken.

Thus we must discard the hypothesis that the sixty-four hexagrams came from the thirty-two pentagrams supplied with a mantic formula or without one. We can only suggest that the hexagrams (which, despite Chu Hsi's opinion, did not come from pentagrams) were at some time all supplied with mantic formulae; and because of the damage to the text, the mantic formulae for a number of hexagrams were either lost or included in the latest layer of text. From the calculations cited above, it is obvious that while the mantic formulae are absent in a number of hexagrams, their terms are included in the basic texts.

However, regardless of such inclusion of mantic terms (and even formulae) in the basic texts, they cannot be considered a united text. In the structure of language, the form of thought, the range of content of hexagram names, and the mantic formulae on the one hand, and the texts to the hexagrams [Judgment texts – Tr.] on the other, are unquestionably two different layers in the basic text. This thesis seems more correct to me, since in the first layer we have the text constructed of variations of the always repeated four terms, *yüan*, *heng*, *li*, and *chen* (if we do not count the names of the hexagrams); the Judgment texts, while they do not lack certain repetitions, are nevertheless not characterized by them. This is especially clear from the complete list of texts cited below which are met in this layer of the *Book of Changes*. (The list is arranged according to O. Rosenberg's system, according to the first character of the text; the numbers to the right indicate the number of the hexagram. Thus it serves as an index to this layer of the text.)

Index to Hexagram Texts

(Hexagrams without [added] texts [of the second layer – Tr.]: 1, 14, 34, 58.)

利西南	40	The southwest is favorable.
利西南得朋， 東北喪朋	2	Favorable. To find a friend in the south-west, to lose a friend in the northeast.
利西南不利東北	39	The southwest is favorable, the northeast is unfavorable.
利有攸往	24	It is favorable to have some place to go.
	41	
	42	
	43	
	45	
	57	
利有攸往亨	28	It is favorable to have some place to go. Accomplishments.
利周獄	21	Favorable for taking advantage of discord.
利涉大川	5	The ford across the great river is favorable.
	13	
	18	
	26	
	42	
	59	
	61	
利艱貞	36	Steadiness in difficulty is favorable.
利建候	3	Enfeoffment is favorable.
利建候行師	16	Enfeoffment and the movement of troops are favorable.
利見大人	6	A meeting with the great man is favorable.
	39	
	45	
	57	
利貞	4	Steadiness is favorable.
	32	
	53	
	59	

61

63

利女貞	37	Steadiness is favorable to a woman.
行有尚	29	Actions will be approved.
其庭不見其人 無咎	52	Going about your court you do not notice your people. There will be no error.
可貞	41	Steadiness is possible.
可小事不可大 事	62	Little affairs are possible; great affairs are not possible.
（亨）	30	[Accomplishment.]
（亨利貞）	45	[Accomplishment. Steadiness is favorable.]
孚號	43	Proclaim with truth.
有言不信	47	There will be words but they are not believed.
有孚窒	6	For the possessor of truth, there is a hindrance.
有孚惟心亨	29	For the possessor of truth, only in the heart is accomplishment.
有孚元亨	5	For the possessor of truth, a great accomplishment.
有孚元吉無咎	41	For the possessor of truth, there is primordial fortune. There will be no error.
有孚顒若	20	Possessing truth, be impartial and strict.
有厲	43	There will be danger.
有攸往夙吉	40	If there is some place to go then there will be fortune in good time.
朋來無咎	24	Friends will arrive. There will be no error.
用大牲吉	45	[For the sacrifice] large animals are indicated. Good fortune.
見大人	46	A meeting with the great man is indicated.

「同人」于野亨	13	[Relatives] in the fields. Accomplishment.
南征吉	46	The campaign to the south brings good fortune.
初筮告再之瀆	4	On the first divination I proclaim; the second and third time he is confused; since he is confused, I do not proclaim.
初吉終亂	63	In the beginning, good fortune; at the end, disorder.
曷之用二簋可用亨	41	What is needed [for sacrifice] two [instead of eight] cups are sufficient for sacrifice.
勿恤	46	Do not grieve.
勿用有攸往	3	Where to go is not indicated.
勿用取女	44	To take a wife is not indicated.
勿憂	55	Do not worry.
揚于王庭	43	You ascend to the king's palace.
惕中吉終凶	6	With trepidation, guarding the center brings good fortune. The extreme brings misfortune.
大往小來	12	The great departs, the petty arrives.
大吉	62	Great good fortune.
大人吉無咎	47	Good fortune for the great man—there will be no error.
棟橈	28	The ridgepole caves in.
康候用錫馬蕃庶	35	The contented prince must grant horses in great abundance.
豚魚吉	61	Good fortune to wild boars and fishes.
震驚百里不喪七鬯	51	Thunder frightens over hundreds of fields, but it does not overturn the spoon [of sacrificial wine].
震來虩笑言啞啞	51	The thunder comes...O, O! [but it goes and] we laugh, Ha-ha!
旅貞吉	56	In wandering, steadiness brings good fortune.

（艮）其背	52	[Concentration] on one's back.
取女吉	31	To take a wife brings good fortune.
反復其道	24	You turn back on your road.
改邑不改井	48	They change the city, but do not change the well.
履虎尾不喫人亨	10	Step on a tiger's tail; if he does not bite [you]—accomplishment.
丈人吉無咎	7	Good fortune to the wise man. There will be no error.
「牝馬之貞」	2	[The steadiness of a mare.]
己日乃孚元亨利貞悔亡	49	If you will be full of truth to the last day, then there will be primordial accomplishment and favorable steadiness. Remorse will disappear.
七日來復	24	After seven days, return.
先甲三日後甲三日	18	[Be watchful] for three days before the beginning and three days after the beginning.
先迷後得主	2	He leads and he will get lost, he follows and he will find his lord.
觀頤自求口實	27	Contemplate the jaws. They themselves seek what fills the mouth.
元吉亨	50	Primordial [good fortune]. Accomplishment.[25]
元永貞無咎	8	Primordial eternal steadiness. There will be no error.[26]
無咎	17	There will be no error.
	24	
	32	
	41	
	52	
無所往其來復	40	If there is no place to go then it [solution]

---

25. No. 50. "Supreme good fortune" in the Wilhelm/Baynes version. Tr.
26. No. 8. In Shchutskii's text the words "primordial" and "steadiness" are in brackets. This seems to be a misprint. Tr.

吉		will come and there will be good fortune again.
無喪無得	48	You will lose nothing, but neither will you gain anything.
無攸利	54	Nothing favorable.
	64	
飛鳥之音	62	The lingering voice of a flying bird.
其瓶凶	48	You will break the jug. Misfortune.
汔至亦來繘井	48	You almost reach the water, but still you do not have enough rope for the well.
不宜上宜下	62	It is not proper to go up, it is proper to go down.
不利君子貞	12	Steadiness is not favorable to the prince.
不利即戎	43	It is not favorable to take up weapons.
不利有攸往	23	It is not favorable to have a place to go.
	25	
不利涉大川	6	The ford across the great river is not favorable.
不寧方來復夫凶	8	Isn't it better to come at once? For the latecomer, misfortune.
不家食吉	26	Eat not [only] from your own home. Good fortune.
不獲其身	52	You do not perceive your own body.
其匪正有眚	25	The one who is not right will have self-caused poverty.
貞吉	5	Steadiness brings good fortune.
	39	
小往大來吉亨	11	The petty leave, the great come. Good fortune, development.
小利貞	33	Steadiness is favorable for the petty.
小亨	56	Accomplishment for the petty.
	57	
	63	
小事吉	38	Good fortune in insignificant affairs.
小狐汔濟濡其尾	64	The young fox had almost swum across but his tail was soaked.

153

女壯	44	The woman has strength.
女歸吉	53	The woman goes away [to her husband]. Good fortune.
安貞吉	2	Abide in steadiness. There will be a good fortune.
(...終凶)	6	The extreme brings misfortune.

There are one hundred twelve texts in all. Of these only ten are repeated. This is too small a percentage to consider them formulae similar to the mantic ones.

From this alone it is clear that part of the text of the *Book of Changes*, which I call the oldest part, is divided into two layers. The first layer consists of only the name of the hexagrams and the mantic formulae. The second layer is the text to the hexagrams [Judgment texts – Tr.] with the citations from the first layer included in it.

I will give here the translation of the first layer of the basic text of the *Book·of Changes* (the names of the hexagrams and the mantic formulae).

1) Creation. Great accomplishment; steadiness is favorable.[27]

2) Fulfillment. Great accomplishment; the steadiness of a mare is favorable.

3) Initial difficulty. Great accomplishment; steadiness is favorable.

4) Immaturity. Accomplishment.

5) Necessity of waiting.

6) Litigation.

7) The army. Steadiness.

8) Drawing near.

9) Rearing of the small. Accomplishment.

10) Stepping.

11) Flowering.

27. It will be noted that the translations Shchutskii uses here for the *yüan, heng, li, chen* formula differ from those he uses further up in the introduction. Tr.

12) Decline.

13) Relatives.

14) Possession of many things. Great accomplishment.

15) Humility. Accomplishment.

16) Freedom.

17) Succession. Great accomplishment; steadiness is favorable.

18) Correction. Great accomplishment.

19) Visit. Great accomplishment; steadiness is favorable.

20) Contemplation.

21) Clenched teeth. Accomplishment.

22) Decoration. Accomplishment.

23) Destruction.

24) Return. Accomplishment.

25) Faultlessness. Great accomplishment; steadiness is favorable.

26) Rearing of the great. Steadiness is favorable.

27) Nourishment.

28) Overdevelopment of the great.

29) Abyss.

30) Radiance. Steadiness is favorable; accomplishment.

31) Combination.[28] Accomplishment; steadiness is favorable.

32) Constancy. Accomplishment.

33) Retreat. Accomplishment.

34) Great power. Steadiness is favorable.

35) Rising [above the horizon – Tr.]

36) Defeat of the light.

37) Household.

38) Discord.

39) Obstacle.

40) Solution.

41) Decrease.

42) Increase.

28. Translating this term in the Line texts (in the untranslated third part) Shchutskii uses "interaction." Tr.

43) Going out.

44) Contraposition.

45) Reunion. Accomplishment.

46) Ascent. Great accomplishment.

47) Exhaustion. Accomplishment; steadiness.

48) The well.

49) Exchange.

50) The altar.

51) Lightning. Accomplishment.

52) Mountain-chain.[29]

53) Current.

54) The bride.

55) Abundance. Accomplishment.

56) Wandering.

57) Penetration.

58) Joy. Accomplishment; steadiness is favorable.

59) Breaking up. Accomplishment.

60) Limitation. Accomplishment.

61) Inner truth.

62) Overdevelopment of the small. Accomplishment; stead-iness is favorable.

63) Already at the end. Accomplishment.

64) Not yet at the end. Accomplishment.

Thus the basic text, which must be separated from the archaic commentatory literature, is divided in turn into three layers:

First layer—the names of the hexagrams and the mantic formulae.

Second layer—texts to the hexagrams [Judgment texts] (including the citations from the first layer.)

Third layer—texts to individual lines (including the citations from the first and second layers).

Although the traditional schools of commentators interpret

29. *Ken* is translated "concentration" by Shchutskii at other places. Tr.

the *Book of Changes* as a unit even to the present, doubts about its monolithic nature were expressed in China and Japan both in the past and in the present. Even tradition itself speaks of the gradual forming of the text; only it does this naively, ascribing to various famous people of antiquity, among them Confucius, the authorship of one or another part, forgetting that Confucius himself emphasized that he was not an author but only the preserver of tradition. The critical line in this question began with Ou-yang Hsiu. The same position was maintained by Lu Chiu-yüan 陸九淵 [30] (this is known, it is true, only according to indirect evidence; the corresponding text [of his] is not preserved). Doubts on the monolithic nature of the text were expressed by P'i Hsi-jui, Tiao Pao, Wang Ying-lin, Itō Tōgai, Torajirō Naitō, etc. The latter points to a number of indisputable interpolations. They and a number of others are taken into account and pointed out in our translation. Matsui Rashu's philologically valuable Japanese commentary[31] sometimes proved to be of help in defining them. The present research rejects the monolithic nature of the basic text of the *Book of Changes*.

30. Lu Chiu-yüan or Lu Hsiang-shan 陸香山 (1139–1192) is a representative of Sung philosophy who came out against Chu Hsi's school. S.

31. Shchutskii has in mind the *Shueki shakuko* 周易釋故, a work by Matsui Rashu, the disciple of Mase Chūshū 眞藝中州 (d. 1817), one of the greatest *I Ching* scholars of feudal Japan, who thought that the known text of the *I Ching* is an incredible conglomeration of very diverse elements which got into the *I Ching* in different times and from different sources. He made it his aim "to return to the ancient *I Ching*" 復古易經. At the same time, Mase Chushu devoted a great deal of attention to the mantic side of this document and founded his own special school in this area. Matsui Rashu's work is, as the author himself says, only a statement of the ideas of his teacher. Both teacher and disciple left behind them an entire series of works on the *I Ching*. K.

CHAPTER 2

Differentiation by Content

The usual tradition divides the *Book of Changes* into two parts. The first is the basic text which is called the *ching* (text) and the second is the traditional commentaries, the so-called *shih-i* 十翼 (Ten Wings). Tradition does not make an internal differentiation of the basic text as was done in the preceding chapter. Tradition seems to sense the absence of a unity in the basic text when speaking of the (in my view, legendary) authors of the *Book of Changes*.

The Ten Wings are traditionally divided into the following parts:

1) *T'uan-chuan* 彖傳 (Tradition of Judgments) in two parts.

2) *Hsiang-chuan* 像傳 [1] (Tradition of Images) in two parts.

3) *Hsi-tz'u chuan* 繫辭傳 or *Ta-chuan* 大傳 (Tradition of aphorisms or the Great Tradition) in two parts.

4) *Shuo-kua chuan* 說卦傳 (Tradition of the explanation of the trigrams).

5) *Hsü-kua chuan* 序卦傳 (Tradition of the sequence of the hexagrams).

6) *Tsa-kua chuan* 雜卦傳 (Various traditions on the hexagrams).

7) *Wen-yen chuan* 文言傳 (Tradition of characters and words).

Usually, commentators not inclined to philological or historical criticism ascribe all Ten Wings to Confucius. Thus, for example, the Sung commentator Hu I-kuei 胡一桂 says

---

1. The Chinese usually use the character hsiang 象 and not hsiang 像 . Tr.

that the *Hsi-tz'u chuan* was created by Confucius, and that therefore, Ssu-ma Ch'ien calls it the *Ta-chuan* (Great tradition) in distinction from other treatises (*chuan*) which were written by Yang Ho 楊何 , Ssu-ma Ch'ien's teacher.

On the other hand, as was pointed out in the first part of the present work, P'i Hsi-jui, denying, like Ou-yang Hsiu and Itō Tōgai, Confucius' authorship of the Ten Wings, thought that he (Confucius) had created the basic text. The argument did not, however, follow the line it should have. If it had been ascertained that different parts of the Ten Wings were randomly divided by tradition, without necessary internal connection between each of the parts, and that either as a whole or in part they are a varied text, then the question of a single authorship, not to mention Confucius, would never have become the basis of the discussion.

The traditional division of the Ten Wings must be seen as groundless because of the following considerations:

1) It was constructed on a mixed methodology. While the *T'uan-chuan* and the *Hsiang-chuan* are related (being line-by-line commentaries) to the basic text and each is divided into two parts just as the basic text is, the *Hsi-tz'u chuan*, not having any direct relation to particular parts of the basic text, is divided into two parts mechanically and without any connection with the two parts of the basic text.

2) Two completely different texts (apparently written at different times) are incorporated in the *Hsiang-chuan*. However, even tradition observes this, since a more accurate classification of texts speaks of two *Hsiang-chuan* commentaries, *Ta-hsiang chuan* (Great tradition of images) and *Hsiao-hsiang chuan* (Little tradition of images). But this division is made not on the basis of size (the *Ta-hsiang chuan* is shorter than the *Hsiao-hsiang chuan*), but rather on the basis of their significance.

3) Two completely different texts are collected under the one name *Shuo-kua chuan*. A small part of it at the beginning comes close to the *Hsi-tz'u chuan* commentary in both form

and content, but the remaining larger part is analogous to the *Tsa-kua chuan*. Thus we read at the beginning of the *Shuo-kua chuan*:

In antiquity when the sages originated [the study of] the Changes, they grasped profoundly the clarity of the spirits and gave birth to the oracle by milfoil.[2] [The number] "3" [they designated as] Heaven and [the number] "2" as Earth and based [the oracle] on numeration.[3] They discerned permutability in [the changing] of dark and light and established symbols [hexagrams – Tr.]; they uncovered the signs[4] in the [alternation] of rigidity and pliability, and created the separate lines [of the symbols].[5] They conformed harmoniously with the absolute Way and its personal acceptance, and arranged [life in accord-

2. Cf. *Hsi-tz'u chuan*, part II, in their own way chapters on the history of Chinese culture from the point of view of the *Book of Changes*. S.

3. Cf. *Hsi-tz'u chuan*, part I, a chapter on the technique of mantic numeration. S.

4. The translation of the term *fa-hui* 發揮 given in Couvreur's dictionary does not take the parallelism into account and is thus incorrect as too summary: "faire connaître." In order to understand the term *hui* 揮 one must take into account:

a) that it is understood now as *chen-tung* 振動 ("to rouse to movement") or *san* 散 ("to scatter");

b) as the rhyme and phonetic analogue of the words *wei* 微 ("elusive," "imperceptible") and *hui* 徽 ("banner," "mark," "sign") in antiquity it had already replaced the second of these characters (for examples of such substitutions and their explanations see *Tz'u-t'ung* 辭通 , vol. I, *chüan* 卷 111, pp. 3–4). The polysemanticism of opposite meanings should not surprise us, for it is enough to remember even such examples as: *ming*, "light" (明)//"dark" (冥); *luan* "disorder" (亂)// "to put in order" (亂)//; *li* "to hold on to something," "to fall into ..." (離)// "to be separated from someone," "to leave ..." (離); *wei* "imperceptible" (微)// *hui* "noticeable" (徽);

c) if the statements in points *a* and *b* are synthesized in one meaning of the term *hui* 揮 , then we can see the following content in it: "to expose something that is not yet exposed";

d) in this context the term *fa-hui* 發揮 is parallel to *kuan* 觀 ("to see change-ability") which is constructed on the formula predicate-object, consequently for 揮 one must choose a nominal and not a verbal meaning: "... revealed the sign. ..." S.

5. Cf. the story in the first part of the *Hsi-tz'u chuan* about the creation of the hexagrams on the basis of observations of the external world. S.

ance] with a feeling of propriety; they fully comprehended the order [of the world], and to the end they knew the conditions [of the soul] and thus achieved [knowledge of] fate.[6]

Just like this first chapter of the *Shuo-kua chuan*, the second chapter also is closely connected with the cycle of questions dealt with in the *Hsi-tz'u chuan*.

In antiquity when the sages originated [the study of] the Changes, they intended to conform to the laws of the essense of [man and his] fate. And thus they established the Way of Heaven: Dark and Light; they established the Way of Earth: Pliability and Rigidity; they established the Way of Man: Love (仁) and Duty (義). They combined these three potentials and doubled them. For this reason in the *Book of Changes* six lines comprise a hexagram, and in it dark and light are divided and pliability and rigidity alternate. Thus in the *Book of Changes*, the six positions make up an entire unit.

Chapter 3 of the *Shuo-kua chuan* still has lines reminiscent of the *Hsi-tz'u chuan*, but the rest of its chapters are analogous to the *Tsa-kua chuan* and are distinguished only by the fact that the latter deals with hexagrams while the second part of the *Shuo-kua chuan* deals with trigrams. But both are only glosses which aim to explain the significance of the names of the trigrams and hexagrams, and also to inform the diviner of the established mantic tradition of associations of various animals, articles, and phenomena with certain trigrams and hexagrams.

4) Similarly, the *Wen-yen chuan* text is not homogeneous. This was already noticed by Wilhelm who, suggesting that the *Wen-yen chuan* was written if not by Confucius then by his closest students, studied the *Wen-yen chuan* more thoroughly than the rest of the Wings. The *Wen-yen chuan* breaks up into four different texts. I think that Wilhelm misjudges this work only by such a close relationship with Confucius. As we shall see below, its entire character is completely alien to

6. The text in the first part of the *Hsi-tz'u chuan* is wholly in the spirit of the gnosiological temperament. S.

Confucius, and had he known it he probably would have declared it heretical, harmful, and not canonical.

5) The closeness of the *Hsi-tz'u chuan* and the *Shuo-kua chuan* was, to a certain extent, remarked by the Japanese *I Ching* expert, Matsui Rashu, who took the risk of completely reorganizing (in a more systematic order) the *Hsi-tz'u chuan* and uniting it with the text of the first chapters of the *Shuo-kua chuan*.

6) Finally, the contents of the texts themselves combined under the general title of Ten Wings are completely different. This combination of different items contradicts both reality and scholarly classification. Actually, they should be divided into three groups: (1) Commentaries (both parts of the *T'uan-chuan* and the *Hsiang-chuan*); (2) Theoretical treatises on the *Book of Changes* as a whole (all of the *Hsi-tz'u chuan* and *Hsü-kua chuan* and chapters 1 and 2 of the *Shuo-kua chuan*); and (3) Glosses to terms of the *Shuo-kua chuan* from chapter 3 on, *Tsa-kua chuan* and the *Wen-yen chuan*.

It must be noted that even within the limits of these three groups the texts are not of the same nature. The *T'uan-chuan* treats the hexagrams as a whole, analyzes the trigrams which compose them, and, proceeding from this analysis, ably explains the Judgment texts. For example, the *T'uan-chuan* commentary to Hexagram 12 (*P'i*. Decline. Judgment: "Decline is improper people.[7] Steadiness is unfavorable for a noble man. The great departs, the small comes"). The *T'uan-chuan* comments:

Decline is improper people. Steadiness is unfavorable for a noble man. The great departs, the small comes.[8] This means that Heaven and Earth are not connected and all creatures do not develop. When

---

7. These words are an interpretation. S. [At this point S. refers the reader to a note to his translation of the second layer which reads: "In contemporary editions the characters *chih-fei-jen* 之匪人 occur at the beginning, but as Matsui shows they are insertions. In addition, according to Matsui, the order of the phrase here is a parallel to the preceding hexagram." Tr.]

8. For a relatively correct sentence sequence in this text see the note to its translation above. S.

2. *Differentiation by Content*

high and low are unconnected then a government does not exist in the Empire.[9] The inner [lower] trigram [here] is dark, and the outer [upper] is light. The inner trigram is pliability and the outer is rigidity. The interior [here] is the commoner and the exterior is the noble man. The way of the commoner is to grow and the way of the noble man is to diminish.

We see here a typical commentary which regards political events from the point of view of cosmic forces.

There is an entirely different technique of commentary and a different intent in the *Ta-hsiang chuan*. Here is what it says about the same hexagram: "Heaven and Earth are not connected: this is decline. The noble man [in such circumstances] avoids difficulties, thanks to virtue and thrift. It is impossible to be honored [here] and through it to get reward." In this commentary we see a moral treatise devoted to a question of ethics, taken dynamically in connection with some situation of life (expressed in the hexagram) and not statically as an ever inviolable dogma. I might mention that for Confucianists the moral norm is expressed in the words: "The Way is that from which one can never deflect even for a moment."

Let us now turn to the *Hsiao-hsiang chuan* commentary. It is distinguished from the *Ta-hsiang chuan* by the fact that it is related to different texts: to the Line texts, not to the Judgment texts. In the majority of cases this commentary turns out to be an academic explanation of the Line texts, taking into account, it is true, the structure of the hexagram and the role of the line in it, but it inclines toward a mantic interpretation of the hexagram. Here is a typical explanation for the *Hsiao-hsiang chuan* (the same hexagram, third line). The Line text: "Hexagram line the third. Be full of shame." Text of the *Hsiao-hsiang chuan*: "Be full of shame, [for] this is not a proper position."[10] Or under the fourth line, the Line text reads: "There will be a command from on high. There will

9. For the state is regarded in the *Book of Changes* as a system of connection between lower and higher. S.

10. It would have been proper if this odd (third) position were occupied by a light line. S.

be no error. In all who are with you will be the grace [of heaven]." Text of the *Hsiao-hsiang chuan*: "There will be a command from on high. There will be no error, [i.e.] aspirations will be realized."

In the last example it is especially evident that the text of the *Hsiao-hsiang chuan* presents nothing of interest. This is typical scholasticism. But its influence lasted for several centuries: the majority of the commentators of the end of the second century A.D. were under the unquestionable influence of this commentary. Wilhelm apparently recognized its small value, for he included it not in the first volume of his translation, but in the third volume with the brief title "Materials."

The text of the *Hsi-tz'u chuan* stands out among the Ten Wings. This is an entire encyclopedia of *I Ching* lore! It is true that it is unsystematic; the alternation of the most different themes in it sometimes produces the painful impression of its mixed character and fortuitousness.[11] Nevertheless, this text was judged to have played the most outstanding role in the development of Chinese philosophy. For it was through this book that the *Book of Changes* and its theory were understood by the brilliant philosopher Wang Pi (third century A.D.), and in essence it was out of this book that the *I Ching*-based doctrines of the Sung thinkers developed, that school in which questions of philosophy were well worked out. In this encyclopedia of *I Ching* lore we find both an ontology (the doctrine of the material substance of the world) and a cosmology (the doctrine of the forces of darkness and light, their rhythmical alternation which begets all the life of the cosmos, and of a number of cosmic forces which produce the growth of plants, etc.), as well as gnosiology (the doctrine of the correlation of words and the recognizable image as its content, etc.) and a "history of culture" (the doctrine of the development of cultural institutions from the point of view of the concepts of the *Book of Changes*, etc.). As we have seen, the

11. A not wholly successful attempt at its systematization was made only once, as far as I know, by Matsui Rashu mentioned above. S.

first two chapters of the *Shuo-kua chuan* are affiliated in significance with the *Hsi-tz'u chuan*. The text of the *Hsü-kua chuan*—the longest of sorites known to me—is an attempt to prove the validity of the arrangement of hexagrams that we find in the *Book of Changes*. This text was analyzed and treated especially systematically by Ch'eng I-ch'uan in the eleventh century. Here is just his beginning:

There is Heaven and Earth and only after this are all things born. What fills all the space between Heaven and Earth is only all things. Thus after [the symbols of Heaven and Earth] [Ch'ien and K'un – Tr.] is placed the symbol Chuan. It means both filling and the first moment of a thing's existence. When, as something is born, it is undoubtedly immature, thus [the symbol "initial difficulty"] is followed by "immaturity." Immaturity is the youth of a thing. If something is young then it must be reared. Thus "necessity of waiting" follows "immaturity." The necessity of waiting is the way of nourishment. For food and drink there is certainly competition. Thus after ["necessity of waiting"] comes "competition." In competition a great number of people certainly rise up, thus after it comes "army." Army is a mass of people. In a mass of people there are certainly those among whom there takes place a drawing near. Thus (after army) comes "drawing near." Drawing near is approach [of one another], etc.

The rest of the Ten Wings are only glosses; thus it is either impossible or pointless to translate them, for the translation of terms is really a problem in comprehending a terminology which represents a selection of synonyms for the compilation of a gloss. Of course, those who wish to study and understand the internal logic of the document and especially to study the Han commentators on the original cannot ignore the reading of these texts. However, our purposes do not demand this. Thus I limit myself to pointing out the character of these texts (the end of the *Shuo-kua chuan*, *Tsa-kua chuan*, and *Wen-yen chuan*.

CHAPTER 3

Differentiation by Techniques of Thinking

I must preface the materials in this chapter with some general statements in order to make clear early what I mean by an analysis of techniques of thinking. In reading this chapter it may appear that in so ancient a work as the *Book of Changes* I find our own contemporary conceptions and ascribe them to authors who lived in a period completely different from ours. In other words, I foresee a reproach concerning the modernization of an archaic document. I would like to clarify this question.

If we speak of beehives, then we must mention that their cells are in hexagonal sections. This is a concept of geometry, but no one will suspect us of an inclination to ascribe to the bees a knowledge of geometry. If the representatives of a culturally backward people know how to construct huts out of logs, this still does not mean that they have a knowledge of such engineering science as the statics of wooden structures or strength of materials. However, if we were to study their technique, we could not avoid these scientific terms to make the results of our studies understandable to contemporary readers. Finally, how many millions of people have played various musical instruments without the slightest knowledge of the laws of acoustics and the theory of music? However, scientifically we can speak of their creativity only from the point of view of contemporary acoustics and the theory of music. Thus, in studying the techniques of thinking reflected in the *Book of Changes*, we must use our present-day techniques of thinking. This does not mean, however, that we see any evidence of equality between the thinking techniques of these texts' authors and our own. On the contrary, the aim of this chapter is to show the peculiarities of the thinking of the authors of the *Book of Changes* in various parts of the document.

The thinking of the authors of the basic text's first layer was still very amorphous. To begin to look for even a hint of logical connection would be in vain. The grammatical relationships in this text are still very unclear. One can recognize only the establishment of terms as the single achievement of thinking at this stage. But these "terms" can be considered terms only with great reservations, for the very characteristic of a term—its definiteness—comes to almost nothing because of their polysemantic nature. There are a number of hexagrams similarly defined by identical mantic formulae. One can only suppose that in the application to different hexagrams they were understood differently. In this regard even the names of the hexagrams are no exceptions. If one takes into account how variously the name of a hexagram is interpreted in the texts of the second, and especially of the third, layer, then the diversity of their concepts emerges graphically. At this stage its thought only begins to elaborate terms. The second and third layers of the basic text do not differ greatly from each other in regard to the technique of thinking, but the thinking operating in them, though primitive, is incomparably more developed than in the first layer. First of all, the struggle with polysemanticism is clearly expressed in them. This struggle basically goes along the line of first creating a context, and then of making the term precise by definition. Apparently, this is explained by the fact that the thinking conditioned by the possibilities of language as an expression of thought could be facilitated in such forms as were present in the amorpho–synthetic Chinese language. The latter, lacking possibilities for conventional word formation, presented wide possibilities for the integration of several words in *composita* and possessed great flexibility in detailed artistic images as a means of expressing thoughts.

Thus the thinking of the authors of the second and third layers developed, not by construction of accurate terms expressing concepts, but by ideas invested in verbal images. Often these images were made precise by a single definition or by a number of its variants and sometimes by entire descriptions. Of course, in this thinking there are also such concepts as "great," "small," etc. But the chief role still belongs to the ideas bearing implied concepts. Such ideas were already developed to the level of symbolic notions, which is the transitional stage to concepts. In this process, of course, thinking is connected with the level of language development which is defined by the level of development of the life of society. The latter conditioned the development of the writing system.

The Chinese character was especially conducive to the development of the symbolic capacity of thinking (for Chinese characters had already lost the direct link with the depiction of objects in distinction from pictures and pictograms) and to schematism (for, in the graphic method, the way from pictograph to ideograph is schematism). While schematism also led to greater common intelligibility of terms, the symbolism still prevailing in them prevented their direct intelligibility. Thus it became necessary to interpret symbolic images which, in my opinion, was one of the reasons which brought the ancient commentatory literature to life. For its realization, thinking had to take a step forward in the direction of conceptual elaboration.

And indeed, in such a text as the *T'uan-chuan* we find thinking which already realized the concept of time. Furthermore, not only was time in general understood, but also understood was its differentiation by the content of life situations extending through time. Often in the *T'uan-chuan* it is pointed out that "time [of some] hexagram [i.e., of some life situation] is significant [an important time]." While in the third layer one can see a flash of the concept of space, such texts as the gloss to the third layer—*Hsiao-hsiang chuan*—have

3. Differentiation by Techniques of Thinking

a manifest indication of space [the so-called position within a hexagram]. Apparently, light and dark at this stage of development of thinking were understood as cosmic forces. Here thought undoubtedly was suited to differentiating antithesis, to understanding antagonism (struggle, movement) and its psychological analogy—impulse of will perceived as aspiration.

Another commentary—the *Ta-hsiang chuan*—is characterized by the specific attitude of the ethical order. In it the thinking is systematically occupied with parallels between the images of the text and ethical norms, as if they were reflected in the texts. The ethical concepts here are perfectly obvious but, in addition, it is impossible not to see in the thinking of the author of the *Ta-hsiang chuan* the latent presence of parallelism without which the concepts of linkage (spatial, temporal, conditional, intentional, causal, etc., relations) cannot develop. Thinking of this type, being raised to the level of ethical concepts, is at the same time attracted by the construction of a copybook morality supported by the authority of a text and its authors, and not based on an integrated world view. In order to correct this shortcoming, the thinking of later authors (*Hsi-tz'u chuan* and the beginning of the *Shuo-kua chuan*) cannot but turn to the elaboration of world views as systems of world judgments. Thus it is not surprising that these texts played a great role in the development of philosophy.[1] But at this level of development thinking lingers temporarily (until the new stage of commentatory literature—until Wang Pi, the precursor of Sung philosophy). Thus nothing new in the realm of thinking techniques can be found in such glosses as the final section of the *Shuo-kua chuan*, *Tsa-kua chuan*, and the latest layers of the *Wen-yen chuan*.

If, regardless of the presence of a developed world view, the *Hsi-tz'u chuan* is far from systematic, this shortcoming is made up by the author of the *Hsü-kua chuan*, who is inclined

1. It is characteristic that in M. Granet's book, *La pensée chinoise*, in discussion of the *Book of Changes*, we most often meet references to the *Hsi-tz'u-chuan*, although this is already far from the basic text. S.

to systematic discursive thinking. At the same time, it was his nature to aim at an integration of the complexes of concepts and ideas for an understanding of a higher order. Finally, the *Hsü-kua chuan* (in the development of the text) is an extensive sorites.

If we turn our attention to how thoughts are combined in different parts of the *Book of Changes*, we shall see great variety. Thus in the first layer of the basic text the link of thought images is almost unnoticeable.[2] In the second layer individual thoughts follow one after another and their interrelations are almost never expressed; their links can be perceived only from the context, from the very synthesis of their sequence. Most often this sequence is such that the first statement seems to be commented on in the second. For example: "With trepidation, guarding the center brings good fortune! The extreme brings misfortune" (Hexagram 6); or "Isn't it better to come at once? For the latecomer, misfortune" (Hexagram 8). But in the overwhelming majority of cases even such commentatory links of thought are not found in the second layer. Most often these are random statements characterizing the given situation from different perspectives. Thus one must suppose that the authors of the second layer were to a certain extent already capable of analytical thinking and possessed an understanding of how the particular might in a consistent way be reflected in the general.

It is this quality of thinking which is reflected with special intensity in the third layer. There, usually isolated texts appear as variants of the basic thesis stated in the second layer. In the selection of variants of the characteristics, thinking at this stage is intensively directed toward analysis of the conceptions. In the majority of cases at this stage, the link between individual thoughts is still not expressed but (as follows from the context)

2. Perhaps the embryo of links can be seen only in the fact that not all the terms combine with each other. Thus, for example, we do not meet the combination *yüan-li*, although *yüan-heng* is often encountered. The terms are seen to be not neutral in their relations with one another. S.

it is undoubtedly present in the mind of the authors. Thus, while the first layer of the basic text is almost wholly amorphous, the second layer is amorphous synthesis and the third layer basically preserves the same amorphous synthesis, but includes the latent links of thought (mainly successive relations of neighboring statements: explanation, comparison, opposition, sequence, spatial links, temporal links, and conditional links). Certain types of thinking already begin to show in the basic text, from the very indefinite polysemantic nature of undifferentiated ideas, through symbolic reasoning, to accurately outlined artistic images. It is obvious that all three layers represent thinking of some common stage which differs more from other stages than the layers differ from one another. This becomes especially apparent if we consider that the thinking underlying all the rest of the texts [the later texts – Tr.] now included in the *Book of Changes* already has clearly expressed thought links. They are no longer latent. Beginning with the *T'uan-chuan* and the latest texts we often meet statements of conditional, temporal, and spatial links. Time is already thought of as a universal category. In connection with the concept of time we even meet induction[3] (generally less intrinsic to Chinese thinking of those times, which was more inclined to deduction). All types of thought links which exist in the previous texts are present also in the Ten Wings; and in them (of course, in a variety of ways)[4] these links, in distinction from the basic text, are as a rule clearly expressed and formed by means of language.

Thus if, in the basic text, thinking was conducted with latent thought links, then for all the oldest commentaries, glosses, and treatises, the exposition of these links is characteristic. Only in the order of hypothesis can one make the first supposition on the date of composition of the basic text and the Ten Wings and date the basic text to no later than

3. See *T'uan-chuan* to Hexagrams 40, 42, 44, etc. S.

4. Thus, for example, for the *Ta-hsiang-chuan* the expression of causal links is typical, for the *Hsü-kua-chuan*, sorites, etc. S.

the seventh century B.C. and the Ten Wings to a time no earlier than the fifth century B.C. I base my conclusions on the fact that the thinking reflected in the basic text is more archaic and less developed than the thinking reflected in such texts as the genuine *Kuan-tzu* (the so-called *Pseudo Kuan-tzu* is excluded), and on the fact that the thinking of the Ten Wings is much more developed than the thinking represented in the *Lun-yü*, *Tao-te-ching*, etc. Of course, this is only an approximate chronology, but it finds support from other aspects, as will be seen later.

CHAPTER 4

Differentiation by Language

While, in the study of non-Chinese written documents from the aspect of their linguistic techniques, the researcher can with sufficient confidence work with the facts concerning the history of morphology, the sinologist, working with the amorphous synthetic Chinese language,[1] lacks such opportunities. The only thing to which he can turn his attention is the syntactical structure of the Chinese language in the text under study. The fact of the matter is that, regardless of the ironclad syntax of the present-day and old Chinese languages, the archaic Chinese language possesses specific peculiarities in the syntactical relationships. In other words, the norms for constructing a sentence in Chinese over the course of its historical development were not invariable. Conrady pointed out the pre-positioning of the predicate in archaic Chinese, suggesting on perfectly good grounds that, for example, the phrase *chien-lung* 見龍 does not mean "appearing dragon" but "the dragon appears." Takada cites a number of sentences with pre-positioned predicates in pre-Chou documents. Furthermore, the present-day and old Chinese norms of pre-positioning the attribute are not so absolute, for the materials cited in great abundance by Takada clearly testify that in the pre-Chou language the norm was just the opposite—post-positioning of the attribute. It is partially preserved up to the present in Tibetan, Burmese, and Thai, and in Vietnamese the post-positioning of the attribute is preserved even as a norm;

1. It must be remembered that Shchutskii is speaking of the language of the time of the *I Ching*, i.e., of the ancient language and thus about its form, which some European sinologues call "archaic." K.

their pre-positioning is met only in comparatively late borrowings from Chinese and (in neologisms) even from Japanese.

In archaic Chinese, as it appears from Takada's materials, there existed even pre-positioning of the object. Such comparative freedom of syntax in archaic Chinese is understandable if we take its phonetic wealth into account: the abundance of closed syllables which was already partially lost in ancient Chinese, or the probability of initial affricates, etc. All this adds great definiteness to the individual word, and hence opens greater freedom for syntactical structures.

Thus we observe in the Chinese language, in the realm of its syntax, a movement toward the stabilization of syntactical constructions because of the disappearance of the pre-posited predicate, the pre-posited object and the post-posited attribute. Consequently, if we study the syntactical structure of archaic Chinese texts, the number of archaic constructions will be directly proportional to the antiquity of the text.

It is known that in Chinese parts of speech are not formally distinguished, but are only a function of the syntactical structure. Gradually in the course of linguistic practice, the quantity of applications of one or another term in the role of some part of a sentence gave it a new quality—a tendency to express a certain definite part of speech. This is evident even from the fact that in present-day Chinese not all words can be substantive, adjective, and verb. This process found its expression in the specialization of the negative: thus the negative *pu* 不 ("not") cannot be applied to a substantive, an entity which is negated with the help of *wu* 無 ("no"). Consequently, the more archaic the text, the less the specialization of the negative is expressed in it. Thus it is almost unnoticed in the second layer of the basic text of the *Book of Changes*, but it is quite appreciable in the later texts. It is not difficult to understand that the more a word was recognized from the point of view of its tendency to fulfill the function of a certain part of speech, the less the possibilities in the language for complex *composita*.

Amorphousness is a special pre-condition of the latter.[2] In general, even the contemporary Chinese language, which is very close to an amorphous synthesis, possesses exceptional possibilities for the construction of *composita* the like of which I have not met in any of the languages of the West and East known to me. Thus in Chinese an entire sentence expressing the function of one member of a sentence without any formal appearance can be integrated[3] into a *compositum*.

This phenomenon is more widespread in ancient Chinese than in the present-day language. Consequently, the more the integration occurs in a text, i.e., the less the standardization of the morphological function of words, the more archaic the text. In view of this, the following phenomena must be taken into account: (1) the difference between simple and complex (integrated) subjects; (2) the language's sensitivity to the place of the predicate (i.e., the difference between the predicate and the pre-posited predicate); (3) the differences between a simple and complex (integrated) object and the possibility of pre-positioning the object; and (4) the presence of archaic post-positioning of the attribute. One can also consider the growth of the number of grammatical indicators.

Such facts permit us to construct a very precise language profile, which turns out to be so characteristic that one can put the texts into a chronological order.

In comparing the syntactical profile it becomes evident that the differentiation of the parts of the *Book of Changes* in terms of content and techniques of thinking finds full substantiation in linguistic facts. It turns out that the differences between the language of the basic text and the language of the Ten Wings is no greater than that between the parts of the basic text itself. Hence there arose the necessity of extending the differ-

2. For example, the internal amorphousness of words in Sanskrit *composita* side by side with the richest morphology of this language. S.

3. On the term "integrated sentence" see B. A. Vasil'ev and Iu. K. Shchutskii, *Uchebnik Kitayskogo yazyka (bay-khua)*. S.

entiation to the basic text itself. It became clear that in the basic text we should distinguish at least three layers of gradual complexity. In the first layer there are only the names of the hexagrams and the multidefined mantic terms *yüan*, *heng*, *li*, and *chen*. These apparently are conventional terms employed in divination up until the time that the text of the *Book of Changes* was elaborated and standardized. The second layer, qualitatively different from the preceeding, is made up of texts on the hexagram as a whole, the so-called *kua-tz'u*. According to the profile of the syntagmata this text is very close to the language of the *Shih-ching*. In this language, archaic constructions are still perceptible, as was noted in European (Conrady) and Japanese (Takada) sinology. The third layer, the so-called *hsiao-tz'u* (the reading *hsiao* is from the K'ang-hsi dictionary; present-day dictionaries also give the reading *yao*) being quantitatively larger, differs greatly from the second layer. This is made up of texts to the individual lines of the hexagrams created at a significantly later time, judging by some of the indications of Wang Ying-lin, Naitō, and others; also according to some facts of the present study, they are not without multiple interpolations. The profile of its syntagmata, although close to the profile of the syntagmata of the *Hsi-tz'u chuan*, still in the area of suffixes and prefixes,[4] the formal appearance differs radically from the latter. It is in this area that a vague demarcation is drawn between the basic text and the Ten Wings.

4. This is what the Russian says. Possibly Shchutskii is referring to the pre-posited and post-posited parts of speech mentioned above. Tr.

CHAPTER 5

Dialect of the Basic Text

As is known, the archaic Chinese language reflected in the ancient classical books is not a purely amorpho-synthetic language, for there already exist in it several formants of the agglutinative type (for example, the formants of adverbs: *jo* 若, *ju* 如, *jan* 然, etc.) However, these are still not fully agglutinative endings, since they preserve their own proper non-auxiliary meaning. This is conditioned by the fact that at this stage of development of the Chinese language we find the process of agglutinative elaboration still in its very beginnings. The technique of using formants of this type and also of some other words which play a dual role—the role of independent words and the role of auxiliary connective for full-value words—is different in texts of ancient written documents. This can be explained only by the fact that these texts were written in different dialects.

All this was unknown to the uncritical readers of ancient China, so it was impossible for them to suspect the conscious falsification of ancient texts or the stylization in some dialect. This supposition is also supported by the fact that the ancient Chinese uncritical readers were inclined not to pass on the dialectical differences of textual terminology, but, on the contrary, to fuse them together in their glosses, explaining the word of one dialect with a synonym from another, better known dialect. The indifference to the characteristic features of dialects could play a negative role only with the possible substitutions of synonyms at the time of the transmission of the text. But these cases of damage to the texts were hardly numerous, since the attitude of the uncritical readers toward the classical (for them almost sacred!) texts is known, as is their urge to copy the texts with slavish fidelity.

All this allowed Karlgren, who noticed the interdialectical differences of the classical texts, to work out, on the basis of statistical counts of these dialect peculiarities, a method of defining a dialect which is expounded in his work on the linguistic critique of the text of the *Tso-chuan*.[1] I used a similar method with regard to the text of the *Book of Changes* and obtained the following results.

I considered: (1) the basic text of the *Book of Changes* (B); (2) the *T'uan-chuan* (T); (3) the *Ta-hsiang chuan* (D); (4) the *Hsiao-hsiang-chuan* (S); and (5) the *Hsi-tz'u chuan* (H) with regard to following words: *jo* 若, *ju* 如, and *jan* 然.

words \ texts	B	T	D	S	H
jo—if	0	0	0	0	0
ju—if	0	0	0	0	0
jo—like	0	0	0	0	0
ju—like	1	1	0	0	0
jo = *jan*	6	(1)	0	0	0
ju = *jan*	19	(3)	0	(3)	0

In addition, this function of *jan* as a formant is met in four cases (three of them in the *Hsi-tz'u chuan*).

words \ texts	B	T	D	S	H
pu-jo	0	0	0	0	0
pu-ju	2	0	0	(1)	0
ju-ho	0	0	0	2	0

1. See B. Karlgren, *On the Authenticity and Nature of the Tso-chuan*. S.

From these facts it is evident that (1) in the *Book of Changes* the conditional phrase does not demand either *jo* or *ju*; (2) we assume *ju*² meaning "like"; (3) both *jo* and *ju* are used as formants (suffixes) of adverbs but with a clear preference for *ju*.

Such a vocabulary is very close to the vocabulary of the *Shih-ching*.³ In this regard, the equation *ju* = *jo* = *jan* is especially characteristic of the *Book of Changes*.

In the overwhelming majority of cases within the basic text, we find *yü* 于, which arbitrarily (though only a few times) is replaced by *yü* 於 and even *hu* 乎 (possibly only as a result of damage to the text). In this, the concurrence with the language of the *Shih-ching* is observable.⁴

There are a few more observations. *Ssu* 斯 in the meaning of *tz'u* 此 is met only twice, while *tz'u* 此 is not met at all.⁵ *Ssu* 斯 in the meaning *tse* 則 is not met, but *tse* 則 in the meaning "..., then ..." is met six times in the basic text (in the *T'uan-chuan* which is twice as small as the basic text, *tse* 則 is met seven times, or twice as often as in the basic text). In other words:

1) The use of the word *ssu* 斯 in the meaning "this" distinguishes the language of the *Book of Changes* from the language of the *Tso-chuan* and brings it close to the language of the *Lun-yü* (although there are only two instances of this usage, yet *tz'u* 此 is completely absent).

2) *Ssu* 斯 in the meaning "..., then ...," as in the language of the *Tso-chuan* but in distinction from the language of the

---

2. According to K'ung Ying-ta, 如 is equal to 同 (Hexagram 35). But even this single instance can be interpreted differently if we do not take into account the facts from the second table, with 如 = *jan*, as Hayashi does: he places a period after *ju* and translates the text: 晋如たれど鼫鼠りなれども屬し . S.

3. On the latter, Karlgren writes (p. 54), "There are no examples of the sense 'if.' In the sense 'like as' is the rule ..." S.

4. Karlgren writes (p. 55), "... 于 is the rule. (Without any special function, quite synonymous with 于) only in certain cases and *here mostly in the Kuo-feng*, *less* strictly normalized than the rest." S.

5. *Ssu* is absent in the dialect of the *Tso-chuan*. S.

Lun-yü, is absent. The first points to the similarity of the language of the *Book of Changes* and the *Shih-ching*, but the second to their difference. Thus, speaking of the similarities of these languages, it is impossible to identify them fully.

In later times the word "..., then ..." was expressed in the overwhelming majority of cases by *tse* 則 and not by *ssu* 斯, i.e., the development of this word in Chinese went from *ssu* to *tse* and not the other way round. Thus one can assume that the language of the *Shih-ching* is somewhat older than the language of the *Book of Changes*. However, the facts cited in the preceding pages, clearly testify to the fact that the language of the *Book of Changes* is rather close to that of the *Shih-ching*.[6] Proceeding from these considerations, it is natural to conclude that the language of the *Shih-ching* and the language of the *Book of Changes* represent two successive stages in the development of the same language. Thus it is not surprising that in the *Book of Changes* there are quotations from the *Shih-ching*, but not the other way round.[7]

6. Since it is known that the *Shih-ching* is not monolithic, it is necessary to stipulate that this closeness is established by us in the part of the *Shih-ching* known as *Kuo-feng*, without taking into account the adverbs and dialects represented in it. S.

7. Honda's hypothesis that the *Book of Changes* and the *Tso-chuan* were probably written by the same person thus no longer is valid. Although Honda stated it on the basis of a comparison of the languages of these texts, this comparison was made only through impressions which the Japanese scholar got from a part of the terminology—from the names of animals. Clearly this is not enough. S.

CHAPTER 6

Chronology of the Parts of the Text

My study of the *Book of Changes*, the results of which are stated in the preceding chapters, leads me to the recognition that not one but several texts are concealed under this collective title. This was acknowledged by the Chinese commentatory tradition, and in this regard I agree with it. I only suggest that at the present level of sinology it has long been necessary to divide the constituent parts of the document independently of the traditional division.

From the considerations which I have given it is evident that the *Book of Changes*, as a document composed of several parts, could not have taken shape at one time, but, on the contrary, is the fruit of centuries of work. In order to determine the dates between which this process took place supplementary researches are necessary. But first we must still establish the sequence of the creational process of the *Book of Changes*, the stages of which were reflected in the various texts. The question is, therefore, the relative age of the separate parts of the document.

Of course, it is good if the document has an accurate indication of the time of its composition, supported by historical cross-testimony. In the practice of philology this is unfortunately rare; however, one need not be disturbed by this for the following reasons.

An absolutely accurate date for the composition of a document is an exceptionally rare phenomenon. We have very few texts in which the year, month, and day of composition are indicated. Such dates are met in official documents, letters, and sometimes poetry, but even then they are comparatively recent. Nevertheless, events of antiquity are dated sometimes accurately enough if we can manage to place them in connection with a solar or lunar eclipse indicated in a corresponding text. Even in these cases, however, there always remains doubt: it may be a mention of an eclipse by means of a later insertion, the more so in China, since astrologers from long ago knew how to calculate the dates of past eclipses.

For later (medieval and later) documents in the countries with hierogliphic cultures there are means to approximate dates from the paleographic studies of the deformation of characters which, according to Chinese custom were subject to conscious alteration if they were part of the name of a reigning emperor. If in a text a character which was part of the name of an emperor reigning in such a year was subjected to alteration under the influence of a taboo, then it is conventionally assumed that this text was written under this emperor or soon after him. If this character is not altered, then the text was written before the emperor, i.e., earlier than a particular year. All the same, even here it is impossible to be absolutely sure, for the alteration of a character under the influence of a taboo could have been introduced into the text by a copyist who lived somewhat later than the author. There are known cases where the text appeared only after the death of the author. On the other hand, the reverse is also possible: a text, written at the court of a powerful feudal lord who did not highly regard his official sovereign, might not have been subjected to alteration due to this taboo. Thus we have here, also, only an apparently precise dating. This is not to mention the falsifications which fill up Chinese literature.

From these pessimistic facts, however, I draw some far from pessimistic conclusions. Does an absolutely precise date exist at all? After all, it is possible that a text reflecting the events between certain years was written and dated only many years after it matured in the author's consciousness, thus reflecting the corresponding time lapse. Thus it is impossible to regard absolute date as a fetish. By this I do not mean to deny that a reliable, absolute date makes it possible to decide many things, but in the overwhelming majority of cases one can get around the matter without any prejudice especially when the text deals with events which took place in the deep past. Still, it is impossible to ignore the time of the appearance of the document, that is the "time" and not the date; i.e., paying greater attention to the epoch than to the year, month, and day. Such a definition of the time can be linked with other events, the time of which is known. On the other hand, each text is composed over a more or less significant stretch of time. Sometimes it is essential to establish a relationship in the times between the individual parts of a text. Such a double determination of chronological relationships I call "chronological coordination."

From what has been said in chapters 1 through 5 of Part II of this work it is evident, as I suggest, that the basic text was created earlier than the commentaries, glosses, and treatises usually called the Ten Wings, and on the basis of chapter 3 one might even suppose that it was created significantly earlier. There is an apparent conflict between the results of the investigations indicated in chapters 3 and 4: according to the techniques of thinking, the third layer of the basic text is significantly more primitive than, for example, the *Hsi-tz'u chuan*, but according to the language profile these texts are closer to each other than the second and third layers of the basic text. This contradiction is resolved by recognizing the preeminence of the facts in chapter 3.

From the entire character of the third layer of the basic text, it follows that it arose in the practice of divination and was intended for divination. Its ideological content is inseparably linked with the activities of shaman-diviners who (according to many evidences, for example, the *Tso-chuan*) played a noticeable role at the court of the ancient Chinese rulers. Subsequently, under the influence of general social development, consciousness reaches a philosophical level. Here a great role was played by Confucianists, Taoists, Mohists, and thinkers of other less widespread schools. The struggle of these schools had especially great significance for the development of philosophy. By the time of the composition of the *Hsi-tz'u chuan* the philosophical thinking of the Confucianists[1] was already so developed that a philosophical interpretation of the *Book of Changes* was needed to supplement the mantic interpretation. This explains the great difference between the technique of thinking in the third layer of the basic text (the mantic text) and the technique of thinking of the *Hsi-tz'u chuan* (the philosophical encyclopedic text).

On the other hand, Confucius passed on to his school an almost fanatic regard for the text, for the literary tradition. He himself said: "I transmit, but do not create, I confide in antiquity and love it" (*Lun-yü*, vii, 1). Later on, Confucianism, conservatism, and the philology of Chinese dogmatists are inseparably linked with each other. Thus it is not surprising that the language of the Confucianists reflected in the *Hsi-tz'u chuan* is consciously placed in close connection with the texts of the *Book of Changes*, and in profile differs little from the language profile of the third layer.[2] While the language profiles of the second and third layers differ from each other significantly, it is only because, in the time which elapsed between their composition, society developed so intensively that a more expressive and harmonious language profile was elaborated.

In addition, we must add that in the text of the *T'uan-chuan* (only once, it is true) we meet something like a mention of

1. The connection of the *Hsi-tz'u chuan* and the entire later fate of the *Book of Changes* with the Confucian school is for me just as much beyond question as is the fact that Confucius himself had nothing to do with the *Book of Changes*. S.

2. The language of the Taoists, little connected with the literary tradition (of course, only in those times), displays a completely different and less ancient profile. Simple familiarity with the language of, for example, the *Tao-te-ching* or especially the *Lieh-tzu* is convincing in this regard. S.

the text of the *Ta-hsiang chuan* (Hexagram 23)[3] and might suppose that the *Ta-hsiang chuan* is older than the *T'uan-chuan*.

Further, we must take into account that the text of the *Wen-yen chuan* is a heterogeneous text. The oldest parts of it, according to the evidence in the *Tso-chuan*[4] were already in use among *I Ching* interpreters before Confucius. The latest parts of this text might be dated according to techniques of language and thinking as well as by the type of text, to the same time and social circle to which the rest of the glosses are dated.

Thus, on the basis of the facts of chapters 1 through 6, the chronological coordination of the texts united in the *Book of Changes* is presented in the following sequence.

1) First layer of the basic text (its sources are lost in the inadequately documented past).

2) Second layer of the basic text (in language it is a younger contemporary of the *Kuo-feng*, or a work of the following generation or generations).

3) The third layer of the basic text, with the exception of interpolations, is close to the second.

4) The most ancient citations in the *Wen-yen chuan*.

5) *Ta-hsiang chuan*.

6) *T'uan-chuan*.

7) *Hsiao-hsiang chuan*.

8) *Hsi-tz'u chuan*, the first three paragraphs of the *Shuo-kua chuan*, and the *Hsü-kua chuan*.

9) *Shuo-kua chuan* beginning with the fourth paragraph, the glosses of the *Wen-yen chuan*, and the *Tsa-kua chuan*.

3. This is possibly a misprint of the hexagram number, as there is no discernible similarity in the *Ta-hsiang chuan* and the *T'uan-chuan* in this hexagram. Tr.

4. See Part 1 of Ou-yang Hsiu's treatise. S.

CHAPTER 7

Problems of Dating the Basic Text

As is known, slave-owning existed in ancient China. It may be that once it played a leading role. However, at the present time our sinology recognizes the existence of feudal relations under the Chou (especially the later Chou) dynasty.[1] It is also beyond question that there were slaves in ancient China. There is no doubt whatsoever that slavery and slave-owning are clearly reflected in the text of the *Shih-ching*. Is it also the same in the *Book of Changes*? The following linguistic and ideological facts answer in the negative.

The social terminology of the basic text of the *Book of*

---

1. In reading this part of Shchutskii's work, the reader should take into account that the historical views of the author were determined as a whole by the state of historical scholarship at the time the work was written, i.e., in the 1920s and 1930s. At that time, historians of China—both in China and in the West—thought that the Chou period was already the epoch of feudalism. Only a very few allowed themselves to disagree with this, suggesting that it was more correct to view the social system of Chou China, in any case in the eleventh–eighth centuries B.C., as a slave-owning one. As is well known, there is no argument about this now. Both students of China and our historians of China unanimously consider this period a slave-owning one. Not being an historian, in his presentations of the history of China, Shchutskii depended entirely on conceptions reigning in historical circles in his time. We retain this section because there are useful parts in it, for example, the list of social terms encountered in the *I Ching*, and the enumeration of historical facts connected with the *I Ching*, although it is impossible at the present state of our scholarship to agree with the interpretation of these facts which Shchutskii presents and those with whom he argues (e.g., Maspero). If we accept, after Shchutskii, that the eighth–seventh centuries B.C. were the time when the *I Ching* took shape, then we must think that this document dates to a period of a slave-owning system and even then an early phase of it. K.

Changes is rather rich. We find the following categories designating persons in one way or another.

1) NEUTRAL TERMS (9)

人	*jen*	person
旅人	*lü-jen*	wanderer
行人	*hsing-jen*	passerby
男	*nan*	man
女	*nü*	woman, girl
男女	*nan-nü*	men and women
大耋	*ta-tieh*	aged man
丈人	*chang-jen*	adult
童蒙	*t'ung-meng*	youth

2) HIERARCHICAL TERMS (9)

上帝	*shang-ti*	supreme ruler, god (?)
聖人	*sheng-jen*	sage person
賢	*hsien*	wise man
賢人	*hsien-jen*	wise person
朋	*p'eng*	friend, associate
朋友	*p'eng-yu*	friend
幽人	*yu-jen*	hermit
元夫	*yüan-fu*	good person
惡人	*e-jen*	bad person

3) KINSHIP TERMS (30)

祖	*tsu*	ancestor
妣	*pi*	deceased mother
考	*k'ao*	deceased father
父	*fu*	father
母	*mu*	mother
父母	*fu-mu*	parents
嚴君	*yen-chün*	parent
父子	*fu-tzu*	father and son
夫	*fu*	husband
丈夫	*chang-fu*	husband
夫子	*fu-tzu*	husband

老夫	lao-fu	old husband
夫婦	fu-fu	husband and wife
夫妻	fu-ch'i	husband and wife
婦	fu	wife
婦人	fu-jen	wife
老婦	lao-fu	old wife
妻	ch'i	wife (second?)
女妻	nü-ch'i	wife
妾	chieh	concubine
子	tzu	children
小子	hsiao-tzu	little children
長子	chang-tzu	older son
弟子	ti-tzu	younger son
女子	nü-tzu	daughter
兄	hsiung	elder brother
弟	ti	younger brother
妹	mei	(younger?) sister
娣	ti	bride
家人	chia-jen	members of the household

4) SOCIAL TERMS (35)

大人	ta-jen	great man//"great people"
小人	hsiao-jen	nobody//"little people"
宮人	kung-jen	royal concubines
邑人	i-jen	townspeople
主人	chu-jen	master
賓	pin	guest
客	k'e	guest
帝	ti	sovereign
天子	t'ien-tzu	son of heaven (king)
王	wang	king
先王	hsien-wang	former kings
王公	wang-kung	king and grand duke
王母	wang-mu	king's mother
王侯	wang-hou	king and (independent) prince
公	kung	grand duke

侯	*hou*	(independent) prince
諸侯	*chu-hou*	independent princes
康侯	*k'ang-hou*	illustrious prince
后	*hou*	sovereign
國君	*kuo-chün*	sovereign of the country
君	*chün*	sovereign
主 *	*chu*	master
士夫	*shih-fu*	man (*vir*); men in service
金夫	*chin-fu*	wealthy man
童僕 *	*t'ung-p'u*	servant; slave (?) (僕 *p'u* is met only twice)
大君	*ta-chün*	great sovereign
臣	*ch'en*	servant → official, vassal
臣妾 *	*ch'en-chieh*	male and female servants (met once)
王臣	*wang-ch'en*	king and vassals
士	*shih*	men in service
武人	*wu-jen*	warrior
君子	*chün-tzu*	princeling → noble person
百姓	*po-hsing*	aristocrats → subjects → people[2] (only in the *Hsi-tzu chuan*)
民	*min*	the people, people
史巫	*shih-wu*	scribes and shamans (primarily shamanesses)

Thus the terms which designate people in the basic text number 83 (100 percent). Of these terms 35 (49.2 percent) concern purely social (besides family) terminology. Of them only three terms (marked with asterisks) can be regarded as terms concerning slavery and slave-owning (8.6 percent of the purely social terminology, or 3.6 percent of all the terms relating to people).

2. As Maspero has shown, this term originally designated courtiers in contrast to the peasantry, who did not have a *hsing* 姓 ("surname"). Only later did this term, through the meaning "people" begin to designate "peasants." S.

Among the purely social terms, the overwhelming majority are terms which concern the feudal system in one way or another. Just such typically feudal contexts as "favorable for the investiture of the prince" (利建侯) are met as citations from the *Book of Changes* in the text of the *Tso-chuan*. In addition, under the same year (534 B.C.) in the *Tso-chuan* there is an entire text testifying that if, on the one hand *p'u* undoubtedly was understood as slave,[3] then on the other, a primary distinction was not made between a "slave" and a subject (*ch'en*) who could also be a (vassal) prince. In other words, while slaves existed then, attention of slave-owners was directed not so much to the institution of slave-owning as toward the typically feudal relationships through the prism of which slavery was regarded. Thus the study of the terminology of the *Book of Changes* leads one to recognize it as a document of feudal literature. For final confirmation, this statement must be supported by the materials and information which we shall give in the following chapter.

The basic social antithesis expressed in the *Book of Changes* is the antithesis *ta-jen* ("great man") and *hsiao-jen* ("nobody") [S. uses the Russian word "nichtozhestvo" – Tr.] In the later development of this term we find its moral interpretation: a "nobody" does not know a feeling of shame or of love (*Hsi-tz'u-chuan*, ch. 2, line 4); they are incapable of true actions (*Chung-yung*, ch. 2); living together, they do not know how to get along with each other (*Lun-yü*, XIII, 23); if they possess courage, they do not know feelings of duty and become "thieves" (*Lun-yü*, XVII, 21); etc., etc. But who are these "nobodies"? While there is a context in the *Tso-chuan* in which *hsiao-jen* can be understood as "slave," this understanding is inaccurate since from the entire context it is clear that it is used just figuratively in this sense: one who draws near the prince

3. In the passage on the guilt of a fleeing *p'u* and on the guilt of a man who concealed such a fugitive, see Couvreur, *Tch'ouen Ts'iou et Tso Tchouan*, III, 129–130. S.

calls himself his "slave" or "serf."[4] In essence, *hsiao-jen* is primarily "man," i.e., peasant. Thus even Confucius (*Lun-yü*, IV, 11) says, "The noble man cares for good deeds, the nobody for the soil."

Who stood in contrast to these "nobodies" (i.e., peasants)? In whose hands was the *Book of Changes*, and who used it? We can obtain full answers to these questions, for in the *Tso-chuan* are registered sixteen instances of divination by the *Book of Changes*. These instances follow:[5]

1) In 671 B.C. the royal scribe divined on the fate of the young son of Prince Li of Ch'en.

2) In 660 B.C. a vassal of the Chin prince Pi Wan (by origin from the royal family) acted, having first divined about his service career.

3) Under 659 B.C. there is a record that King Huan, before the birth of his son Ch'eng-chi, divined concerning his future fate.

4) In 644 B.C. the diviner T'u-fu divined on King Mu of Ch'in's campaign against Chin, where he was forbidden by the Prince of this state to buy grain.

5) Under 644 B.C. there is a record that earlier King Hsien of Chin divined on the future marriage of his daughter Chi with the King of Ch'in.

6) In 602 B.C. one of the rulers of Cheng in an interview with the king of this realm, Wan-man, referred to the *Book of Changes*.

7) In 596 B.C. one of the vassals of Chin in an opinion on a war with Ch'u, in which he participated, referred to the *Book of Changes*.

8) In 574 B.C. the King of Chin ordered his scribe to divine on a strategic plan in a difficult battle with the troops of Ch'u.

4. Couvreur, II, 458–460. S.

5. Couvreur, I, 179, 180, 212–214, 217–218, 294–296, 304–305, 591, 612–618; II, 132–133, 236–237, 419–421, 501–504; III, 35–39, 150–152, 450–455, 479–482, 657–658. S.

9) Under 563 B.C. there is a record that Mu Chiang, the mother of Prince Ch'eng of Lu died in the Eastern palace, before her removal to which she had ordered the scribe to divine on the *Book of Changes*.

10) In 547 B.C. one of the vassals Ch'i, Ts'ui Wu-tzu, ordered the scribes to divine on the widow of the ruler of T'ang, whose beauty captivated him.

11) In 544 B.C. Tzu T'ai-shu (Yu Chi), vassal of the Marquis of Cheng, in giving an account of a mission to Ch'u, referred to the text of the *Book of Changes*.

12) In 540 B.C. the royal physician of Ch'in referred to the *Book of Changes* in a diagnosis of the illness of the Prince of Ch'in.

13) In 534 B.C. the minister of Wei, K'ung Ch'eng-tzu, divined on the state of health of the son of Chou-e, the concubine of Prince Hsiang of Wei.

14) In 512 B.C. allegedly "a dragon appeared" in Chin. The scribe Ts'ai Mo referred to the text of the *Book of Changes* in speaking of it.

15) In 509 B.C. the same scribe and astrologer (Ts'ai) Mo, in speaking of Chi P'ing-tzu who had been elevated to vassal, referred to the *Book of Changes*.

16) In 487 B.C. Yang-hu, a vassal of Chao Yang of Chin, divined for him whether or not it was possible to join with Cheng in its war with Sung.

From the examples cited we can see the different objects of divination: from affairs of state to personal and intimate matters (no. 10). But the initiators of divination are invariably the same: the feudal lords of the Chou dynasty. Thus it becomes perfectly obvious that the *Book of Changes* is a document of feudal literature not only in terms of time, but also in terms of the class which used it.

Furthermore, there is yet one more essential observation that can be made on the basis of these references in the *Tso-chuan*. Throughout the course of the seventh century B.C. the feudal lords used the *Book of Changes* exclusively as a divinatory text.

In this regard usually they did not divine themselves, but employed the services of one or several diviners. Only in 602 B.C. was the *Book of Changes* not used for divination: it is referred to as a doctrine containing a certain world view. Further, although it remains a text intended for divination, more and more perceptibly there appears the tendency to use it, with the help of a judgmental faculty, for explaining the world and the phenomena which occur in it. Thus during the sixth and fifth centuries B.C. the *Book of Changes*, while preserving its mantic significance, comes to be understood as a philosophical text. Sometimes Japanese sinologues (for example, Takeuchi Yoshio 武內義雄 in his article on the development of Confucian ideas)[6] points to the role of Confucius, who turned the course of China's intellectual development from divination about the world to introspection of the individual, as a result of which supposedly arose ideas about the world which corresponded to thinking and not to divination. From the materials cited above we can see that the opinions of the Japanese sinologue are true only in part. It is true that about the sixth to fifth century B.C. a crisis occurred in the mantic world view in China, but it is not true that it was the result of Confucius' activities, for the replacement of divination by judgments began long before Confucius. It is, however, impossible to deny that Confucius played an eminent role in this process, although he was not the only one. It is clear, therefore, that it is not the philosopher who creates the epoch, but that the epoch creates the philosopher, and he can only influence his contemporaries and descendants.

On the basis of the *Tso-chuan* materials one can maintain that the *Book of Changes* already existed in the seventh century B.C. as a text which enjoyed great authority. Of course it is impossible to think that the text was preserved in absolute inviolability; of course it was developed. But these changes, as far as can be seen, are of only four types: (1) commentatory

6. "Jukyō shichō" 儒教思潮 . S.

additions, subsequently taken as the basic text and merged with it (these are in the majority); (2) insignificant omissions in the text; (3) transpositions of adjacent phrases (indicated in the translation); and (4) changes in the language associated with its development. These hardly play a significant role, for the rate of development of the Chinese written language is comparatively slow. The following can serve as an example of such linguistic changes. The *Tso-chuan* preserved older (less morphologically developed) versions[7] of those phrases which are included in the *Wen-yen chuan*.

In the *Wen-yen chuan* text, after the subjects *yüan, heng, li, chen*, comes the marker *che* 者 . For the rest, the phrases correspond. Thus sometimes the change followed only the lines of a morphological definition of a sentence achieved with the help of a formant. But since the text is not rich in formants, such modernization of the text took place only in rare instances.

While the *Tso-chuan*, as Karlgren has shown, was written between 468 and 300 B.C., the *Book of Changes*, even if regarded most skeptically, must be dated to an earlier time, apparently no later than the seventh century B.C. And since the divinatory inscriptions on bones, which come down to the eighth century B.C., represent a more archaic form of the language than that in the oldest parts of the *Book of Changes*, it is most natural to establish the time of its creation between the eighth and seventh centuries B.C.

Endō Ryūkichi 遠藤隆吉[8] has shown that objects of nature are richly represented in the *Book of Changes*, but objects of the sea are not.[9] Thus Endō supposes that the *Book of Changes* was evidently created in Central Asia.[10] To say in Western China

---

7. 元，善之長也。亨，嘉之會也。利．義之和也。貞，事之幹也 . S.

8. *Eki no shosei tetsugaku* 易の處世哲學 , pp. 18–22. S.

9. We must keep in mind that Taoist literature, for example, is filled with images of the sea, especially *Chuang-tzu* and the *Shan-hai ching*. S.

10. In the Pamirs, in Endō's opinion. I think that this is not so much the influence of reality as it is the influence of Indo-Germanistics, which apparently had an impact on the Japanese sinologist. S.

would seem more accurate, for even the materials of the *Tso-chuan* are such that one cannot but notice the especially strong popularity of the *Book of Changes* in the states of Chin and Ch'in. Apparently they are the place of its creation. And since at bottom it was born in an agricultural environment,[11] this also inclines one to recognize Chin or Ch'in as the place of origin of the *Book of Changes*.

Thus the basic text of the *Book of Changes* is originally a divinatory and subsequently a philosophical text which took shape from the materials of agricultural folklore in the Chin or Ch'in territories between the eighth and seventh centuries B.C.

11. The basic antithesis: Light (sun) and Dark (the thickness of the earth in which grain sprouts), the attention to the growth of crops, and many other characteristic features of the document incline me to this assertion. S.

CHAPTER 8

Commentatory Studies

As is known, since ancient times the *Book of Changes* has occupied first place among the classical books of Confucianism. And for this reason it could not fail to attract the attention of Chinese philologists. Furthermore, in language and content, it likely belongs to the most mysterious of the classical texts, so no matter how many times commentators interpreted it, it remained in a certain sense obscure, and again and again attempts have been made to explain it. Such new attempts are undoubtedly connected with the general course of development of China's philosophy and philology. Thus it is not surprising that a voluminous commentatory literature developed around the *Book of Changes*. To judge its extent it is enough to point out that the *Ssu-k'u ch'uan-shu tsung-mu* mentions about five hundred works devoted in one way or another to the *Book of Changes*. There are commentaries, subcommentaries, systematic treatises, general theories, and discourses about individual aspects of these theories; there are works devoted to the *Book of Changes* itself and works about the apocryphal literature which formed around it. Some authors of commentaries appear only as authors, others appear only as compilers of the commentaries of past generations. Some authors emphasize the "objectivity" of their opinions, others the "subjectivity."

And this is not all that has been written in the Far East about the *Book of Changes*, for the *Ssu-k'u ch'uan-shu tsung-mu* does not take into account the great number of Taoist works on this theme included in the *Tao-tsang* (the Taoist canon). And they do not take into account the works of Japanese *I Ching* experts, who were also numerous. Thus the literature on the *Book of Changes* is an entire library of rather impressive size. It is impossible to deal with it in every detail even in specialized works, but it is also impossible to ignore this truly voluminous literature.

The process of the development of Chinese philosophy, as with the entire historical process, is so multifaceted that one can study its most varied aspects in greater or lesser detail. For our purposes it is enough to mention that this process is not absolutely regular, but develops at varying speeds in certain stages.

Against the background of the developing feudal society of China, the literature on the *I Ching* took shape in the following manner. In the sixth century B.C. to the first century A.D., in the classical period of Chinese philosophy, during the formation of the various feudal schools, the Ten Wings appeared as the anonymous product of the *I Ching* experts. Tradition, as we have seen, ascribes some of them, or even the Ten Wings as a whole, to Confucius. I have already discussed briefly the complete falseness of this ascription, for the ideology of the *I Ching* tradition and the doctrine of Confucius are mutually exclusive doctrines in their fundamental assumptions. It is very important to understand that the Ten Wings is commentatory literature and not the basic text, but very early (probably as early as the first to fourth centuries A.D.) they were so closely associated with the *Book of Changes* itself that from this time they merged together in the notions of nonreflective tradition, a point already made by Ou-yang Hsiu. In the second to fifth centuries the mantic school of commentators was formed, to a certain extent connected with the creation of religious, mystical, and occult literature, which is characteristic of this period. However, with this form of expression of commentator's thoughts, philosophical attempts to comprehend the document begin. In this regard, much was done by Wang Pi, Han K'ang-po, and Cheng Hsüan. The first usually is opposed to the mantic school. This seems relatively correct, for his commentary did not enjoy any success among the diviners of his time. However, Wang Pi was in error when he sharply opposed his predecessors. An acquaintance with his commentaries and with the commentaries of his predecessors leads one to the conclusion that basically he did not manage to transcend the *Book of Changes*' commentatory forms contemporary with him; nevertheless, he surely anticipated the future path of its understanding.

It is usually supposed that the Han *I Ching* experts founded a purely mantic school, and those of the Sung, a purely philosophical interpretation. This is incorrect, for the Han *I Ching* experts had something of a philosophical concept of the document, and the commentary of the Sung philosopher and philologist Chu Hsi was demonstratively close to the mantic.

In the second through sixth centuries A.D., with the creation of the religious philosophy of Taoism (and later on of Buddhism as well) symbolic thought played a great role. Ideas were mainly clothed in symbolic images (Ko Hung is typical in this regard). Thus it is not suprising that even the Han *I Ching* experts in the overwhelming majority of cases interpret the text from the point of view of the symbolics of trigrams, hexagrams, and individual lines, etc. (even Wang Pi was not free from this, and subsequently even Matsui Rashu systematically added to his basically philosophical commentary the interpretation of these symbolics).

In the eighth through tenth centuries Buddhist scholasticism had so developed the techniques of thinking (both conceptual and abstract) that the Sung *I Ching* experts could no longer be satisfied with such primitive methods of interpretation as glosses to the symbols and numerical combinations. They needed to interpret the texts philosophically in order to be in a position to put their school in opposition to the elaborate and complex Buddhist philosophy. It is true that such an interpretation achieved its highest point only after Wan I, who inherited as a whole the tradition of the Sung school and significantly enriched it. He managed this by a synthesis of the Sung school and Buddhism, for he himself was a Buddhist and is known as the author of one of the famous commentaries to the *Vijñapti-mātratāsiddhi trimsikā* (The thirty principles of achieving cognition). A commentary to the *Book of Changes* was written by Wan I in 1641.

For a more precise and concrete definition of the foregoing I will cite several commentaries to the *Book of Changes*. Here, for example, is what we read in the commentatory literature on the first words of the book: "Creation (*Ch'ien*). Beginning, penetration, definition, stability." [1]

Tz'u-hsia chuan (probably Han):

Beginning (元) is conception (始), penetration is penetration,[2] definition is harmonization, stability is correctness.[3] The Hexagram Ch'ien is caused by the pure force of light, thus it can precede all that exists. It can always be primary, begin development, combine harmoniously, and solidly and firmly not lose what is proper. Thus even the noble man, conforming with Ch'ien realizes [its] four qualities. Thus it is said: Beginning, penetration, definition, stability.[4]

WANG PI:

This is discussed fully in the commentary *Wen-yen-chuan*.[5]

1. For a discussion of these terms, see pt. I, ch. I. Tr.
2. The Russian terms are *pronitsanie* and *proniknovienie* which have the same root and are both equally rendered as "penetration." Tr.
3. A typical gloss which is almost untranslatable. The need for such glosses arose because of the absence of dictionaries. S.
4. This is not such a typical place. In later aphorisms, even more symbolic explanations are encountered. But here the hexagram itself emerges as a symbol which actually exists (the symbol of Heaven). S.
5. In the *Wen-yen chuan* we read: "The primordial means the beginning of good. The all-penetrating means the unification of all that is beautiful. The harmonious means the harmony of meaning. The stable means the existence of cases. The noble man, embodying compassion, is worthy of standing at the head of people. Beauty, bringing forth the totality [of its qualities], is worthy to be in full accordance with the highest order [in the conduct of people]. The presence of the order of individual objects is worthy of being [the expression] of the harmony of ideas. The presence of stable reliability is worthy of being [the soil] for the potentialities of cases. The best people realize these four higher qualities of the soul; thus it is said of them in the text: primordial, all-penetrating, harmonious, stable as the eternal heaven." S.

K'ung Ying-ta:

Creation is the name of the hexagram. The hexagram is a symbol which expresses a given thing in order to show it to people. Although a combination of two lines can express the forces of Light and Darkness, they still cannot be a graphic expression for all that exists. They still do not make up a symbol. Three lines are necessary to symbolize the three world potentials. They [these three lines] descriptively express the images of Heaven, Earth, Thunder, Wind, Water, Fire, Mountains, and Marshes and thus make up symbols.

In this sense the *Hsi-tz'u chuan* says: "Eight trigrams are arranged in order and the images are included in them." However, in the beginning when there were only trigrams, although they expressed the images of all existing things, they were still inadequate for the expression of the regularity of the metamorphosis of all existing things. Thus they doubled them, and in this fashion they obtained hexagrams in which are fully expressed all existing things, and by the comprehensive images all the possible events in the world are given. Thus the six lines comprise a symbol. This symbol "Creation" in essence expresses Heaven. Heaven is generated by the full gathering of all forces of light. Thus this symbol is composed of six lines of light. It is called not Heaven, but Creation, because heaven means a concrete object, but creation means both the object and its action. Thus in the *Shuo-kua chuan* it is said: "Creation is production." That is, production is the action of heaven as a concrete object. The sages produced the *Book of Changes* so as with its help to show man that in his actions he should take as a model the image not of heaven as an object, but the action of heaven. Thus they called this symbol not Heaven, but Creation.

Itō Tōgai:

When one line is drawn it symbolizes light and is called "odd." [Together with the divided, dark, even line – Tr.] This is a symbol derived from basic polarity. When another such line is added above it, this symbol is called "great light." It is included in a series of four symbols. When still another such line is added above it, this trigram is called "Ch'ien (Creation)." With the help of these combinations of three lines, the eight basic trigrams are expressed. This is what is meant in the basic commentary: "Below is creation, above is creation."

When on top of this trigram still another such trigram is drawn, then the whole is also called "Creation." This is the first of the sixty-four hexagrams. Thus it is called "Creation" in the basic text. The lines of the hexagrams are built up from the bottom and the lower trigram is the internal and the upper is the external. All six lines of this hexagram are light; both the internal and the external in it are creation. This is the pure force of light, the apogee of Production. It is called creation and its image-bearing expression is heaven. The primordial is great; the all-penetrating is penetrating; the stable is proper; the inviolable is correct.

In essence, this means that the characteristics of highest energy are with the necessity to achieve the [capability] of the all-penetrating and to preserve its inviolable correctness. The judgment takes this as the absolute Way of Heaven, and in this sense "primordial" is the beginning of the eternal world. This means a single primordial life force, spreading, penetrates everything without obstruction, and every reality in its birth receives in each individual case this force and possesses its potentials. This essence which is granted is unchangeable. Conforming to it (the primordial force) the sages approach the world. Thus the birth and completion of all categories of existence in the last analysis are subordinated to its metamorphoses. In my opinion, "primordial, all-penetrating, stable, inviolable" are at the basis of the mantic aphorism [of the first hexagram – Tr.]; it is a stroke of luck for one who obtains this aphorism in divination. This formula is met four times in all of the *Book of Changes*. Only in the judgment texts of the hexagrams Creation and Fulfillment [Hexagrams 1 and 2 – Tr.] is it said that these two are "primordial"[6] as praise for the absolute way in which heaven grants and earth grows. Although this is not the basic meaning of these words, all the same it deserves to be understood. In the hexagrams "Plenitude" and "Succession" the terms are interpreted in connection with the context, which, of course, does not injure the case.

Ch'eng I-ch'uan:

When in deep antiquity the sages drew the eight symbols of three lines for the first time, then in them were already expressed the three world potentials, Heaven—Earth—Man. Starting with them, they

6. Itō appears to be in error here. See table, p. 139. Tr.

doubled these trigrams in order to express fully what occurs as the transformations in the world. Thus the symbols of the *Book of Changes* are composed of six lines each. The doubling of the trigram "Creation" forms the symbol "Creation." It is Heaven. But Heaven is only the external aspect of it (the symbol). Its essence is creation. This is production, but a kind of production which does not cease even for a moment.

If we are to speak of heaven in general terms, then it is the Way of the world from which it is impossible to deviate. If we are to speak of it in detail, then as a formed body it is heaven; as the sovereign of the world, it is the deity; as a force with visible success, it is demons; as a force with incomprehensible form, it is the spirit; as an essence, it is Creation. Creation is the beginning of all being. Thus it is heaven and light and father and sovereign. "Beginning, penetration, definition, stability"—these are its four supreme qualities. Beginning is the conception of all that exists; penetration—this is the development of all that exists; definition—this is the appearance of all that exists; stability—this is the completeness of all that exists. These four supreme qualities are inherent only in the symbols of Creation and Fulfillment. In other symbols they are transformed depending on conditions. Thus Beginning is basically the grandeur of good, and Definition is mainly unvarying steadiness. Penetration and Stability, according to the places which they occupy here, are predicates of the preceding concepts. Oh, how wide and great is the idea of these Four Qualities.

Chu Hsi:

The hexagrams are symbols which were drawn by Fu Hsi. A solid line is odd, the number of Light. Creation is production, the essence of Light. The word "Creation" in the basic commentary is the name of the trigram. The lower is the symbol of the internal and the upper is the symbol of the external. The word "Creation" in the text itself is the name of the hexagram. Fu Hsi contemplated what was above and what was below and saw that even and odd were the numbers of the forces of dark and light. And so he symbolized light with a single odd line and dark with a broken even line. Seeing that above each line of light and dark appeared still another line of light or dark, therefore, working from bottom to top, he added another and still another line of light or dark, and thus composed the eight trigrams.

Seeing that the essence of the force of light is production and that the greatest body was heaven, he called the trigram composed of three lines of light Creation and assigned it to heaven. When the trigrams were prepared he added to them three more lines each so that hexa-grams were composed; and it happened that above each of the trigrams was added still another entire trigram, and the sixty-four hexagrams were arrived at. In this hexagram all six lines are odd and light; above and below are creation; this is the purest force of light and the highest development of production.

Thus the name "Creation" and the image "Heaven" are immutable. "In the great penetration, steadiness is useful." This is the text added by King Wen to determine the fortune or misfortune of the whole symbol. This is the so-called Judgment. "Beginning" is great; pene-tration is development; useful is proper; steady is true and inviolable. King Wen thought that the Way of creation is great development, which is correct in the utmost. Thus when this hexagram occurs in divination and not one line in it changes, then this means that for the diviner a great development is in prospect in which there must be correctness and inviolability in order for the action to be useful. Only in this way can it be carried out to its end. That is why the sages created the *Book of Changes*, to teach the people divination by which they could [understand] the very meaning of the appearance of things and the completion of affairs. Such is also the case with the rest of the hexagrams.

Tiao Pao:

The first thought with which this book begins is a discussion of the Creative way from which proceeds all that exists. Thus the *Shu-ching* begins with Yao. This is the beginning of the succession of our kings. The *Shih-ching* begins with the [wedding] song "Kuan-ch'ü." This is the beginning of human relations. The *Ta-ya* begins with the rites of deference. This is the beginning of rites. The *Ch'un-ch'iu*[7] begins with spring. This is the beginning of the year. The *Ch'un-ch'iu* begins with a reference to the king as the leader of the people. This is the general method which was used by the sages of ancient times. The word "Creation" is well discussed in the commentary [of Ch'eng I-ch'uan; here follows the quotation cited before]. Such a quotation

7. Probably the *Lü-shih ch'un-ch'iu* is meant here. Tr.

can just continue [the tradition of – Tr.] the sacred text. Who among the people of later generations can add even a word to it? "Beginning, penetration, determination, steadiness" were called the Four Qualities even from the time of Mu Chiang [mentioned in the *Tso-chuan*, S.]. Confucius cited them in his commentary *Wen-yen chuan* and revealed their meaning in detail. Only Chu Hsi thought they were a divinatory text and said: "great development in which correctness and inviolability are useful." I would prefer to return to the Four Qualities since it does not hurt them to be divinatory texts. I have doubts about Chu Hsi's words when he says that "usefulness consists of correctness and inviolability"; the fact is that supposedly during the phases of beginning and penetration there is not yet correctness; supposedly it is still necessary to strive to be right.

Here there is some ambiguity. Philological works sometimes say that all six lines in this hexagram are pure light and that it can only pertain to heaven, only to the Sage, that only the enormous, infinite heaven can contain this beginning, this penetration, this determination, and this steadiness. There are not enough words to glorify it! Why is there still a warning here? Both these versions are reasonable, but on the whole one must retain from them only the fact that the quality of creation differs from the qualities of the other hexagrams. If we explain the word "beginning" as "great" then this is not enough. For the judgments speak of the "Beginning of Creation" and the "Beginning of Fulfillment." Hu's commentary says that the sovereign of the people abides in the beginning; his advisers obey the beginning; Shun's codes speak of the initial day, i.e., the beginning of the annual cycle of the cult; the *Ch'un-ch'iu* speaks of the initial year; and on the founding of the Yuan dynasty, Liu Pin-chung proposed that they name it Yuan, "Great beginning."

In all these instances the word "beginning" is taken in the sense in which it is applied in the *Book of Changes*, as a creative beginning, that is the beginning of production. If, like Chu Hsi, it is only to explain his word "great," then the explanation cannot develop. Confucius says, "The Beginning of creation is the beginning after which development follows." This explains the matter. Ch'eng-tzu (Ch'eng I-ch'uan) in his commentary says, "Beginning is the birth of all that exists." That is an explanation of the *Book of Changes* in the style of Confucius. Further on in Confucius it is said, "Development is the growth of all that exists, but determination is what invariably follows after it. Steadiness is the final completion of all that exists." These explanations are so solid you cannot change one character. For my own part I would add only that beginning is that moment when we aspire to the higher qualities, penetration is their development, determination is their augmentation, and steadiness is their inviolable existence. Of course, all this I draw from Ch'eng-tzu's commentary.

WAN I (Buddhist commentary in the spirit of the Ch'an doctrine):

All six lines are light lines, thus the name Creation. Creation is production, in heaven it is light, on earth it is tension, in man it is wisdom and the sense of duty, as an essence it is radiance, on the spiritual path it is contemplation. Furthermore in the sensual world it is the desire of the consciousness to conceal one's bad karma; among organs it is the head. This is the heavenly sovereign. In the family it is the master, in the state it is the king, in the Empire it is the emperor; but in general it is mistaken to explain this position from the point of view of the heavenly way or from the point of view of the way of the king. Since here is production, there cannot be any sensual obstacles in it, therefore the text speaks of beginning and penetration. However, one must keep in mind also what the created is; it is to this end that the warning about determination and steadiness is given.

The sages point this out to students as that which is important here; this is a lesson for people who follow the spiritual path. For if production were directed toward the ten sins of the higher order, then man would fall into hell; if toward the ten sins of the middle order, then man would be reborn as an animal; if toward the ten sins of the lower order, then man is reborn as a *preta* (evil spirit). If production is directed toward the ten good deeds of the lower order, then man is reborn as an *asura* (demon); if toward the ten good deeds of the middle order, then a man in his future remains a man; if toward the ten good deeds of the higher order, then a man is reborn as a *deva*; but for this it is necessary that he follow the path of contemplation and concentration, and after that he will certainly be reborn as a *rūpadhātu* (an element possessing form) and an *arūpadhātu* (an element without form); if he will perfect himself in contemplation of the four truths and the twelve *hetupratyaya* (attendant causes), then

205

he will certainly find the fruits of Hinayana and Mahayana [the two largest schools of Buddhism]. If his production is directed toward the ten good deeds of the very highest order and he can be useful for himself and for others, then he will be called a *bodhisattva*; if his production is directed toward the ten good deeds of the very highest order and if he definitively comprehends that the ten good deeds are *dharmakāya* (the essence of the law) and the essence of Buddha, then he fully receives the *anuttara-samyak-sambodhi* (the highest complete enlightenment).

Therefore in the ten worlds everything is beginning and penetration, but with the three sins this is heresy and with the triple good this is true belief. On the sixfold path *kleśa* (suffering) there is heresy; in Hinayana and Mahayana with *akleśa* (liberation from suffering) this is true belief. Even in them when there are egoistic limitations, this is heresy, but for the *bodhisattva*, who saves people, this is orthodoxy —with the full return of the self by one of the two *yana* (Mahayana and Hinayana) it is heresy; and on the middle path, *buddha-dhātu* (element of enlightenment) it is true belief; with the distinction of the middle and deviation there is heresy, with the absence of everything that is not on the middle path there is true belief. Such is the precept of determination and steadiness. Following this, one must realize production.

Thus it must be said that the *Book of Changes* was understood differently in different times. Such schools of commentators must be differentiated, as we shall see from the following chapters.

CHAPTER 9

Commentatory Interpretations

The dogmatism of medieval Chinese scholastic education is well known. Because of this, Chinese feudal philosophy is richer in commentaries than in independent statements by individual authors. Philosophers of feudal China more often took recourse to deduction than to induction. Therefore, it usually happened that in Chinese scholastic compositions the main position is expressed at the beginning and then its commentatory elaboration follows.[1] This is peculiar to the Confucian school most of all, and to Confucius himself as its prototype, and thus enormous significance was attached to the document in question. It is essential to turn our attention to the first lines of a composition. Here is how the standard commentary to the *Book of Changes* written by Chu Hsi begins:

"Chou" is the name of a dynasty. "Changes" is the name of the Book. Its symbols were drawn by Fu Hsi and have the significance of mutual change and changeability. Thus [the Book] is called "Changes." As concerns the texts, they were appended by King Wen and the Duke of Chou. Thus ["Changes"] is called "Chou."

Here we read firsthand the standard, traditional opinions of Chu Hsi, who was, nevertheless, a brilliant philologist and critic of the text, as shown in his aphorisms on the *Book of Changes* (the so-called *Ho-wen*) and in his remarkable researches on such difficult texts as the *Ch'u Tz'u, Chou I ts'an-t'ung-ch'i*, etc. But in this standard commentary Chu Hsi is

1. The *Ta-hsüeh* and *Chung-yung*, treatises most important for Confucianism, were written in this way. S.

primarily a pedagogue, not wanting his philological researches to confuse the student.[2]

This is how the commentary written by Itō Tōgai begins:

I has the meaning "transformation." In deep antiquity when there were not yet any characters, symbols were drawn in order to express fully the images of the change of decrease and increase of dark and light in order to divine [following them] the success and failure of the activities of people. Thus [this book] is called "Changes." Before the transition between the Yin and Chou dynasties it was furnished with texts. Thus it is called *The Chou [Book of] Changes* in distinction from the *Changes* of the Hsia and Yin dynasties.

Of course, Itō Tōgai did not subject all problems to serious criticism, but in any event he regarded the "authors" of the book critically. Thus Itō's work is something of a step forward compared with Chu Hsi's.

The passages I have selected to illustrate Chu Hsi and Itō Tōgai are not the only commentaries. They are, rather, two opposite types of investigators. From their examples we can see that two schools of interpreters existed: the traditional school and the critical school. To the first school we must assign such authors as K'ung Ying-ta, who worked on government orders, and to a lesser extent Ch'eng I-ch'uan and Chu Hsi as well. The second school is represented in the works of Ou-yang Hsiu, Tiao Pao, Itō Tōgai, and others. In general, the commentaries on the *Book of Changes* do not at all clearly express the differences of these schools. We must keep in mind that commentatory eclectics always existed.

We have already seen that the Ten Wings are a collection of glosses, commentaries, and treatises devoted to the basic text of the *Book of Changes*. Still our opinion of them, as of the most ancient commentaries (but not of the basic text),

---

2. The fact that Chu Hsi introduced the theory of the *Book of Changes* into pedagogical discipline is clear, if only because he wrote a special textbook, *Chou I ch'i-meng* (The Chou I for beginners), which played a great role even after his time in classroom studies of the *Book of Changes*. S.

emerges more prominently out of consideration of their utilization in the latest commentaries.

In fact, the variety of traditions reflected in the Ten Wings served as a prototype for different commentaries, and the lack of unity in the understanding of the *Book of Changes* in the Ten Wings served as fertile ground for the diverse personal opinions of even the latest commentators.

The parallel study of the Ten Wings along with a number of later commentaries led me to the observation that some commentaries are more closely connected in their conception of the *Book of Changes* and its methods of study with certain texts from the Ten Wings, and others with others. The results of this work can be expressed in the chart on p. 211.

From this chart it is evident what a great role Wang Pi played as a link connecting the treatises from the Ten Wings with the Sung (in this case philosophical) school of commentators. Thus it is necessary to point to but a few prototypes of his commentary found in the *Hsi-tz'u chuan* and *Shuo-kua chuan, I.* Thus in the *Hsi-tz'u chuan* we read:

The teacher said, "Writing does not express speech exhaustively as speech does not express thought exhaustively. But if this is so, would there not have been thoughts of the sages not pronounced exhaustively?" The teacher said, "The sages created images in order to express thought exhaustively in them. They established symbols to express exhaustively in them the influence of the world on man and man on the world. They appended texts to express their speech exhaustively. . . ."

As is known, Wang Pi also worked on the relations of words, images, and thought. Later, Wang Pi was much occupied by the questions of the "cognition of ideas." Here is the prototype of his reasoning which is found in the *Shuo-kua chuan I:* "Get to know all ideas, comprehend all the essence, then you will approach an understanding of fate."

On the other hand, Wang Pi still did not exhaustively understand and express the object and its idea. The Sung philosophers fully understood this distinction and, for example, Ch'eng Yi-ch'uan wrote in his commentary:

The idea is incorporeal. Thus its significance is expressed through an image. [The idea] of Creation is expressed in the image of a dragon, for it is such that its wonderful transformations are incomprehensible. That is why as an image it expresses the metamorphosis of the creative way, the increase and decrease of the force of light, the advance and retreat of the Sage. . . .

Thus we see that Wang Pi is a link connecting the oldest treatise on the *Book of Changes* with the Sung commentaries. It is these commentaries which created the philosophical conception of the *Book of Changes*, just as Wan I raised it to a high level of philosophical understanding and on the basis of its materials worked out the relationship of a new act of conception to the content of the previously accumulated knowledge. The Sung authors, and especially Wan I, can be used for a critical interpretation of the *Book of Changes*.

Influencing \ Influenced	Han commentators	Cheng Hsüan	Wang Pi	Han K'ang-po	K'ung Ying-ta	Chou Tun-i	Ch'eng I	Chang Tsai	Shao Yung	Su Shih	Su Che	Lu Chiu-yüan	Chu Hsi	Wan I	Tiao Pao	Itō Tōgai	Matsui Rashu	Manchu Versions	P'i Hsi-jui
Tsa-kua	X				X								X						
Wen-yen	X		X		X								X						
Shuo-kua 2	X				X				X				X						
Hsü-kua		X	X				X		X										
Shuo-kua 1			X				X												
Hsi-tz'u 1, 2			X			X	X	X	X	X				X	X	X			
Hsiao-hsiang												X							
Ta-hsiang						X	X								X				
T'uan						X									X				
Han Commentators			X														X		
Taoism		X	X			X		X	X	X									
Buddhism						X		X							X				
Wang Pi				X	X		X									X			
Han K'ang-po																X			
K'ung Ying-ta																			X
Chou Tun-i							X	X											
Ou-yang Hsiu												X	X			X	X		
Su Hsün										X	X			X					
Ch'eng I												X	X						X
Chang Tsai													X						
Shao Yung												X	X						
Su Shih											X								
Su Che										X									
Lu Chiu-yüan																X			
Chu Hsi																		X	

Influence on Chinese Philosophy

Confucius said, "I do not speak about the supernatural, violence, disturbances, or the spirits" (*Lun-yü*, VII, 21). But in the
Shuo-kua chuan we read, "In antiquity when the sages created
the [doctrine of] Changes, they went deeply into the lucidity
of the spirits and engendered the oracle with milfoil." It is
perfectly obvious that the rationalist Confucius had nothing
in common with irrational mantics, which was at that time
the main content of the *Book of Changes*. Thus the Japanese
sinologue, Tsuda Sōkichi 津田左右吉, is perfectly right
when he maintains that the *Book of Changes* was not accepted
by Confucius, but by Confucianists many years after his
death.[1] And indeed, the world view of Confucius—who
demanded primarily "rectification of names," i.e., who once
and for all established the relationship between nomenclature
de jure and *de facto*, always desiring the immutability of a
document—is completely different from the basic conception
of the *Book of Changes:* transformation.

Even in regard to language, the same must be recognized.
We have already seen that the language of the *Book of Changes*
is a completely different dialect from that of Confucius. And,
in the time of compilation, the basic text of the book was
created long before Confucius, but the Ten Wings were
created after him. This is perfectly natural, since in his *Analects*
Confucius does not say a word about the *Book of Changes*,
though he very definitely spoke of other classical books, the
Shu-ching and the *Shih-ching*. These classics are full of his-

---

1. *Dōka no shisō to sono kaiten*, p. 567. S.

toricisms; they were undoubtedly documents, and the documentary occupied for Confucius a gnosiological basis of
knowledge, since Confucius was not concerned especially
with a theory of knowledge. Thus the *Book of Changes*, being
not documentary evidence of any definite historical facts,
but rather a document of speculative creation, even if it had
been known to Confucius, would have been subjected to
attacks on his part. While Ssu-ma Ch'ien speaks of the "zea-
lous" occupation of Confucius with the *Book of Changes*, it is
impossible to regard this with confidence, for Ssu-ma Ch'ien
was not accurately informed on the times of Confucius. He
himself says this clearly at the end of his biography of Lao-
tzu. However, on the basis of these words of the great Chinese
historian we can suppose that by his time the *Book of Changes*
was already completely accepted by Confucianists. When
might this inclusion of the *Book of Changes* into the circle of
Confucianist literature have taken place? In this regard, if we
trace the texts of that time (from Confucius to Ssu-ma Ch'ien)
we find the following.

1) Neither in the *Ta-hsüeh*, the *Chung-yung*, nor in Mencius
is there any mention of the *Book of Changes*.

2) It is mentioned in the *Tso-chuan* and in *Hsün-tzu*, but
not as a Confucian classical text.

3) In the *Pseudo Chuang-tzu* and the *Lü-shih ch'un-ch'iu*,
the school of *I Ching* scholars and the Confucianist school are
mentioned as two independent schools.

4) In the burning of the Confucianist books in 213 B.C. the
Book of Changes was not subject, but was preserved.

5) The eclectic[2] Chia I 賈誼 (200–168), who was inclined
primarily to Confucianism, accepted the *Book of Changes*[3]
and later on, Han Confucianists (even Tung Chung-shu and
others) considered it a Confucian classical book. Thus it was
apparently adopted by Confucianists between 213 and 168
B.C., and from this time invariably enjoyed recognition among

2. *Ibid.*, p. 504. S.
3. Forke, p. 16. S.

them.[4] Wang Pi's philosophy as a whole grew from the *Book of Changes*. The Sung school, completely inseparable from the *Book of Changes*, developed its conceptions to a philosophical level.

The terminology, images, and conceptions of Chou Tun-i, or Chang Tsai or, still more, Shao Yung, were all very closely connected with the *Book of Changes*. Perhaps it is not for nothing that Chou Tun-i's *T'ung-shu* (The Book of knowledge) is sometimes called the *I-t'ung* (Encyclopedia of the I Ching).[5] Therefore, Chou Tun-i exclaimed: "Oh, how majestic the *Book of Changes*" (see *T'ai-chi t'u-shuo*), and "Oh, how majestic the *Book of Changes*. It is the source of essence and life" (*T'ung-shu*, ch. 1). All of Chang Tsai's cosmology is based on the conceptions of the *Book of Changes* (strictly speaking, the *Hsi-tz'u chuan*).

The typical representative of the Sung school did not merely borrow the ideas of the *Book of Changes* and admire it. A contemporary of this school, one of the greatest poets of China, Su Shih (1036–1101), mastered as a whole the basic conception of the book—the conception of changeability, immutability, and their direct ties. To him belong the words:

Oh, my guest, do you really not know this water and the moon? How they rush, but do not disappear; how the moon changes, now full, now in decrease, but in the end it can neither perish nor change its size. When we observe changeability, then even the whole world cannot last a moment; when we observe immutability, then there is no end to either us or the world. Whom do you envy then?[6]

4. Only rarely did they, all the same, indicate its irrationality and incomprehensibility. See for example, Forke, p. 76, on the conversation of Liu Hsiang and Yang Hsiung and also the treatise by Su Hsün (eleventh century). S.

5. It is possible, incidentally, that the *I-t'ung* is a separate treatise lost by Chu Hsi's time. In any case, the very presence of the *I-t'ung* among Chou's works points to his connection with the *Book of Changes*. S.

6. See my translation of this essay in *Vostok*, pp. 205–208. S.

The Confucianists not only studied the *Book of Changes*, they sometimes imitated it. Such, for example, is the *Book of the Great Mystery* (*T'ai-hsüan ching*) of Yang Hsiung—a very difficult text which has not been unriddled up to the present. In it there are the same symbolic linear figures apropos of which texts are pronounced; only these figures are composed of four lines, of which there are three types: solid, broken, and twice broken. Thus there are eighty-one symbols in the *Book of the Great Mystery*. I will cite as an example the translation of the first chapter and the first two symbols of Yang Hsiung's *Book of the Great Mystery*.

Book of the Great Mystery

"Heads" of the Mystery

O Harmonious Mystery!
As Chaos acts and does not have end
Spontaneously it represents itself as heaven.
Light and Dark are side by side as two and three.

As soon as the one Light stands above all development
Then all being finds corporeality through it.

Worlds and lands, kingdoms and families[7]
In the threefold extension they find their completion.

And there I spread out that nine of nines,
In it is the origin of numerology.

In the strophes I finish off the system of multitudes
And multitudes I unite in names.

In eighty-one heads
The events of the year abide completely.

---

7. These are the names for the four lines of Yang Hsiung's tetragrams. As to the "threefold extension" in the next line, it is a term used in Han political philosophy to illuminate the hierarchical structure of social relationships. Tr.

"Solutions" of the Mystery
Oh plentitude! Oh sun!
In it brilliance, light, lucidity, vividness
Five colors shine purely!

Night . . . I solve it as Dark,
Day . . . I solve it as Light.
The solution of day and night
Now in evil, now in good.

Light puts forward the five blessings.
They are related to ascent,
Dark conceals six extremes
They are related to descent.

If ascent and descent are in relationship
Then the Great Steadiness moves without obstruction.[8]

Warp—in it are South and North,
Woof—in it are West and East.

[Sun] moves along the six transitions
And goes to meet the heavenly dipper.

In the reckoning of time the years record themselves,
And the hundred cereals ripen in good time.

No. 1 ≡ *Chung* 中

Core

HEAD:

The pneuma of light, being submerged, sprouts
In the yellow hall.
The true cannot be
In[9] the core.

---

8. These last two lines were omitted by Shchutskii in the original. Tr.
9. This seems to be a slip for "outside of." Tr.

(STROPHES)

1) Chaos—abyss; expanse—space!
   The concealed!

SOLUTION:
   Chaos—abyss, expanse—space,
   This is the abode of thought.

2) The spirits fight in the secret,
   Their ranks, Dark—Light.

SOLUTION:
   The spirits fight in the Mystery,
   This is good and evil, one beside the other.

3) The dragon comes out of the core
   Fully visible from head to tail,
   One might take it for a prototype.

SOLUTION:
   The dragon comes out of the core,
   His affairs become apparent.

4) The low and futile lack cause
   For great acceptance of nature and fate,
   Evil.

SOLUTION:
   Evil of the low and futile,
   This is impossibility of great acceptance.

5) The sun is in the zenith, blessing;
   Profit by this light of dawn
   And become chief.

SOLUTION:
   The sun is in the zenith,
   This is a noble in a befitting place.

6) The moon loses its roundness
   Is it not better for it to reveal its light to the West.

SOLUTION:
   The moon loses its roundness,
   This is the mean beginning to retreat.

7) The fulfillment of fulfillment.
Fire—as a star, feed [by it]!
Water—as an embrace, be firm!

SOLUTION:
From "fulfillment of fulfillment" to "embrace"
Rely on the statutes.

8) The yellow does not yellow
And is covered with (decay) usual for autumn.

SOLUTION:
The yellow does not yellow,
This is the loss of the force of the core.

9) The plunged soul
The pneuma [of life] and the body[10] disperse.

SOLUTION:
The dispersal in the plunged soul,
This is the invincibility of time.

No. 2 ☰ *Chou* 周

Rotation

HEAD:
The pneuma of Light rotates its spirit
And returns to the beginning.
The creatures follow [it] according to [their] type.

STROPHES:
1) You return to the heart of heaven.
Such pretense of [personal] powers!
Evil!

SOLUTION:
The evil of the return to the heart [of heaven],
This is intolerance of the core.

2) You erect the axis of the core.

---

10. The Russian word *teplo* is probably a slip for *telo*. Tr.

In the rotation there are no angles.
SOLUTION:
> Erect the axis of the core,
> Establish the principal thought.

3) Issuing from yourself, retiring into yourself
   [You] polar star of happiness and unhappiness.
SOLUTION:
> In issuing from oneself and retiring into oneself,
> It is impossible not to be watchful.

4) You gird yourself with a leather belt and buckle,
   On it attach a jasper ring.
SOLUTION:
> You gird yourself with a leather belt and buckle,
> You restrain yourself, you bind.

5) In the center of the earth is your hut,
   Prepare your golden chariot.
   But even this advice will pass.
SOLUTION:
> The advice of the hut and the golden [chariot] will pass,
> [For] the nobody is in no position [to preserve it].

6) Trust in rotation, its truth!
   Upward you penetrate to heaven.
SOLUTION:
> Trusting rotation, its truth,
> The ascent upward will open.

7) In extraordinary excess you see a friend
   And you return to ignorance,
   He is in no position to accompany [you.]
SOLUTION:
> In extraordinary excess you see a friend
> He cannot accompany [you].[11]

---

11. The text is clearly incomplete. The lacuna is noted even in the commentatory literature. S.

8) Again you cross over beyond the borders of the personal,
   But the misfortune from this is not great.
SOLUTION:
   Again you cross over beyond the borders of the personal,
   Misfortune will not be in the center (i.e., will not be
   major).

9) You return toward destruction
   Or you will take to flight.
SOLUTION:
   You return toward destruction,
   Your way has come to the end.[12]

Another type of independent work which developed on
the foundation of the *Book of Changes* is the *Forest of Changes*
(*I-lin*) of Chiao Hung of the Han (the exact dates of his life
are unknown). This is an attempt to consider each hexagram
by itself and in its relationship to each other hexagram. Thus
the text considered four thousand ninety-six[13] possible combinations, and for each of them verse was written. Unfortunately, the understanding of these verses is lost and they are
a completely enigmatic text.

The reflection of the *Book of Changes* in Taoist literature is
of interest. The *Book of Changes* cannot be considered a Taoist
text, and it is impossible even to bring it close to ancient
Taoism, as has been done by Yamasato Motō 山里,[14] for
example. From his comparison emerges especially graphically
all the cardinal differences between Taoism, which believes in
the absolute outside of the world, and the world view of the
I Ching, which does not go beyond the borders of the world,
and was thus, in the end, accepted by Confucianism. Therefore, it is not surprising that the Taoists themselves did not
identify their school with the *I Ching* school, and during the

12. On Yang Hsiung, see Forke (above, n. 3), pp. 74–100. S.

13. I.e., 64^2 S.

14. Yamasato Motō 山里 , *Rōshi to Ekikyō hikaku kenkyū*, 老子と易經比較
研究 . S.

times when the *Book of Changes* did not enjoy recognition as a classical text its influence on Taoism, if there was any,[15] was only episodic. It is perfectly understandable that in the *Pseudo Chuang-tzu* (ch. 33) Taoism is contrasted with the doctrines of the *I Ching*.

However, from the first century B.C. until the seventh century A.D., Taoist authors began to experience the strong influence of the *Book of Changes*. Its basic position—transformation—furthered to the greatest possible extent the theoretical foundation of alchemy, which was widespread among Taoist writers. Thus the famous text *Chou I t's'an-t'ung-ch'i* 周易參同契 ("On the reuniting of the three equals [from the point of view of] the Chou *Book of Changes*"), attributed to Wei Po-yang 魏伯陽, was, as its title indicates, most closely connected with the *Book of Changes*; and, indeed, it was written almost entirely in the terminology of the *I Ching* and with the implicit acceptance of its ideology.[16] The cos-

15. For example, the terms *yin* and *yang* in the *Tao-te-ching*, the cosmology in ch. 1 of *Lieh-tzu*, etc. S.

16. Thus, for example, in this document the most important place for us, a description of a work of alchemy on the "philosopher's stone" [understood in the form of cinnabar] is expressed not without some terms as Light and Dark, otherwise called "the two tendencies." They in turn are connected with the representation of the sun and moon, fire and water, i.e., just as in the *Book of Changes* (or, more accurately, in the *Hsi-tz'u chuan*). Here are the verses:

巨勝尚延年
還丹可入口
金性不敗朽
故爲萬物寶 ·
術土服食之 ·
壽命得長久 · · ·
二氣元且遠 ·
感化尚相通 ·
何況近存身 ·
切在于心胸 ·
陰陽配明
水火爲效微 ·
耳目口三寶 · ·
國塞勿發揚 · · ·

mology of the Taoists, especially as it is expressed in Ko Hung, in the *Kuan-yin-tzu*, in Tu Kuang-t'ing, etc., is fully borrowed from the *Book of Changes*. Especially connected with the latter are the multiple schemes and sketches[17] included in the *Taoist Canon*. Thus even O. Johnson repeatedly had to refer to the *Book of Changes* and to its terminology in his work on Chinese alchemy.[18] In all this, however, one must keep in mind that the greater influence of Taoism was exercised, not by the basic text, but by the *Hsi-tz'u chuan*, which in general played an apparently very great role in the spreading and popularization of the *Book of Changes*.

As far as is known to me, the *Book of Changes* exerted a lesser influence on Buddhism. Only rarely in Buddhist treatises (mainly of the Chen-yen 眞言 school) do we meet *I Ching* terms, and then usually only when the Buddhists were pole-micizing with the Confucianists and Taoists, as for example, in the well-known Buddhist treatise of Tsung Mi 宗密, "On Man" 原人.[19]

> Our century lengthens the sesame.
> The wizard puts the cinnabar in his mouth.
> The essence of gold is alien to decomposition;
> Thus it is the most precious of all.
> And if the alchemist partakes of it,
> Then he can prolong his longevity . . .
> The two tendencies are remote from time immemorial
> But still they penetrate each other.
> It is easier to find them in the self,
> Then closely intertwine them in the heart, the breast.
> As with the Sun, with the Moon—Light-Dark,
> So [in the heart] are Fire and Water fused.
> The treasure—ear, eye, mouth—
> Let them be immovably concealed forever! S.

[See complete English translation by Wu and Davis in *Isis* 18 (1932), 210–289. Tr.]

17. For a list of them see Wieger, *Le canon Taoiste*. S.
18. O. S. Johnson, *A Study of Chinese Alchemy*. S.
19. Tsung Mi (780–841) is one of the greatest figures of the Hua-yen-tsung 華嚴宗 sect in China, a representative of that line of its doctrine which affirmed

However, the Buddhists, though they carefully defended their doctrine from "heresy," i.e., from any non-Buddhist philosophy, finally in the person of the aforementioned Wan I, came to recognize the *Book of Changes* as a philosophical text, which in the skillful hands of the adept could play a role in the introduction to Buddhist philosophy. Such, in any event, is the explanation of the causes which prompted Wan I to write his valuable commentary. He spoke of this quite clearly in the preface to his commentary.[20]

All the same, it must be recognized that the main influence of the *Book of Changes* was exerted on Confucianism, less, though significantly, on Taoism, and almost unnoticably on Buddhism, which had its own extraordinarily elaborated philosophy.

---

the inseparability of "doctrine" 教 and "meditation" 禪 . The treatise "On Man" is the most popular of his works. K.

20. See his preface to 周易彈解 , dated 1641. S.

Problems in Translating the Book

We can regard the *Book of Changes* first as a document from a definite period, and second as a divination text. We cannot ignore either one. In the first sense, we must cleanse the basic text, as much as possible, of the layers of later centuries. In the second sense, we must take the whole *Book of Changes* as it exists at the present time in the Far East, with all its Ten Wings, and with all its textual mistakes. In the first sense there should be displayed the highest criticism possible at the present state of sinological techniques. In the second sense we must refrain from any criticism so as not to distort the naive, realistic conception of the *Book of Changes*. In the first sense the translation should be furnished only with philological notes, following the line of textual criticism for, as we have seen, all commentators looked through the eyes of their time and class. In the second sense we must give an interpretive translation of the *Book of Changes* from the point of view of the oral tradition and its understanding in China and Japan.

Consequently, the *Book of Changes* should be translated twice. However, the interpretive translation from the point of view of the present oral tradition has already been completed by Richard Wilhelm. Thus there is no need to repeat his work, in spite of the errors he tolerated.

The present work is accompanied by a philological translation of the basic text.[1] However, it is enough to have even a superficial acquaintance with it to be convinced of the obscurity

1. [See Introduction to the English edition. The translation is not included here.]

of the *Book of Changes*, an obscurity already noticed by Liu Hsiang. Nevertheless, as we have seen, the *Book of Changes* existed in China and Japan as a text open to understanding, even though varied. Hence, beside a philological translation, we still need an interpretive translation different from Wilhelm's, constructed with a due regard for a sufficiently significant commentary. This commentary should be taken alone or perhaps with several commentaries, but they must be of the same school: an unprincipled interpretation through many commentaries, from which the translator selects only those sentences easiest to understand is inadmissible.

In such a case the question of selection of a commentary arises. It is well known that Ch'eng I-ch'uan is considered the greatest authority in the Far East. However, my experience inclines me to select the more critically tempered Wan I. His commentary was written in the terms and expressions of Buddhist philosophy. Buddhist terminology, in view of its great precision and mastery within European Buddhological literature and Japanese Buddhological lexicography, makes possible an understanding of Wan I's commentary without allowing the slightest ambiguity. Thus, on the basis of his commentary, one can accurately establish his understanding of the *Book of Changes*. Of course, this is also possible with other commentaries, but such a work would demand incomparably greater effort and time, without creating at the same time confidence in the objective correctness of the interpretation. In the interpretive translation which is appended to the present work, proceeding from what has been said above, I base my translation on the commentaries of Wang Pi, Wan I, and Itō Tōgai.

The philological translation of the basic text without interpretive notes will be little understood by European readers, as, incidentally, the basic text without commentary is little understood, if at all, by the Chinese or Japanese reader not prepared for the reading of this text. However, sinologists, regardless of nationality, who have mastered the system of the *Book of*

Changes, undoubtedly can understand the basic text both in the original and in the translation. What makes it understandable? The knowledge of its system, the ability to find the explanation of one place in other places. Thus, in reading the basic text, it is necessary to keep the following in mind:

1) Each hexagram is a symbol of some life situation which develops in time. Each text to a hexagram is a short characterization of this situation, basically or completely. Each text to a line is a concrete characterization of some stage in the development of the given situation. With this, one must take into account that, in view of the authors' level of thinking and language techniques, such characterizations almost never are expressed in the form of precise ideas. The elements of the *Book of Changes* are elements of imagery. Instead of speaking of the appropriateness of collective action, the *Book of Changes* says, "When the reed is plucked, the other stalks follow after it, since it grows in a bunch. Firmness brings happiness. Development."[2] Instead of speaking of the vanity of an undertaken action, the *Book of Changes* says, "The nobody has to be powerful; the nobleman has to perish. Firmness is terrifying. When the goat butts the fence, its horns stick in it,"[3] etc.

Furthermore, in the basic text we meet standardized images like formulae: "Auspicious is the ford across the great stream"; i.e., the situation is predisposed to some great undertaking. Or, "Auspicious is the meeting with the great man," an indication of the possibility of help from a powerful person.

2) As we pointed out above, the texts to individual lines narrate the sequence of the situation's development. The first position characterizes only the very beginning of the given process, when it still has not appeared with all its typicality. The second position characterizes the apogee of the internal development of the given situation, just as the fifth position is the maximal exposure of it externally. The third position characterizes the moment of crisis, the transition from internal

2. See Hexagrams 12, 1. S.
3. See Hexagrams 34, 3. S.

to external. Thus, if one reads in succession all of the texts of the third position, regardless of all the laconism sometimes encountered, their common feature, that is, the dangerousness of the situation, emerges. For example: "Waiting in the mud. The arrival of brigands draws near" (Hexagram 5). "A cart of corpses may be in the army. Misfortune" (Hexagram 7). "Even the blind can see! Even the lame can walk! But if you step on the tail of a tiger so that it bites you, there will be misfortune. The soldier nevertheless acts for the sake of a great sovereign" (Hexagram 10). "The rafter caves in. Misfortune" (Hexagram 28). "For him who is connected with runaways there will be sickness and danger. For him who has male and female servants, good fortune" (Hexagram 33), etc., etc. The fourth position characterized the beginning of the appearance of the given situation in the outside. Thus it is as little typical as the first. However, it is favorably influenced by the proximity of the fifth position. Thus the aphorisms to the fourth position are not as gloomy as the preceding. The fifth position has already been mentioned in connection with the second position. The sixth position is the completion or overdevelopment of the process of the given situation, in which it either loses its typicality or turns into its opposite. The latter is very characteristically expressed particularly in Hexagrams 11 and 12.

3) One must always keep in mind that the basic text is very intimately connected with the hexagrams, trigrams, and lines which constitute it. Thus, in order to consider a text, it is essential to examine it with regard to their symbolics which were pointed out in the introduction to the present work.

4) The connection of the texts with each other and their shift of position must be considered the concretization of the seven basic positions of the *Book of Changes*, inherited from the real text by the entire group of commentators, in spite of all their differences indicated above. These seven positions most clearly emerge in the *Hsi-tz'u chuan*; however, with sufficient reflection one can be convinced that they are in a·way overtones inherent in the basic text. Here they are in general terms:

(*a*) the world is both changeability and immutability and, what is more, the natural unity of them; (*b*) at the basis of this lies the polarity which runs throughout the world, the antipodes of which are as opposed to each other as they are attracted to each other: in their relationship the world movement appears as a rhythm; (*c*) thanks to the rhythm, that which has been established and that which has not yet been established unite into one system, according to which the future already exists in the present as a "sprout" of coming events; (*d*) both the theoretical understanding and the practical realization of this are necessary and, if the activity of a person is thus normal, then he harmoniously takes part in his environment; (*e*) thus is excluded the conflict of internal and external, and they contribute to the development of each other only by the fact that the internal is defined by the external and is creative in the external; (*f*) in this way the personality devotes sufficient attention to itself and to the society around it, and being satisfied with its position, finds the possibility of higher forms of creation: creation of the good and not just the fulfillment of any copybook morality; (*g*) thus, thanks to the sustaining unity of abstraction and concreteness, the full flexibility of the system is achieved.

It can be shown that these positions are expressed in very contemporary language. However, among the tasks of the author of the present study is the making understandable, as much as possible, to the reader what is not understandable to him when confronted with the original text. If one is to master these instructions the *Book of Changes* will hardly be so incomprehensible—of course, only with the reader's active attention to the text. A passive reading of the *Book of Changes*, as of a diverting piece of *belles lettres*, is an idle waste of time.

CHAPTER 12

Reflection in Artistic Literature

It can be said that almost all writers of ancient China from the time of the Han canonization of the classics were in one way or another acquainted with the *Book of Changes* as the most important of classical texts. Thus it is not surprising that it exerted an appreciable influence on them. Primarily, it affected their education and hence their ideas and terminology, whatever the differences in various periods of Chinese literary history. However, in this area the influence of the book is no greater than the influence of any other classic.

Alongside such saturation of ideas of the *Book of Changes* into Chinese literature, there also exist a number of works devoted to the book itself, and in them the book found its literary reflection. Both prose essays and verse were devoted to it.

Below, as an example of such literature, I cite Su Hsün's essay and several poems. Su Hsün was very well acquainted with the *Book of Changes*, and his statements on separate places in the text are accepted first by Wan I, whose commentary is the basis of my interpretive translation. Thus I find it useful to give the translation of this essay. In it Su Hsün gives the clear contrast of the *I Ching* and the *Li-chi*. His son, Su Shih (Su Tung-p'o) also wrote an essay with the same title, but I do not translate this since it considers questions of an exclusively mantic character: the symbolism of the numbers six, seven, eight, and nine which designate the lines of hexagrams in divination.

The lyrics devoted to the *Book of Changes* are not, of course, the best verses from the treasure house of Chinese poetry. Thus I cite only a very few of them only so that the reader can form some idea of this area of Chinese poetry and what emotions the *Book of Changes* provoked in Chinese poets. The translation of more extensive material might have been made the basic theme of my work, for its quantity is enormous: it occupies several volumes of the encyclopedia *T'u-shu chi-ch'eng*.

In the majority of cases the lyrics repeat the imagery of the naive tradition of the *Book of Changes*. As to the poets, of course, Confucius studied the book so zealously that the leather straps on his copy broke three times. And naturally, he wrote the Ten Wings, and Fu Hsi (or Pao Hsi-shih) drew the trigrams, etc., etc. Only the critically tempered Ou-yang Hsiu left us a poem in which a satirical attitude toward the *Book of Changes* shows through. Incidentally, in his poems he is more occupied with the unsuccessful turn of his career than with the book itself. "I am in disfavor. Why not study the *Book of Changes*!" Thus we can paraphrase the basic attitude of his verses. Meng Chiao's poetry might serve as another attitude toward the *Book of Changes* as toward a treasure of universal secrets. Such an attitude can be found in numerous pieces of rhyme-prose (*fu*) which are so verbose and grandiloquent that they say little to contemporary readers. Therefore, I do not translate them. As concerns their content, it can be expressed in the famous exclamation of Chou Tun-i: "Oh, how majestic the *Book of Changes*! In it is the source of essence and fate."

I avoid notes to keep them from overshadowing the text. Let the Chinese poets speak for themselves!

Su Hsün (1009–1066)

Discourse on the *Book of Changes*

When the Rites were adopted into the doctrine of the sages, people came to believe in it; when the Changes were adopted, people honored it. Believing in it they could not reject it; honoring it they did not dare to reject it. The doctrine of the sage was not rejected because the Rites gave it clarity and the Changes gave it profundity.

When people first appeared there was neither noble nor base, neither high nor low, neither elder nor younger. They did not plow, but they did not starve; they did not make silk, but they were not cold. Thus the people were free.

The people complain about labor and rejoice in freedom as water flows downward. But then it was the Sage only who established sovereign and subject among them, so that the nobles in the Empire subordinated the commoners to themselves; he established fathers and sons among them so that the fathers in the Empire subordinated sons to themselves;[1] he established elder and younger brothers among them so that the elder in the Empire subordinated the younger to themselves. [The Sage did this so that] they began to dress only after they made silk and began to eat only after they cultivated the land. Guiding the Empire, the Sage gave it labor.

However, the strength of one sage, of course, was insufficient to cope with the great number of people in the Empire. And if he could take their joy from them and change it into their bitterness, it is because the people of the Empire followed after him in this and agreed to reject freedom and to begin their work, to accept with joy and respect the sage and honor him as lord and teacher and act according to his laws and institutions—the Rites led to all this.

As soon as the sage created the Rites, in his explanation of them he said that if there were not noble and base, high and low, elder and younger in the Empire, then people would kill each other without end; if they did not cultivate the land, they would eat the meat of animals and birds, and if they did not make silk they would dress in the hides of animals and birds; then animals and birds would be eaten by people without end.[2] If there are noble and base, high and low, elder and younger, then people will not kill each other. If people eat what they cultivate on the land and dress in the silk which they have made, then animals and birds will not be eaten by the people.

People love life more than freedom and hate death more than labor. The sage took freedom and death from them and gave them labor and life. In this way, even little children know what to strive for and what to avoid. Thus in the Empire they trusted in the doctrine of the sage and could not reject it because the Rites made it clear.

However, what is clear is easily understandable and what is easily

1. The Chinese texts read, "That the high in the Empire subordinated the low to themselves." S.'s rendering might just be a slip. Tr.

2. According to the Chinese text, this involves mutual consumption. Tr.

understandable is profaned, and what is profaned can easily be rejected. The sage feared that his doctrine would be rejected and that the Empire would return to chaos. So he created the Changes. Having considered the images of heaven and earth, according to them he constructed the individual lines; having grasped the transformation of dark and light, according to it he constructed the hexagrams; having deliberated the trends of demons and spirits, according to them he constructed the texts.[3] Then people in their youth began to study the Changes, but even with whitened heads they did not reach its sources. Therefore, in the Empire they gazed at the sage as at the depth of the spirit, as at the heights of heaven, honored this man and in consequence also honored his doctrine. Thus in the Empire they honored the doctrine of the sage and did not dare to reject it because the Changes made it profound.

In general, if people give credence to something, it is because there is nothing in it which they cannot unriddle; if they revere something it is because there is something in it which they cannot see through. Thus there is nothing in the Rites which cannot be unriddled, but there is something in the Changes which cannot be seen through. Thus the people of the Empire came to believe in the doctrine of the Sage and revered it. And if it were not so, how could it be that the Changes were what the Sage labored on to create, something unprecedented, strange, mysterious, and fantastic in order to glorify himself in future generations?

The Sage could spread his doctrine only by means of what is most wonderful in the Empire. Divination by tortoise shell and divination by milfoil are what is most wonderful in the Empire. But divination by tortoise shell is ordained in heaven and is not foreseen by man. In divination by milfoil Heaven decides it but man shapes it. Tortoise shell is smooth and there are no regular lines on it. But when they heat the rod and pierce the shell with it and get the crack: "Corner" or "Brace" or "Fork" or "Bow,"[4] all are done only by the rod and what can man foresee in them? The Sage said, "This art belongs exclusively to Heaven. Can such an art really be spread by my doctrine?" And he took to the milfoil. But in order to get an odd or even

---

3. A phrase has been omitted here in S.'s translation. Tr.

4. Technical designations for special types of oracles. The third term is Russian is *rogatka*, which can mean horn-shaped stick, or slingshot. Tr.

bunch in milfoil stalks, the person himself has to divide the entire bunch of stalks in two. In the beginning we shall take one stalk [of all fifty] and comprehending that it is one stalk, put it to one side. Then [of the two bunches which we divided] we count the stalks by fours and comprehend that we count by fours; the remainder we take between our fingers and know that what is left is either one or two or three or four, and that we selected them. This is from man. But dividing all the stalks in two parts, we do not know [earlier] how many stalks are in each of them. This is from heaven. The Sage said, "This unity of heaven and man is [my] doctrine [Tao]. In it is what spreads my teachings." And then proceeding from this he created the Changes to inspire the ears and eyes of the Empire, and his doctrine is thus honored and not rejected.

Thus the Sage employed these means to capture the heart of the Empire and spread his doctrine to infinity."

Fu Hsien (Third Century)

Poem on the *Chou Changes*

Let the low, in order to save[5] himself
   Revere the high and he will bring fame to himself.
In the urge toward good, toward perfection of affairs
   There is an invariable law from time immemorial.
It will again and again shine,
   Lighting up all from all sides.
It is impossible for the nobody to act now,
   Just the way of the nobles will be extended.

Meng Chiao (751–814)

After Hermit Yin Explained the *Book of Changes*
I Send This in Parting with Him

Heaven and Earth were revealed to me in the teacher's
   story

5. S. might have misread here the Chinese term. The rendering is ours. Tr.

As if the magic oracle was speaking with me,
Mystery of mystery which men do not know,
All are confirmed to me from each word.[6]
The white night was lit by the autumn moon,
The fresh breeze rhymes with limpid brook.
Only just penetrated, suddenly I seem to be in the
    distance.
With the spirit I feel . . . in silence there is no speech.
With the first awareness all fetters are dissolved.
In evening thought I incline toward a troubled morning.
The boat of the wanderer has no stop on the waves.
The horses neighed, the shafts were removed here.
My teacher, the hermit Yin Ch'in, who lives in the
    thicket
Knows that there is a friend who understands him.

Ou-yang Hsiu

I Read the *Book of Changes*

Let white-haired men be at the vermillion helm.[7]
Here in Tung-chou, kindness is shown to a sick servant;
On this endless day to give oneself up to the zither and
    wine,
To light the incense and read the *Book of Changes* in late
    spring . . .
He wore the attire of the sages but is discarded like
    slippers now.
He was abandoned by waves and wind on the earthly
    path.
Now if they say: Who is this hermit-gentleman?
His name forever astonishes everyone!

---

6. S. misread this word. Tr.
7. The Chinese term here means the carriages used by the nobility. Tr.

Chu Hsi

The *Book of Changes*

I immerse myself in the book later than the doubling of
    the trigrams,
But to see the ages before they were drawn, there are no
    obstacles to my eyes.
I understood the Great Limit; in it both forms are rooted.
The leather straps on the book just now broke!

Inspiration

I have heard that in former times Pao Hsi-shih originated
Creation and Fulfillment for the first time.
The action of Creation echoes the power of Heaven,
and Fulfillment agrees with the signs of Earth.
In the heights he perceived the circle of initial chaos.
In a single moment he dashed a thousand *li*,
In dales he noticed the form of motionless peace,
Antiquity is preserved in the complacent thickness of
    earth.
Having understood the meaning of these images, never
    stable,
We enter the gates of good in unity with it.
Application to this should never run short,
And in admiration of its thought we will be strengthened!

Ch'iu Ch'eng (Twelfth Century)

I Consider Lines of the *Book of Changes* and Show them to Cheng Tung-ch'ing

Clear thought is lodged in images in the Changes,
But no one can discover it in some lines.
He who does not know the meaning of the line,
    Interprets it in vain;
Just as if he paints an invisible whirlwind with colors.

Bibliography

Entries preceded by asterisk (*) indicate titles in Shchutskii's
original bibliography. All other titles were added by Konrad.

*Barannikov, A. P. *Khindustani* (*Urdu i Khindi*) [Hindustani
(Urdu and Hindi)] Leningrad, 1934

Barde, R. "La Divination par le Yi-King (I-ching)," *Monu-
menta Serica.*

————. "Recherches sur les Origines Arithmétiques du Yi-
King (I-Ching)" *Archives internationales d'Histoire des
Sciences* (Continuation of *Archeion*, 1952).

Behm, B. *I Ging. Das chinesische Orakellbuch.* In *Der Bear-
beitung von Bill Behm.* Klagenfurt: Leon sen, 1940.

*Bunakov, Iu. V. *Gadatel'nye kosti iz Khe-nani* (*Kitay*). *Ocherk
istorii i problematiki v sviazi s kollektsiei IKDP.* (Oracle
Bones from Honan [China]). Sketch of the history and
problems connected with the collection of the I[nstitute of]
B[ooks,] D[ocuments and] L[etters], *Trudy I[nstituta]
Ia[zyka i] M[yshleniia im. N. Ia. Marr*], III. Leningrad,
1935.

Chang Hsueh-ch'eng 章學誠. *Wen-shih t'ung-i* 文史通義
(General interpretation of the literary and historical documents). Ku-chi ch'u-pan-she 古籍出版社. Peking, 1956.

*Chao Lan-p'ing 趙蘭坪. *Chung-kuo che-hsueh-shih* 中國哲
學史 (History of Chinese philosophy). Shanghai, 1925.

*Chavannes, Edouard (trans.). *Les mémoires historique de Se-Ma
Ts'ien*, vol. v, Paris, 1905.

Ch'en Che-chung 陳哲中. "Chou I kai-shou" 周易概說
(General explanation of the Chou I), *Kuo-k'ao Yueh-k'an*
國考月刊, ch. 5, nos. 3–5 (April 1937).

Chiang Shao-yuan 江紹源. "Chou I K'un kua ti-san yao-

tz'u hsin-chieh" 周易坤卦第三爻辭新解 (A new explana-
tion of the line text to the third line of the hexagram K'un
in the *Chou I*), *Pei-p'ing Hua-pei Jih-pao Chung-kuo ku-chan-
pu-shu yen-chiu* 北平華北日報中國古占卜術研究, no. 28
(1937).

————. "Chou I Po shang-chiu yao-tz'u 'Shih kuo pu shih
chun-tzu te yu hsiao jen pao lu' hsin chieh" 周易剝上九爻
辭'碩果不食君子得輿小人剝廬'新解 (New explanation of
'Shih kuo pu shih chun-tzu te yu hsiao jen pao lu' the line
text for nine in the top place in the hexagram *Po* of the
Chou I), *Pei-p'ing Hua-pei Jih-pao Chung-kuo ku-chan-pu-
shu yen-chiu* 北平華北日報中國古占卜術研究, no. 21
(1937).

————. "Chou I Sung kua-tz'u hsin-chieh" 周易訟卦辭新解
(New explanation of the text to the hexagram *Sung* in the
Chou I), *Pei-p'ing Hua-pei Jih-pao Chung-kuo ku-chan-pu-
shu yen-chiu* 北平華北日報中國古占卜術研究, no. 27
(1937).

————. "I kua ju-ho te ming" 易卦如何得名 (How the I
hexagrams got their names), *Pei-p'ing Hua-pei Jih-pao
Chung-kuo ku-chan-pu-shu yen-chiu* 北平華北日報中國古占
卜術研究, no. 22, (1937).

Chiang Ts'an-nei 江參內. "Sung kua ti-erh yao-tz'u hsin-chieh
pu" 訟卦第二爻辭新解補 (A supplement to the new
explanation of the line text to the second line of the hexagram
Sung), *Pei-p'ing Hua-pei Jih-pao Chung-kuo ku-chan-pu-shu
yen-chiu* 北平華北日報中國古占卜術研究, no. 26 (1937).

Ch'ing-ju Hsüeh-an 清儒學案 (Intellectual biographies of
Ch'ing Confucianists). Shanghai: Wen-jui-lou, 上海 : 文
瑞樓, n.d.

Ch'iung Shao-yuan 邛邵願. "Chou I ti-liu-kua Sung kua
liu yao-tz'u   hsin-chieh"   周易第六卦訟卦六爻辭新解
(New explanation of the line text to the sixth line of hexagram six, "Sung" of the Chou I), *Pei-p'ing Hua-pei Jih-pao
Chung-kuo ku-chan-pu-shu yen-chiu* 北平華北日報中國古
占卜術研究, no. 24 (1937).

————. "Chou I ti-liu-kua Sung liu yao-tz'u hsin-chieh pu-ch'ien" 周易第六卦訟六爻辭新解補遺 (Addendum to the new explanation of the line text to the sixth line of hexagram six, "Sung," of the Chou I), *Pei-p'ing Hua-pei Jih-pao Chung-kuo ku-chan-pu-shu yen-chiu.* 北平華北日報中國古占卜術研究 , no. 25 (1937).

Chou I cheng-yi 周易正義 (The correct meaning of the Chou I). In *Shih-san-ching chu-shu* 十三經注疏 , Chung-hua Shu-chü 中華書局. Peking, 1957.

*————. In *Shih-san-ching chu-shu* 十三經注疏 . Chiang-hsi, Nan-ch'ang 江西南昌, 1815.

Chu Chun-sheng 朱駿聲 *Liu-shih-szu kua ching-chieh* 六十四卦經解 (Explanation of the 64 hexagrams). Ku-chi ch'u-pan-she 古籍出版社. Peking, 1958.

**Chung-kuo jen-min ta-tz'u-tien* 中國人民大辭典 (Chinese people's dictionary). Shanghai: Shang-wu yin-shu-kuan 上海商務印書館 , 1914.

*Conrady, A. "Yih-king Studien. Herausgegeben von Eduard Erkes," *Asia Major* VII (1931/1932), 409–468.

*Cordier, Henri. *Bibliotheca Sinica*, vol. II. Paris 1905–1906.

*Couvreur, S. (trans.) *Tch'ouen Ts'iou et Tso Tchouan.* 3 vols. Ho Kien Fu, 1914.

*Edkins, J. "The Yi King with notes on the 64 kwa," *China Review* XII (1883–1884).

*Endō Ryūkichi 遠藤隆吉 . *Eki no shosei tetsugaku* 易の處世哲學 (Philosophy of behavior in the I). 2d ed. Tokyo: Waseda Daigaku 東京: 早稻田大學 , 1925.

Fan' Ven'-lan' [Fan Wen-lan]. *Drevniaia istoriia Kitaia ot pervobytnoobshchinnogo stroia do obrazovaniia tsentralizovannogo feodal'nogo gosudarstva.* (Ancient history of China from the primitive social structure to the formation of a centralized feudal state.) Moscow, 1958.

*Forke, Alfred. *Geschichte der alten chinesischen Philosophie.* Hamburg, 1927.

*————. *Geschichte der mittelalterlichen Chinesischen Philosophie.* Hamburg, 1934.

*Giles, Herbert A. *A History of Chinese Literature*. London, 1901.

*Granet, Marcel. *La pensée chinoise*. Paris, 1934.

Han-i araha inenggidari giyangnaha I-Dzing-ni jurgan-be suhe bithe. Wood-block ed., 1963.

Han-i araha ubaliyambuha Jijungge nomun. Wood-block ed., supposedly 1765.

*Harlez, Charles de. *Le Yih-King*. *Texte primitif, rétabli, traduit et commenté*. Brussels, 1889.

*————. *Le Yi-King, traduit d'après les interprètes chinois avec la version mandchoue*. Paris, 1897.

*Hauer, Erich. Review: "I Ging. Das Buch der Wandlungen, aus dem Chinesischen verdeutscht und erläutert von Richard Wilhelm . . . 1924," *Ostasiatische Zeitschrift* (Berlin, Leipzig, 1925).

*Hoang Tsen-yue. *Étude comparative sur les philosophies de Laotseu, Khongtseu, Motseu*. Lyon, 1925.

Huang Chih-liu 黃之六. "Tsai yu Huai-hsuan Hsien-sheng lun I-hsiang-shu" 再與槐軒先生論易象書 (Further discussion with Mr. Huai-hsüan of the I image text), *Pei-p'ing Ch'en-pao I-t'uan* 北平晨報藝團, 10 May 1937.

Huang Shou-ch'i 黃壽祺. "Yü Shang Huai-hsuan Hsien-sheng lun I ti-san-shu" 與尙槐軒先生論易第三書 (Discussion with Mr. Shang Huai-hsuan of the third book of the I), *Pei-p'ing Ch'en-pao I-t'uan* 北平晨報藝團, 2 June 1937.

The I Ching or Book of Changes. The Richard Wilhelm Translation rendered into English by Cary F. Baynes. 2 vols. Princeton, 1951.

I Ching 易經. In *Chung-kuo shih-hsüeh lun-wen so-yin* 中國史學論文索引, vol. 2. Peking: K'e-hsüeh Ch'u-pan-she 北京：科學出版社, 1958.

*Itō Tōgai 伊藤東涯. *Shūekikyō yoku tsūkai* 周易經翼通解 (Commentary on the Chou I Ching Wings). Tokyo: Goshi kaisha 東京：合資會社, 1916.

*Itō Zenshō 伊藤善韶. Preface to *Shūekikyō yoku tsūkai* 周易經翼通解 (Commentary on the Chou I Ching Wings).

Tokyo: Gōshi kaisha 東京 : 合資會社, 1916.

"I-tszin" (I Ching), *Bol'shaia Sovetskaia Entsiklopediia*, 2nd ed., vol. 19, pp. 167–168.

*Johnson, O. S. *A Study of Chinese Alchemy*. Shanghai, 1928.

*Kanno Michiaki 簡野道明. *Rongo kaigi* 論語解義 (Explanation of the Lun-yü). Tokyo: Meikatsu Shoin 東京 : 明活書院, 1928.

Kao Heng 高亨. *Chou I ku-ching t'ung-shuo* 周易古經通説 (Explanation of the ancient classic the Chou I). Peking: Chung-hua Shu-chu 北京 : 中華書局, 1958.

*Karlgren, Bernard. "*On the Authenticity and Nature of the Tso-chuan*." Goteborg, 1926.

Kishimoto Suigetsu 岸木翆月. "Shūeki tetsugaku ni arawareru banyū dōsō shisō" 周易哲学に現れる万有同相思想 (Universal thought reflected in Chou I philosophy), *Shinkon* 新墾, no. 18. 10 (1948).

Kobayashi Ichirō 小林一郎. *Ekikyō daikōza* 易經大講座 (Lectures on the I Ching), vols. 1–10. Tokyo, 1940–1941.

*Krause, F.S.A. *Ju Tao Fo. Die religiosen und philosophischen System ostasiens*. Munich, 1924.

Ku Tzu-lin 古子霖. *Chou I chih hsin yen-chiu* 周易之新研究 (New studies of the Chou I). Ch'eng-tu 城都, 1939.

*Kumazawa Banzan 熊澤蕃山. *Shūgi washo* 集義和書 (Collections of Japanese Commentaries). Tokyo, 1921.

Kuo Mo-jo 郭沫若. *Bronzovyi vek*. (Bronze age), Trans. from the Chinese. Moscow, 1959.

———. *Chou I te kou-ch'eng shih-tai* 周易的構成時代 (The Chou I's time of formation). Shanghai: Shang-wu Yin-shu-kuan 上海 : 商務印書館, 1940.

*Legge, James. *Lun Yü. Confucius Analects. Chinese Text with English Translation*. Shanghai, 1935.

*———. (trans.). *The Yi King*. Sacred Books of China, Part II. Oxford, 1882.

Li Ching-ch'ih 李鏡池. "Chou I kua-ming k'ao-shih" 周易卦名考釋 (Examination and explanation of the hexagram names of the Chou I), *Lingnan Hsueh Pao* IX. 1 (1948).

————. "Chou I wu-tz'u hsu-k'ao" 周易筮辭續考 (Further study of the Chou I divination texts), *Lingnan Hsueh Pao,* VIII.11 (1947).

*Li Kuang-ti 李光地 (ed.). *Chou I che-chung* 周易折中 (The correct text of the Chou I), 1715.

*Li Kuo 李過. *Hsi-ch'i I-shuo* 西谿易說 (Hsi-ch'i's explanation of the I). Shanghai: Shang-wu Yin-shu-kuan 上海 : 商務印書館 , n.d.

Liu Pai-min 劉百閔. "Chou I hsi-tz'u-chuan jen-shih-lun-ti k'ao-ch'a" 周易繫辭傳認識論底考察 (Examination of the epistemology of the Hsi-tz'u chuan in the Chou I), *Tung-wen Wen-hua* 東文文化 , II.1 (1955).

————. "The epistemology of the 'Great Appendix of the Yi-Ching," *Journal of Oriental Studies*, no. 2 (Hong Kong, 1955).

*McClatchie, T. *A Translation of the Confucian Yi-king.* Shanghai, 1876.

————. "Phallic Worship," *China Review* IV (1875–1876).

————. "The Symbols of the Yih-King," *China Review* I (n.d.).

*Maspero, Henri. *La Chine antique.* Paris, 1927.

Müller, R. *I Ging. Das Buch der Wandlungen, aus dem Chinesischen verdeutscht un erläutert.* Jena, 1937.

*Nagai Kimpū 長井金風 . *Shūeki jigi* 周易時義 (Contemporary Interpretations of the Chou I). Tokyo, 1924.

*Naitō Torajirō 内藤虎次郎 "Ekigi" 易疑 (Questions about the I). *Shinagaku* 支那學 III.7 (1923), 1–16.

Needham, J., and Wang Ling. *Science and Civilization in China,* vols. 1–3. London, 1956–1959.

*Ou-yang Hsiu 歐陽修 . "I t'ung-tzu-wen" 易童子問 (Questions of a Youth about the Book of Changes) in *Sung Yüan Hsüeh-an* 宋元學案 (Intellectual biographies of the Sung and Yuan). Shanghai: Wen-jui-lou 上海 : 文瑞樓 n.d.

Petrov, A. A. "Ocherk filosofii Kitaia" (Sketch of China's philosophy) in *Kitai* (Moscow, 1940), pp. 248–272.

*————. *Van Bi (226–249). Iz istorii kitaiskoi filosofii.* (Wang

Pi [226–249]. From the history of Chinese philosophy). Moscow-Leningrad: Academy of Sciences, 1936.

*Phan kê-Binh. *Wiêt Hán văn khảo.* Hanoi, 1930.

*Philastre, P. L-F. (trans.). *Tscheou Yi: Le Yi: King ou livre de changements de la dynastie de Tscheou, traduit pour la premièr fois en français avec les Commentaires traditionnels complet de T'schèng Tsé et de Tshouli et des extraits des principaux commentateurs par Philastre.* Annales du Musée Guimet VIII, XXIII. Paris, 1885–1893.

*P'i Hsi-jui 皮錫瑞. *Ching hsueh t'ung-lun* 經學通論 (General treatise on the study of classical books). 1907.

Radul'-Zatulovskii, Ia. B. *Konfutsianstvo i ego rasprostranenie v Iaponii* (Confuciansism and its spread in Japan). Institut Vostokovedeniai AN, SSSR. Moscow-Leningrad, 1947.

————. "Materialisticheskaia filosofiia Ito Dzinsai" (The materialistic philosophy of Itō Jinsai), *Sovetskoe Vostokovedenie* II (1941).

Rai-ki 禮記 (Li-chi). In *Kokuyaku kambun taikei* 國譯漢文大系 XVIII, ch. 16. Tokyo: Taiden Goshisha Toyamabo 東京: 大傳合資社富山房 , 1928.

Shang Chieh-chih 尚節之. "Tsai ta Huang Chih-liu lun I shu" 再答黃之六論易書 (Another answer to Huang Chih-liu's letter on the I), *Pei-p'ing Ch'en-pao I-t'uan* 北平晨報藝團, 4 June 1937.

Shang Ping-ho 尚秉和. "Ta Huang Liu-chih lun I shu" 答黃之六論易書 (An answer to Huang Liu-chih's letter on the I), *Pei-p'ing Ch'en-pao I-t'uan* 北平晨報藝團, 10 May 1937.

*Shchutskii, Iu. K. "Iz Kitaiskoi esseisticheskoi literatury" (From Chinese essay literature), *Vostok*, first collection (Moscow-Leningrad, 1935), pp. 190–200.

*————. "Sledy stadial'nosti v kitaiskoi ieroglifike" [Traces of the phasic in Chinese characters] *Iafeticheskii sbornik* VII (Leningrad, 1932), pp. 81–96.

"Shūeki ni-tsuite" 周易につぃて [On the Chou I], *The Kwaitoku*, no. 26 (October 1955).

*Skachkov, P. E. *Bibliografiia Kitaia* (Bibliography of China). Moscow-Leningrad: Sotsekgiz, 1932.

*Ssu-ma Ch'ien 司馬遷. *Shih-chi* 史記 (Historical records). T'ung-jen-t'ang, 同人堂, 1806.

Suvarnāprabhāsottamasūtra. Das Goldglanz-Sūtra. Ein Sanskrit-text des Mahāyāna-Buddhismus. I-Tsing's chinesische Version und ihre tibetische ubersetsung. Hrsg. von J. Nobel. 2 Bde: Tsing's chinesische Version ubersetzt usw 1958; II Die tibetische Ubersetsung mit kritischen Anm. hrsg. 1958.

*Takada Tadasuke 高田忠周. *Koryūhen* 古籀篇 (Dictionary of ancient pictography). Tokyo, 1925.

*Takase Takeshirō 高瀬武質郎. *Eki sen yū* 易闡幽 (Expounding the hidden meaning of the I). Osaka: Bungaku jitsu koen Shū 大阪：文學術講演集, 1925.

Takeuchi Yoshio 武内義雄. *Eki to Chūyō no kenkyū* 易と中庸の研究 (Study of the I and the Chung Yung). Tokyo: Iwanami Shoten 東京：岩波書店, 1946.

*————. "Jukyō shisō" 儒教思想 (Confucian thought), *Sekai shisō* 世界思想, nos. 1–5 (1928).

*Tao-meng-chi Hsien-sheng 刀蒙吉先生. *Tu-I-fa 'I-cho'* 讀易法"易酌" (Considering the I': A method of reading the I). Ch'i-yang: Shun-chi-lou 祁陽：順積樓, 1843.

*Terrien de la Couperie. *The Oldest Book of the Chinese (The Yh King) and Its Authors. Vol. 1: History and Method.* London, 1892.

*Tetsugaku daijiten 哲學大辭典 (Dictionary of philosophy). Tokyo, 1912.

Thang Yung-thung, "Wang Pi's New Interpretation of the I Ching and Lun Yü," *HJAS* 10 (1947) 124–161.

Ting Ch'ao-wu 丁超五. *K'e-hsueh-te I* 科學的易 (The scientific I). Shanghai: Hua-tung Yi-yuan 上海：華東醫院, 1953.

Toda Toyoo 戶田豊郎. "Ō Hitsu, Ekichū teihon ni tsuite" 王弼，易注底本について (On the original text of Wang Pi's I-ching commentary), *Tetsugaku* 哲學, 5 March 1955.

Toda Toyosaburō 戶田豊三郎. "Ekiden no seiritsu ni tsuite

———Fukuda Yamashita ryōshi no ronsō o yomu" 易伝の
成立について一福田山下両氏の論争を讀む (On reading
the debate between Fukuda and Yamashita concerning the
establishment of the I tradition). *Shibun* 史文, no. 55 (Sept
1955).

Ts'en Chung-mien 岑仲勉. "Chou I kua-yao piao-hsien-che
shang-ku-te shu-hsueh chih-shih" 周易卦爻表現着上古的
數學知識 (Ancient mathematical knowledge revealed in
the hexagrams and line texts of the Chou I). In his *Liang
Chou Wen-shih Lun-yeh* 兩周文史論叢 (Essays on the literature and history of the Two Chou's). Shanghai: Shangu
Yin-shu-kuan 上海: 商務印書館, 1958.

*Tsuda Sōkichi 津田左右吉. *Dōka no Shisō to sono kaiten*
道家の思想と其の開展
ment). Tokyo: Tōyō Bunko 東京: 東洋文庫, 1927.

*Ueda Mannen 上田万年. *Dai jiten* 大字典 (Big dictionary).
Tokyo: Kaizōsha 東京: 改造社, 1928.

*Vasil'ev, B. A., and Shchutskii, Iu. K. *Stroi kitaiskogo iazyka.*
(Structure of the Chinese language) Leningrad, 1936.

*———*Uchebnik kitaiskogo iazyka* (*bay-khua*) (Textbook of
Chinese [pai-hua]). Leningrad: Leningrad Oriental Institute,
1935; 2nd ed., rev. and supp. Leningrad, 1935.

Vsemirnaia istoriia (World History), vol. 1. Moscow, 1955.

*Wang Pi 王弼. *Chou I lueh-li* 周易略例 (General examples
of the Chou I), *SPTK*, 1928.

*Wieger, Leon, *Taoisme*, vol. 1. London, 1911.

*———*Histoire des croyances religieuses et des opinions philosophi-
ques en Chine depuis l'origine, jusqu'à nos jours.* Hsienhsien:
Mission Press, 1917.

Wilhelm, Hellmut. "I-Ching oracles in the Tso-chuan and
Kuo-yu." *JAOS* LXXIX. 4 (October–December 1959),
275–278.

———. *Klassiker, Chinesische I-Ching, Die Wandlung, Acht
Essays zum I Ging.* Zurich, 1958.

———. "Leibniz and the I Ching," *Collectanea Commissionis
Synodalis in Sinis*, no. 16 (1947).

————. *Die Wandlung: acht Vortrage zum I-Ging* (*I Ching*). Peip'ing: Vetch, 1944.

*Wilhelm, Richard. *Geschichte der chinesischen Kultur*. Munich: Bruckmann, 1928.

*———— (trans.). *I Ging. Das Buch der Wandlungen*. 2 vols. Jena, 1924.

*Yamasato Motō 山里. *Rōshi to Ekikyō hikaku kenkyū* 老子と 易經比較研究 (Comparative study of Lao-tzu and the *I Ching*). Tokyo, 1927.

Yamashita Shizuo 山下靜雄. "Keijiden-ni okeru, henka no riron no tenkai" 繫辭傳における, 変化の理論の展開 (The development of the theory of transformation in the Hsi-tz'u chuan), *Bulletin of the Educational Research Institute, Faculty of Education, University of Kapochina*, vol. 7 (1955).

Yan Iun-go (Yang Yung-kuo). *Istoriia drevnekitaiskoi ideologii* (History of ancient Chinese ideology), trans. from the Chinese. Moscow, 1957.

Yan Khin-shun. *Drevnekitaiskii filosof Lao-tszy i ego uchenie* (The ancient Chinese philosopher Lao-tzu and his doctrine). Moscow-Leningrad, 1950.

*Yao-chiang Huang-li-chou Hsien-sheng 姚江黃梨洲先生. *Ming-ju hsüeh-an* 明儒學案 (Intellectual Biographies of Ming Confucianists). Shanghai: Wen-jui-lou 上海: 文瑞 樓, n.d.

Yi-Ching: A Concordance to Yi Ching (in Chinese). Harvard-Yenching Institute, Sinological Index Series, supplement no. 10.

*Yu Yung-liang 余永梁. "I kua yao-tz'u-te shih-tai chi ch'i tso-che" 易卦爻辭的時代及其作者 (The date and authorship of the I Ching's hexagram and line texts). *Bulletin of the Institute of History and Philology of the Academia Sinica*, vol. 1, no. 1 (1928).

Yuan-Kuang (Le Maître) *Méthode pratique de divination chinoise par le "Yi-King" Avec un important introduction, préface et notes explicatives*. Traduit par Tchou-Houa et Charles Canone. Paris, 1952.

*Zakharov, I. *Polny man'chzhursko-riisski slovar'* (Complete Manchu-Russian dictionary). St. Petersburg: Academy of Sciences, 1875.

*Zottoli, A. *Cursus literaturae sinicae*, vols. 1–5. Shanghai, 1879–1882.

Zurcher, Eric. *The Buddhist Conquest of China: The Spread and Adaptation of Buddhism in Early Medieval China.* 2 vols., Leiden, 1959.

Index

Library of Congress Cataloging in Publication Data

Shchutskiĭ, IUlian Konstantinovich, 1897–1937
    Researches on the I Ching.

    (Bollingen series; 62.2)
    Translation of Kitaĭskaia klassicheskaia Kniga
peremen.
    Includes bibliography and index.
    1. I ching. I. Title. II. Series.
PL2464.Z7S4713 1978   299'.5128'2   78-63600
ISBN 0-691-09939-1